Adventism Confronts Modernity

Adventism Confronts Modernity

An Account of the Advent Christian
Controversy over the Bible's Inspiration

Robert J. Mayer

FOREWORD BY
Garth M. Rosell

PICKWICK *Publications* · Eugene, Oregon

ADVENTISM CONFRONTS MODERNITY
An Account of the Advent Christian Controversy over the Bible's Inspiration

Pickwick Publications
An Imprint of Wipf and Stock Publishers
199 W. 8th Ave., Suite 3
Eugene, OR 97401

www.wipfandstock.com

PAPERBACK ISBN: 978-1-4982-9526-0
HARDCOVER ISBN: 978-1-4982-9528-4
EBOOK ISBN: 978-1-4982-9527-7

Cataloguing-in-Publication data:

Names: Mayer, Robert J. |

Title: Adventism confronts modernity : an account of the Advent Christian controversy over the Bible's inspiration / Robert J. Mayer, foreword by Garth M. Rosell

Description: Eugene, OR: Pickwick Publications, 2017 | Includes bibliographical references.

Identifiers: ISBN 978-1-4982-9526-0 (paperback) | ISBN 978-1-4982-9528-4 (hardcover) | ISBN 978-1-4982-9527-7 (ebook)

Subjects: LCSH: Adventists—Doctrines. | Bible—Criticism, interpretation, etc. | Bible—Inspiration.

Classification: LCC BX6154 M2 2017 (print) | LCC BX6154 (ebook)

Manufactured in the U.S.A.   02/15/17

To my wife Renee Mayer, with great appreciation and love.

Contents

Foreword

THE PUBLICATION IN 1980 of George Marsden's pioneering volume, *Fundamentalism and American Culture: The Shaping of Twentieth-Century Evangelicalism*, marked an important historiographical watershed in the study of the modern evangelical movement.[1] His "sweeping work of synthesis," as one scholar phrased it, produced both a flurry of fresh interest in the study of American evangelicalism between 1870 and 1925 and the publication of a growing body of scholarly literature not only exploring many of the issues that had been raised by Marsden's work but also illuminating additional aspects "of twentieth-century evangelical history."[2] Bob Mayer's fascinating study, *Adventism Confronts Modernity*, provides a valuable new addition to that scholarly conversation and it also offers a fresh vantage point from which to view and evaluate the twentieth-century evangelical terrain.

Using the Advent Christian Church (a relatively small Christian denomination with historical roots in the Millerite movement) as his primary point of reference, Mayer examines the bitter debates over the authority of Scripture that broke out within the denomination during the 1960s. While these debates were initially centered within the Advent Christian's two

---

1. George M. Marsden, *Fundamentalism and American Culture: The Shaping of Twentieth-Century Evangelicalism: 1870–1925* (New York: Oxford University Press, 1980).

2. Barry Hankins, "Marsden and Modern Fundamentalism," in Darren Dochuk, Thomas S. Kidd and Kurt W. Peterson, eds., *American Evangelicalism: George Marsden and the State of American Religious History* (Notre Dame, IN: University of Notre Dame Press, 2014), 141–65.

colleges, Aurora and Berkshire, the deepening divisions over the nature and role of the Bible in the church quickly spread to touch congregational life as well.

There are important differences between the first half and the second half of the twentieth century, to be sure. Yet there are also some striking similarities between the controversies described so vividly by Marsden in the first decades of the twentieth century and those that are described so powerfully by Mayer in the last half of the century. By providing us with a well researched, reliable and delightfully readable account, Mayer has offered his readers a glimpse into a fascinating new world—a world that may be filled with lots of unfamiliar faces and some interesting new venues but that is also populated by a multitude of familiar issues. By helping us to view old issues through new lenses, we might just be able to see them more clearly.

So prepare yourselves for a feast!

Written June 27, 2016

Dr. Garth M. Rosell

Senior Research Professor of Church History
Gordon-Conwell Theological Seminary
130 Essex Street
So. Hamilton, Massachusetts 01982

Preface

My exposure to the Christian faith and to the Advent Christian Church began over fifty years ago in San Francisco, California. Unlike many Advent Christians who trace their relationship to the denomination back one or more generations, none of my ancestors was associated with any branch of the Adventist movement. My association and appreciation for Adventism has grown from the fact that it was through an Adventist denomination that I first heard the gospel and learned of Christian faith.

During the mid-1960s, I discovered that Advent Christians were engaged in a major debate over the nature of the Bible and its role within the church. I also discovered that much of the debate centered on the two Advent Christian-related colleges, Aurora University and Berkshire Christian College. It became obvious that Advent Christians, at least in my part of the country, had strong opinions and even some division within their ranks. Since that time, I have remained fascinated with the Advent Christian debate over the Bible's inspiration.

Parkside Community Church, the Advent Christian congregation in San Francisco, was the place where I developed much of my love and appreciation for the Advent Christian Church and for the historical heritage of Adventism. High school and college brought me into contact with the larger world of evangelicalism through ministries like Young Life and the Mount Hermon Christian Conference Center. Through their influence, I sensed God's calling to Christian ministry and entered Fuller Theological Seminary. I continue to be grateful for the profound influence of these congregations and ministries both on my theological pilgrimage and my Christian life.

There are a number of people to whom I must express appreciation. I am grateful to the Advent Christian pastors and leaders who agreed to be interviewed for this work, and who took time to respond to my written inquiries. Transcripts of their interviews are on deposit at the Adventual Collection, Goddard Library, Gordon-Conwell Theological Seminary in S. Hamilton, MA. Several people not only responded with encouragement, they opened their file drawers and supplied me with correspondence and reports that make up many of the primary source materials used in my research. Three I want to specifically mention are Dr. Clyde Hewitt, longtime professor of history at Aurora College, Dr. Roland Griswold, director of church expansion for the Advent Christian General Conference, and Dr. Carlyle Roberts, one of the core faculty at Berkshire Christian College during the mid-twentieth century. They died during the most intensive stage in the research and writing of this project and now rest in the care of Christ. They influenced the Advent Christian Church in important ways and I am privileged to have known each of them.

Garth Rosell, professor, mentor, friend, and colleague supervised the original research and writing of this work. Not many people have the privilege of having their dissertation supervisor later become a trusted friend and colleague, and I am grateful to Garth for his ongoing friendship and his encouragement to revise this for publication. Thank you, Garth. Freeman Barton, my library colleague at Gordon-Conwell Theological Seminary, has gone above and beyond the call of duty several times in providing valuable research help. Freeman has also been a friend and mentor as I entered the field of theological librarianship. Thank you, Freeman.

Dorothy Crouse, the widow of Dr. Moses Crouse, provided me with copies of Dr. Crouse's MA thesis and PhD dissertation. Without her help, completion of this work would have been much more difficult. Oral Collins provided valuable insights into the Cleveland Conference. He also provided a major correction in chapter 6 that saved this writer a significant embarrassment. David McCarthy provided important guidance as I sought to navigate the issues and the personalities involved. All three of these individuals have died since the research was completed, and this writer is grateful for their lives, their love for Christ, and their help.

David A. Dean graciously read each of the chapters and has offered his perspectives on the events described in this work. I am grateful for his friendship and scholarly insight. Don Fortson read through the most recent draft and suggested several important revisions. My mother, Nova Mayer, instilled in me a love for reading and learning that I will always appreciate. My wife, Renee, has not only helped with the initial typing and proofreading, she has patiently encouraged me to continue when the stress of work and research seemed almost insurmountable. It is to her that this book is dedicated.

While I am thankful for the help of so many, I recognize that they may draw different conclusions about these events and their meaning, and any mistakes in the text or errors in judgment are mine. My hope is that this work will enable further reflection on the important issues of theology and praxis that emerged among Advent Christians during the first two-thirds of the twentieth century, issues that Christians of all persuasions continue to grapple with. I also hope that this work will reflect the love and appreciation that I have for the two movements that have shaped my Christian pilgrimage—evangelicalism and Adventism. Some may still view them as mutually exclusive. I do not, and I am grateful that God has used both of them in my life.

Introduction

"THERE WAS A FEELING in the air that I never felt at General Conference before—like the night before the mother of all battles." Those words from one pastor captured what everyone attending the 1964 Advent Christian denominational convention must have felt on that warm June evening in Montreat, North Carolina. "You got all the troops in their little squadrons gathering and talking. And you can just feel the tension in the air."[3] After years of discussion, debate, and dissention, the moment had arrived. Since the mid-1950s, this small denominational family rooted in the Adventist movement established by William Miller had publicly struggled with conflict over how best to understand the inspiration of the Bible and its role in the life of the church. That conflict was compounded by the reality that the two colleges that prepared Advent Christian clergy and lay leaders held strong differences of opinion—differences that emerged within the leadership of the denomination based on college loyalties. Now the time had finally come. The Advent Christian Church would finally resolve this conflict over the Bible. Or would it?

Until recently, many historians have viewed the controversies between fundamentalists and modernists as largely focused in time (1910–1930) and place (among Baptists and Presbyterians). During the last thirty-five years, that perspective has been altered. We now see that these long-running debates over the Bible's inspiration and authority have impacted many Protestant communions and continue in different configurations even into

3. Oral history interview, David S. McCarthy, November 24, 1995.

the early twenty-first century. While this writer uses military metaphors with great reluctance, perhaps the best way to view these debates is as a multi-layered conflict with battles on many fronts, and each front with its own generals, captains, foot-soldiers, and supply lines.

This work focuses on one of those fronts, a small denomination born out of the disappointment of its founder, William Miller, and his Adventist followers during the early 1840s. The Advent Christian Church was one of several denominations that grew out of the Great Disappointment of 1844, the failed prediction that Jesus Christ would return personally and visibly during October of that year.[4] One-hundred-and-twenty years after the Great Disappointment, this small denomination would find itself locked in a controversy over the Bible's inspiration and authority. For a denomination that prided itself on its distinctive understanding of biblical truth,[5] it was ironic that it now experienced the same struggles that had plagued Northern Baptists and Northern Presbyterians two generations earlier.

4. For accounts of the life of William Miller and the founding of the Advent Christian Church, see Hewitt, *Midnight and Morning;* and Knight, *Millennial Fever and the End of the World.* For a more recent biography of William Miller, see Rowe, *God's Strange Work.*

5. For a description of Advent Christian distinctive doctrinal teaching, see Dean, *Resurrection Hope.* Advent Christians have historically maintained three distinctive doctrines that touch on the areas of theological anthropology and eschatology. The first, commonly called "conditional immortality" by many Adventists but termed "annihilationism" by others (including some critics), is the belief that God alone is naturally immortal (see 1 Tim 6:13–16) and that human beings do not necessarily possess immortality, but ultimately receive it through faith in Jesus Christ. Therefore, those without Christ will not suffer conscious eternal torment, but will be judged, punished according to their sins, and ultimately destroyed.

The second distinctive, popularly called "soul-sleep," interprets the intermediate state between physical death and the return of Christ as a period of temporary unconsciousness. In their third distinctive, Advent Christians interpret the last portion of Revelation as teaching that God will destroy the earth by fire and establish his eternal kingdom on an earth made new.

Advent Christians have also taken pride in their heritage rooted in the Adventist movement of the 1830s and 1840s and its teaching regarding the imminent personal return of Jesus Christ. Baptist lay-preacher William Miller originally predicted that Jesus Christ would return to earth around the year 1843. Subsequently, some Adventists revised those predictions and embraced October 22, 1844 as the precise date (a view that Miller himself only accepted weeks before the October date). These mistaken attempts at date-setting combined with what some interpreted as religious fanaticism, caused a number of churches to disenfranchise many of their Adventist members. Many who became part of the Advent Christian Church and other Adventist bodies were those who suffered this disenfranchisement and it became integral to their distinct ecclesial identities.

What makes the Advent Christian controversy an important story is not the size of the denomination. Other small denominations have faced similar struggles. The importance of the Advent Christian story rests in its historical context as a uniquely American denomination with roots firmly in the Restorationism of America's Second Great Awakening. Studying the Advent Christian conflict over the inspiration and authority of the Bible can help us gain insight into the role and function of Scripture in a restorationist context. It helps us look at how denominations and associations of churches that combine non-creedal approaches toward Christian theology with a congregational form of church government resolve or fail to resolve important theological and organizational differences.

At this point, a word about how we seek to understand Christian history and the events contained in it is essential. This work is shaped by three assumptions about writing history that can be described with three words: evidence, context, and people.[6] Writing history involves interpretation, and while historians cannot totally divorce their work from their assumptions about life and meaning, interpretation must be grounded in evidence grounded in primary sources. This writer hopes that the evidence offered in the narrative and the accompanying notes will not only demonstrate the validity of the interpretations offered, but will invite others to explore that evidence and offer their own interpretations of these events.

Writing history involves context. Events have a variety of contexts—ecclesiastical, geographic, economic, cultural, and theological to name a few. Understanding the Advent Christian controversy over the Bible's inspiration involves understanding how this small somewhat obscure group of congregations and individuals fits into the larger context of American Protestantism from the 1840s to the mid-1960s. Protestantism in the United States changed dramatically during that 125-year period, and despite the best efforts of Adventists to isolate themselves from the rest of American Protestantism, especially in doctrinal and theological terms, complete isolation was simply not possible. Therefore, this work surveys significant change in American (and to a lesser degree, European) Protestantism especially as it relates to how the Bible and its teachings should be understood and practiced within Christianity, and addresses how those changing understandings influenced Advent Christian theologians, pastors, and denominational leaders.

6. For more information on historical method and writing history, see Bebbington, *Patterns in History*; and Wood, *The Purpose of the Past*.

Writing history involves understanding people at the heart of events. One of the most important developments in historical writing over the past fifty years has been the development of writing history from the "bottom up" as opposed from the "top down." In other words, historians have learned that we can discover fresh perspectives on events in the past by viewing them through the eyes of people and groups who may not seem significant to the casual observer. So, when we tell the story of American Christianity we focus not only on those individuals and groups we deem important by their popularity or social standing. We address the concerns of people and groups who may seem marginal at first.

While this had led to fresh original thinking, the danger comes if we think we can tell the entire story only through those individuals and groups. For example, we cannot fully tell the story of Christian involvement in the American Civil War only through the lives of individual enlisted soldiers, as important as their stories are. Our historical narrative would be woefully incomplete without significant attention to Abraham Lincoln, Jefferson Davis, Ulysses Grant, Thomas "Stonewall" Jackson, and others.

This work takes advantage of both perspectives by viewing the important twentieth century American Protestant debates over Holy Scripture through the lives of significant individuals within a Christian denomination that at first glance appears marginal. Moreover, writing in this denominational context is even more challenging given that Advent Christian denominational polity is fiercely congregational, making it even more difficult to say that certain individuals can speak with any sense of authority in this denominational framework. But that is where this study is of greatest value. It is easier in denominations and organizations with a more connectional polity to identify the major actors, both in terms of individuals and agencies. It is not so easy in organizations and movements where authority is not structural but implied, where people are free to recognize their leaders (or not), and where those called to leadership must demonstrate that calling not through structural appointment but through sustained action and relationship. Often times, personal relationship becomes the key deciding factor in conflicts within the congregation or association. This writer believes that congregational life in the twenty-first century will become less connectional and more associational, hence this study sheds important perspective regarding how doctrinal and theological disagreements are handled in these associations.

In the pages that follow, we will describe the Advent Christian conflict over the Bible's inspiration and authority. To do this, we will explore the historical and theological roots of Adventism and the Advent Christian Church, and discuss ways that they impacted the controversy that emerged within the small denomination during the 1950s and early 1960s. We will address the mechanics of the conflict itself, measuring its impact on the Advent Christian Church and observing the lessons that all Christians and Advent Christians today can learn.

CHAPTER ONE

Restorationists, Modernists, and Adventists

THE ROOTS OF THE Advent Christian conflict over the inspiration of Holy Scripture lie in two important areas: the unique theological foundations of Adventism as one of several powerful restorationist movements that swept through the United States between 1790 and 1850, and the colli- sion between evangelical orthodoxy and the modernist impulse that be- gan with Charles Darwin's *On the Origin of Species* in 1859 and reached its crescendo with the fundamentalist-modernist controversies of the early twentieth century. The early foundations of Adventism were anti-modern and restorationist. William Miller and his early followers had one essential desire: to overturn the postmillennial consensus that dominated much of early NINETEENth century American evangelicalism and replace it with a premillennial belief in the almost immediate return of Jesus Christ. The United States, in the view of Miller and the early Adventists, was not the vehicle that God would use to usher in his millennial kingdom. No human being or nation, according to Miller and his followers, could accomplish that. Instead, in their view, the Bible clearly taught that Jesus Christ would return to earth suddenly, visibly, and personally before the inauguration of the millennium.[1]

---

1. In Rev 20:1–6, John the Elder speaks of a one-thousand-year period of time dur- ing which Satan is bound in captivity and Christ reigns. Throughout church history, Christian theologians have offered several interpretations of this passage. The dominant interpretation among American Christians during the early nineteenth century was

1

The Restorationist Impulse
in Early American Christianity

The American War of Independence ushered in a half-century of democratic revolution (1790–1840) that altered the shape of major institutions and the lives of people in the young nation. With independence from Great Britain came widespread rejection of the British cultural notions of class, culture, and hierarchy in favor of a growing egalitarianism that allowed common people to independently forge their identities and destinies. Nowhere was this democratic impulse felt more profoundly than in the churches of the early American republic.

In England, as in other European nations, church and government were fused in ways that tied both to the preservation of political and cultural heritage. While the fusion of church and state meant that clergy of the established church were socially and culturally part of the ruling class, it also meant that individuals and congregations who dissented from the theological and doctrinal positions of the state church were in many cases denied civil liberties and even persecuted for their convictions. During the two centuries before the American Revolution, England (and much of Europe) had been rocked by one religious controversy after another. Because the British colonies in North America had become home to thousands of men and women from a variety of denominations and traditions fleeing religious tyranny, those who inhabited the colonies were forced to wrestle with how to live peaceably together despite their different convictions.

After independence from Great Britain had been won, American politicians such as Thomas Jefferson and James Madison argued that the only way to guarantee religious freedom and avoid the type of bloodshed that had plagued Europe was to separate the functions of church and state. All citizens should be allowed to worship God according to the dictates of their

---

postmillennialism, the view that through the influence of Christian faith and ideals, humanity would progress and the millennium would be ushered in before the return of Christ.

Miller and his Adventist followers articulated *premillennialism*, the notion that Christ must return to earth visibly and personally before the millennium. In Miller's view, at the return of Christ, "the dead saints or bodies will arise, those children of God who are alive then, will be changed, and caught up to meet the Lord in the air, where they will be married to him. The World and all the wicked will be burnt up . . . and then Christ will descend and reign personally with his Saints; and at the end of the 1000 Years the wicked will be raised, judged and sent to everlasting punishment." Miller quoted by Knight *Millennial Fever*, 17.

conscience. The federal government should not favor one Christian church or communion over another and moreover should not adjudicate church disputes nor support monetarily or otherwise the work of the church.[2]

The impact of this new approach to the relationship between church and state was immediate and dramatic. Christianity in its American context began to move away from centralized ecclesiastical structures and comfortable associations with high culture. In the aftermath of the Revolution, the European state churches that enjoyed the privileges of establishment in their home countries now struggled to compete both with each other and with a host of new Christian movements indigenous to American soil. Anglicans, Presbyterians, Lutherans, and Roman Catholics in the new United States found themselves forced to adjust to a new situation where they could no longer depend upon privileged status. Americans who found themselves dissatisfied with their present religious traditions were free to join another or to start their own.

That is what many chose to do. American Christianity was now wrapped up in the democratic convulsions that swept the new nation from 1790 to 1840. During this period, common people began to play significant roles in American religious life.[3] While Congregationalists, Presbyterians, and Anglicans found themselves struggling to maintain their once dominant roles, people outside the upper classes of American life like Francis Asbury, Elias Smith, Barton Stone, Alexander Campbell, Joseph Smith, and William Miller were establishing new religious movements (or, in the case of Asbury, Americanizing an eighteenth-century British movement) independent of established elites and in tune with the currents of American democracy. These new leaders derived their authority not from education, status within society, or state support but from their ability to persuade people and retain their confidence.

At the heart of these popular expressions of Christianity stood a desire to bypass the received traditions of European church history in an effort

2. For a description of the Jefferson/Madison notion of the separation of church and state and how it came to be expressed in the United States Constitution, see Gaustad, *Neither King Nor Prelate*, 36–58.

3. Hatch, *Democratization*, 3–16. Hatch argues that to properly understand Christianity in the United States, one must grasp the impact of how revolutionary the years 1790–1840 were in American life, thought, and culture. Religious freedom as expressed in the separation of church and state combined with a democratic impulse toward egalitarianism led to "an unexpected and often explosive conjunction of evangelical fervor and popular sovereignty."

to recover or "restore" the purity of New Testament church life. While each of these movements expressed a distinctive theological tone, they gave common expression to what is best termed the "restorationist impulse" within American Christianity.[4] Most of these indigenous American denominations shared several important restorationist tendencies. First, they believed that after the apostolic age, a massive falling away from true Christianity had taken place and that the church had become hopelessly corrupt. Even the Protestant Reformation had not brought full and true reform.[5] Second, recovery of first-century biblical Christianity would mean the outright rejection of all creeds and traditions. While some restorationist movements, most notably the Mormons, argued that God had revealed new scripture in the American context, for others, "No creed but the Bible," was the operative watchword for the formulation of doctrine and theology.[6]

On the surface, this catchy phrase appears to be a crude, but accurate way of expressing the Reformation notion of *sola scriptura*. However, restorationists like Campbell, Elias Smith, and Miller had something much different in mind. Interpretation of Scripture was not to be left to theologians or to clergy with academic degrees. For restorationists, the Bible was seen as a "self-interpreting" book and common people had an obligation to interpret the Bible for themselves using the principles of reason and common sense.[7] Moreover, the ultimate authority in all matters of religious belief and practice was not found in traditions, creeds, or hierarchical church structures but in the private interpretation and judgments of the individual Christian. In the restorationist vision, interpreting the Bible was a democratic task and the individual was the final authority both in church and society.[8]

4. For descriptions of Restorationism, see Hatch, *Democratization*, 17–46; 167–70; and Gaustad *Neither King nor Prelate*, 98; 119–33.

5. Hatch, *Democratization*, 167.

6. Ibid., 179–83. See also, Knight, *Millennial Fever*, 38–40.

7. Restorationism cut across the lines that divided Evangelicals and Unitarians at the turn of the nineteenth century. Thomas Jefferson argued that religion must return to the "plain and unsophisticated precepts of Christ" and sought to use the interpretive principles of enlightenment rationalism to achieve that end. See, Gaustad *Neither King nor Prelate*, 97–107.

8. The importance of how restorationists understand the task of interpreting Holy Scripture is a neglected issue in discussions surrounding the Bible's inspiration, authority, and inerrancy. There is a fundamental tension between the historic Protestant understanding of *sola scriptura* and the restorationist notion that private interpretation of Scripture is the final authority for all matters of faith and practice.

Finally, the majority of restorationist movements practiced a democratic form of congregationalism.[9] Local churches conducted their business by democratic means and were to be independent of any outside ecclesiastical control. Pastors served at the pleasure of the congregation and any associations with organizations or agencies outside of the congregation were to be strictly voluntary. Pastors led by the force of their personalities and by their ability to move and persuade their congregants.[10]

The Restorationist Vision of William Miller

Between 1790 and 1845, the first generation of restorationist Christianity rolled in several waves across the American landscape. Under the direction of Francis Asbury, Methodist circuit riders extended the Wesleyan expression of Christian faith into the western reaches of the new republic. Elias Smith, Alexander Campbell, and Barton Stone challenged the Calvinist orthodoxy of the Presbyterian and Congregational churches and sought to be known simply as "Christians" with no denominational ties. The Baptist John Leland reacted passionately against those within his communion who desired respectability. African-American Baptists and Methodists articulated a distinctive Christianity that addressed their unique cultural position as slaves and second-class citizens in a nation whose constitution guaranteed freedom and equality. Joseph Smith, an impoverished preacher and visionary from upstate New York, developed a unique spirituality that saw America as the final piece of God's redemptive purpose and plan.[11]

These movements represent the earliest (and probably the most powerful) wave of Restorationism in American church history. In the late nineteenth and early twentieth centuries, a new generation of movements with restorationist overtones would emerge in Dispensationalism and Pentecostalism, both of which would have a large impact on twentieth-century evangelicalism.[12] An important bridge between these two generations of

9. Notable exceptions were the Methodists and the Mormons.

10. For an example, see Knight, *Millennial Fever*, 68. The author points to the Christian Connexion, a restorationist sect that developed in New York and New England after the turn of the nineteenth century. "The movement emphasized Christian freedom by avoiding all church organization above the congregational level."

11. For a description of each of these restorationist movements, see Hatch, *Democratization*, 67–122.

12. For a description of dispensationalism, see Marsden, *Fundamentalism and American Culture* 48–71. This author's contention is that in their early configurations,

Restorationism lies in an early to mid-nineteenth-century movement start-ed by a self-educated farmer from the small upstate New York town of Low Hampton. William Miller grew up in an obscure, poverty-stricken family and had limited opportunity for formal education. Lack of educational op-portunity did not quash his intellectual curiosity and his love for reading. After marrying Lucy Smith and moving to Poultney, Vermont, (where his wife's family lived) in 1803, Miller immersed himself in books and in the philosophical literature of Voltaire, David Hume, and Thomas Paine. The influence of these writers combined with that of the educated men he met in Poultney led him to embrace deism as opposed to orthodox Christianity.[13]

After serving as a U.S. Army captain in the War of 1812, Miller reached a point of spiritual crisis that culminated on September 16, 1816.[14] "Jesus Christ became to me," in Miller's words, "the chiefest among ten thousand, and the Scriptures, which before were dark and contradictory, now became a lamp to my feet and a light to my path."[15] Miller's words point to the importance of understanding his spiritual crisis and subsequent conversion in its intellectual and philosophical as well as its emotional and spiritual contexts. For Miller, faith in Jesus Christ meant conversion from the tenets of deism to the embrace of Scripture as the true revelation of God.[16]

Unlike many of his earlier restorationist counterparts, Miller's tem-perament was reserved and rational, not demonstrative and emotional. Soon after Miller's conversion, a friend challenged his belief in the truthful-ness of the Bible. "I replied," Miller wrote, "that if the Bible was the Word of God, everything contained therein might be understood, and all its parts made to harmonize; and I said to him that if he would give me time, I

---

both Dispensationalism and Pentecostalism shared the essential characteristics of Resto-rationism: the need to recover the Christian faith and practice of New Testament times, a deep suspicion of academic theology, the notion of "no creed but the Bible," and a democratic congregational approach to church governance.

13. Dean, "Echoes," 12. In Dean's words, "Miller's inclination towards scepticism led him to deism rather than toward atheism or agnosticism . . . Deism ruthlessly criticized the Bible for its irrational miracles, unreliable prophecies, and unbelievable complication of universally obvious truth; in its place deism offered simple faith in the goodness of man, rational morality, and recognition of a First-Cause of all things."

14. For a description of Miller's conversion experience, see Knight, *Millennial Fever*, 32–35; and Hewitt, *Midnight and Morning*, 15–18.

15. Miller quoted by Knight, *Millennial Fever*, 34.

16. Dean, "Echoes," 23. On pp. 10–95, Dean offers a survey of Miller's intellectual and theological development from his conversion in 1816 to his death in 1849, especially in terms of Miller's understanding of Scripture and his hermeneutical methodology.

would harmonize all these apparent contradictions, to my own satisfaction, or I would be a deist still."[17] That challenge led Miller to a two-year verse-by-verse intensive study of the Bible, a study aided only by his *Cruden's Concordance.*

Miller came away from that study convinced that the Bible was the written Word of God and that it contained a system of truth that was clear and comprehendible to anyone willing to undertake serious study. He came away convinced of something else that would dramatically impact Christianity in the United States during the first half of the nineteenth century. As Miller worked to harmonize the teaching of the Bible, his study of Old Testament prophecies, especially the book of Daniel had convinced him that Jesus Christ would return visibly and personally to earth on or about the year 1843.[18] Miller realized that this radical conclusion was out of step with the postmillennialism that permeated much of American Christianity during his time. While by 1823 he was convinced that his conclusion about Christ's return was biblically sound, Miller did little to propagate his views except to speak with friends and neighbors, and pray that God would raise up one or more clergymen who would reach the same conclusions and communicate them through the pulpit.[19] Miller's reluctance to personally propagate the results of his study began to change in the early 1830s with his first pulpit lectures and with the publication of his views in the *Vermont Telegraph,* a Baptist newspaper. As Miller's message gained popularity and followers during the 1830s and early 1840s, Adventism began to emerge as a distinct movement within American Christianity.[20]

The character and tone of this emerging Adventism was distinctively restorationist. As the movement grew, William Miller was convinced that God had called him and his followers to restore the true New Testament teaching of the second coming of Jesus Christ to the church. Moreover,

17. Miller quoted by Dean, "Echoes," 23. Dean comments on what he sees as a shift in Miller's understanding of Scripture. While at the time of his conversion, Miller had grounded the validation of Scripture in the authority of God, now he would attempt, in Dean's words, "to undertake some rational proof which will satisfy the demands of his own intellect for demonstration that the Bible can be trusted."

18. Knight, *Millennial Fever,* 36. Dean presents a detailed exposition of Miller's argumentation for the 1843 date. See Dean, "Echoes," 76–87.

19. Knight comments, "Apparently his fear of rejection by people outweighed his fear of God. For another eight years (1823–1831) the reluctant prophet continued to resist what he believed to be the unction of the Holy Spirit." See Knight, *Millennial Fever,* 43.

20. The story of the Adventist movement is well told in several books most notably, Knight, *Millennial Fever;* Hewitt, *Midnight and Morning;* and Nichol, *The Midnight Cry.*

Miller's understanding of Christian faith and his usage of Scripture were replete with restorationist overtones. As his rules for interpreting the Bible demonstrate, Miller was deeply suspicious of traditions and creeds and strongly believed that the Bible was a self-interpreting book that could be understood by all Christians who approached the Scriptures with sacrificial faith.[21] Even after the 1844 Great Disappointment, Miller and other Adventist leaders were reluctant to form any organization, even a voluntary one, because of their strong commitment to the autonomy of individuals and congregations.[22]

The restorationist impulse had a powerful impact on Christian faith and practice in the new United States. William Miller and his fellow Adventists shared the assumptions articulated in one form or another by the various restorationist movements of the first half of the nineteenth century. However, Adventism was different from other restorationist groups in three important ways. First, unlike Methodists, Mormons, and the various Christian associations that established separate organizations, many if not most Adventists (at least until October 1844) desired to reform the established churches through the restoration of what they believed was the scriptural doctrine of Christ's return. Second, Adventism was the first major premillennial movement in American Christianity. While the dispensational-premillennialism of John Nelson Darby would become popular among evangelical Christians in the aftermath of the Civil War, Adventism represented the first major assault against the postmillennial consensus that guided much of pre-Civil War American Christianity. Third, unlike the other restorationist movements, Adventism was forced to confront failure. Jesus Christ did not return in either 1843 or 1844. Adventists became subject to ridicule within the churches and scorn in the larger society. Adventist leaders scrambled to make biblical and theological sense of what had failed to happen.

21. See Appendix One for William Miller's fourteen rules of interpretation with attention to rules three, four, five, and fourteen.

22. For a brief sketch of the October 22, 1844 Great Disappointment, see Dean. "Great Disappointment," 6. Before October 1844, William Miller and other Adventists declared on numerous occasions their desire not to establish a new denomination. Even after the events of October 1844, Adventists organized local congregations only after individual Adventists were excommunicated by their churches. Associational and denominational organizations would not be established until the late 1850s and early 1860s.

The Advent of Modernism
in American Christianity

After 1845, Adventism essentially went into exile. As early as July 1843, Charles Fitch, a Presbyterian who had joined Miller three years earlier, urged Adventists to, in his words, "come out of Babylon." While most Millerites understood this as referring to the Roman Catholic Church and its papacy, Fitch extended its meaning to include the established Protestant churches who opposed the Adventist understanding of Christ's return.[23] In the aftermath of the Great Disappointment, as their excommunication from Protestant congregations grew and continued, Adventists began to view the established Protestant denominations as essentially apostate. From that point on, Adventism was for the most part isolated from the rest of American Christianity for the balance of the nineteenth century. Adventism would fracture into several associations, each with its unique understanding of the meaning of the Great Disappointment.[24]

While Adventists struggled from 1845 on to establish their identity, from 1860 on, the mainstream of American Christianity would enter a period of extended crisis that would ultimately fracture it into two opposing and contentious parties. Charles Darwin's *On the Origin of Species*, published in 1859, has been called the most significant book of the nineteenth century for a variety of reasons. Its implications went far beyond biological science and in George Marsden's words, "sparked an intellectual crisis for Christians that no educated person could ignore."[25] Darwin's theory of natural selection challenged for many the Genesis account of creation and seemed to deny God's providential design in creation.[26] Earlier in the century, scientists had reconciled Genesis with the "old-earth" findings of nineteenth-century geology. But the successive attempts to harmonize Darwin's findings with the Genesis account would at best meet with only limited success.

The reason for this was that Darwin's work represented only one aspect of a dramatic intellectual shift that began to build in the second half of the nineteenth century. In Germany, historical studies had undergone

23. Knight, *Millennial Fever*, 153–56.

24. Ibid., 245–325. Knight describes the different ways that Adventists attempted to understand the Great Disappointment and how the different Adventist denominations organized.

25. Marsden, *Understanding Fundamentalism*, 12–13.

26. Longfield, *Presbyterian Controversy*, 12.

dramatic change. Grounded in an idealism which suggested that God could be best seen within the processes of history, the new historical consciousness, to use Marsden's words, "shifted the emphasis in human thought from the perennial quest for timeless truths to explaining how human belief changes and progresses."[27] The study of history was no longer a search for fixed historical truth, but the use of scientifically critical historical methods to determine "what actually was."[28]

Historicism was being applied to biblical studies by Julius Wellhausen, David Friedrich Strauss, and others. Through their application of literary analysis, comparative linguistics, and archeology, the German critics questioned the Mosaic authorship of the Pentateuch, the historical reliability of Job, the dating of Daniel, and the authenticity of significant portions of the Gospel narratives. By the late 1800s, theologians at Union Theological Seminary (New York), the University of Chicago, Harvard, and other important theological institutions were rapidly adopting the methods and views of the emerging higher criticism. As a result, "a nascent theological movement, billed as the New Theology was making a serious bid for the hearts and minds of American Christians."[29] For a growing number of academics, biblical scholars, and pastors, the Christian faith had to be reconciled with what they considered the indisputable results of biblical criticism and evolutionary thought.

The rise of historical-critical studies fostered another important theological development—the advent of the study of comparative religion. The Christian faith would no longer be seen as superior to all other religions, but simply one of many equally valid religious expressions. This was no doubt the spirit behind the 1893 World's Parliament of Religions held in Chicago.

These and other intellectual developments contributed to a sense among American evangelicals in the late 1800s that the Christian way of life they believed and propagated was under attack. Notions of absolute truth were questioned. Traditional moral and social standards were challenged. The Bible was seen not as a special revelation of God, but as a cultural product just like any other book.[30]

---

27. Marsden, *Soul of the American University*, 20–67.

28. For discussion, see ibid., 25n17. This phrase is a translation of the words of German historian Ranke, "wie es eignetlich gewesen."

29. Longfield, *Presbyterian Controversy*, 19.

30. Marsden, *Soul of the American University*, 207.

The unease felt by American evangelicals was compounded by the experience of rapid and dramatic social change within the United States during the last third of the nineteenth century. The physical and economic devastation of the Civil War (1861–65) caused many to question the post-millennial optimism that was part of America's Puritan and older evangelical heritage. By the dawn of the twentieth century, westward expansion was virtually complete.[31] Technological advance led to industrialization and dramatic improvement in transportation and communications. As the factory grew in economic importance, jobs began to move from the countryside to the city. The United States was becoming more urbanized and more diverse socially and ethnically.[32] While African-Americans continued to face the legacy of slavery and the reality of bigotry and prejudice, immigration from abroad exploded. Fourteen million European immigrants, many from the Roman Catholic regions of Ireland, Eastern Europe, and Southern Europe, came to the United States between 1860 and 1900. By the turn of the century, immigrants and their children made up one-third of the U.S. population.[33] Protestant Americans (and Adventists) watched as the Roman Catholic Church grew dramatically.

Industrialization not only fueled urbanization and immigration, but led to a dramatic increase in wealth and materialism on the one hand and poverty on the other. Large corporations grew to dominate their industries and make their owners wealthy men, while many laborers (including women and children) toiled sixty hours each week and earned only a few hundred dollars per year.[34]

The dramatic change in economic life meant an expanded role for American education. After the Civil War, American higher education was affected by a series of changes including importation of the German university model, the expansion of professionalism and specialization, and new ways of funding colleges and universities that embraced government and philanthropic support.[35] While as late as 1850, most American colleges

31. For a valuable discussion of how the American understanding of land and property influenced westward expansion and continues to influence the worldview of European-Americans, see Dyrness, *How Does America,* 29–59.

32. Longfield, *Presbyterian Controversy,* 15. By 1900, city dwellers made up forty percent of the population. By 1920, that figure passed 50 percent.

33. Ibid., 16.

34. Ibid., 14.

35. Ibid., 16–17.

had been church-related, by the end of the century the study of religion and theology was no longer at the heart of academic life.

What was happening at American colleges reflected the growing secularization of late-nineteenth- and early-twentieth-century American life. Protestant Christians during this time faced a world very different from that of their grandparents, and their responses to the intellectual and social challenges of this time would not be unified. The evangelical consensus that had shaped much of American Christianity since the early 1700s would finally be broken. While the restorationist impulse of the first half of the nineteenth century had shattered any hope for organizational cohesion within American Christianity, the emerging modernist impulse would fracture its doctrinal and theological unity regarding the essentials of Christian faith.

As secular tendencies and understandings began to make significant impact on American intellectual and social life, a number of Christians, especially influential pastors and college teachers, began to suggest that Christian theology must be brought into harmony with the new understandings of scientific and historical method. By the early twentieth century, what William Hutchison has termed "the Modernist Impulse" within American Protestant Christianity would reach full flower as a powerful force.[36]

In Hutchison's view, three principles were the focal point of the Modernist impulse:

1. "[T]he conscious intended adaptation of religious ideas to modern culture."

2. "[T]he idea that God was immanent in human cultural development and revealed through it."

3. "[T]he belief that human society is moving toward the realization (even though it may never attain the reality) of the Kingdom of God."[37]

The Modernist impulse built on the postmillennial understanding of Christian history that had been part of American evangelicalism since the time of Jonathan Edwards. From Edwards to Charles Finney,

36. Hutchison, *Modernist Impulse*. Hutchison traces the history and growth of this theological movement within American Protestant Christianity.

37. Ibid., 2.

the postmillennial notion that the Holy Spirit would use the preaching and teaching of the gospel to shape a new world marked by righteousness, peace, and prosperity that would lead to the return of Jesus Christ, provided the dominant eschatological motif. Unlike their evangelical postmillennial predecessors, this growing group of modernist Christian thinkers viewed the millennial kingdom as arriving through God's presence in and activity through the great forward movements of humanity.[38] Human culture and activity are not alien to the Christian faith. God's work is not found outside of human activity, but within it. Moreover, his purposes and plans are revealed in human historical and scientific progress.

Advent Christian Organizational and Theological Direction

By the time Darwin's original work on evolution appeared, the theological fracture within the Adventist movement was essentially complete. In the aftermath of the Great Disappointment, the fundamental theological issue within the Adventist movement focused on how to interpret (or reinterpret) the meaning of what for all intensive purposes looked like a failed prophecy. With the death of William Miller in 1849, that struggle became all the more acute. In the aftermath of Miller's death, Adventism had fractured into two broad coalitions.[39]

The first (sometimes called the "moderate") faction argued that William Miller had the right event but the wrong time. In other words, Miller's message that the visible, premillennial return of Jesus Christ would soon occur was essentially correct. The fact that Christ did not return to earth by October 22, 1844, meant that there were obviously aspects of the Bible's message about the return of Christ that Adventism had failed to fully grasp. Therefore the Adventist task was twofold: further study of the Bible and continued proclamation of the need for people to prepare for the second coming of Christ.

38. Ibid., 6.

39. Knight, *Millennial Fever*, 217–325. According to Knight, by the end of 1845, "two separate strands of Adventism had developed, and there was no middle ground between them" (239). But within each strand, there were a variety of theological and doctrinal nuances and positions. The restorationist notion that theological authority rested with the people, not with clergy or movement leaders was practiced widely among Adventists in the aftermath of the Great Disappointment and plays an important role in the further fragmentation of the movement.

The second (or "Sabbatarian") faction took a different course and argued that Miller had the right date but the wrong event. The event foretold in Daniel 8:14[40] was not the return of Jesus Christ, but the beginning of a second phase of Christ's ministry in the heavenly realm.[41] In that context came a new program of Adventist ministry, the recovery of Sabbatarianism as the sign of God's faithful remnant people. Influenced by Joseph Bates, and James and Ellen White this faction organized into what is now Seventh-day Adventism. These three individuals gave this Adventist faction an especially strong organizational and theological cohesion, to the point that when the Seventh-day Adventists formally organized, they became the only Adventist denomination not to practice a purely congregational form of church polity.

While Seventh-day Adventism has a fascinating theological and social history,[42] after the 1850s there was minimal contact between it and the denominations that emerged out of the first Adventist faction described above. In addition, while Seventh-day Adventism developed a strong theological and organizational cohesion, the "moderate" faction was fraught with several theological voices and controversies, the most serious being a dispute over the doctrine of conditional immortality.[43] This theological belief was pioneered among Adventists by George Storrs, a former Methodist who had joined the Adventist movement in 1842. Even though this doctrine was opposed by William Miller and other Adventist leaders, Storrs propagation of conditional immortality had wide influence within the movement, even before the Great Disappointment of October 1844.[44]

---

40. This passage reads "He said to me, 'It will take 2,300 evenings and mornings; then the sanctuary will be reconsecrated'" (NIV).

41. For a concise description of this theme and the development of what would become the theological position of the Seventh-day Adventist Church, see Knight, *Millennial Fever*, 304–19.

42. For a survey of that history, see Land, ed. *Adventism in America*.

43. A brief description of this doctrinal belief is found in the first footnote of the introduction. For a contemporary defense of the doctrine of conditional immortality, see Fudge, *Fire That Consumes*. For an account of this doctrine's roots in the thought of several of the early church fathers, see Banks, "Rise and Growth," 74; and McGrath, ed. *Christian Theology Reader*, 355.

44. Dean, "Echoes," 111–13; Knight, *Millennial Fever*, 19–49. The only senior Adventist leader to accept belief in conditional immortality before October 1844 was Charles Fitch. (Fitch would die after baptizing a number of new converts in frigid Lake Ontario waters just days before the Great Disappointment.) The initial depth of opposition to this doctrine among the upper echelon of Millerite leaders was reflected in an Adventist

The acceptance of the conditionalist doctrine among the "moderate" faction demonstrated the power of the restorationist impulse within this branch of Adventism. The leadership of the movement and the editorial position of its leading publication, the *Advent Herald*, remained firmly committed to the more traditional view that the human soul was naturally immortal and that the destiny of the wicked (those without Christ) was conscious eternal punishment for their sin.[45] Among rank and file Adventists however, the conditionalist position continued to gain strength during the late 1840s and early 1850s to the point where by 1856, it was the position held by a strong majority of moderate Adventist clergy and laity. The formation of doctrine and theology was seen not as the providence of an elite leadership, but part of a democratic process where the opinions and beliefs of ordinary Christians could play a determinative role. With the refusal of the *Advent Herald*, the publication with the closest ties to the elite within moderate Adventism, to allow for publication of conditionalist views on their pages, the moderate faction would become further fragmented.

Because publications played a vital role in Adventism, it was common for Adventist believers to identify themselves by their loyalty to a given publication. Thus, to be a *Herald* Adventist was to identify with the theological position of that weekly publication. In 1858, the "Herald Adventists" organized the American Evangelical Adventist Conference, the first "denomination" to organize out of the moderate faction.

With the transfer of the Advent Herald to the new organization, that publication became even more forceful in its antagonism toward the conditionalist position. In response, the bulk of moderate Adventists with conditionalist leanings gravitated toward an Adventist publication established in 1854, the *World's Crisis*.[46] Thus, by 1858 the *Crisis* Adventists would be the largest moderate Adventist faction, and in 1860 they would organize the Advent Christian Association.[47]

---

publication established by Josiah Litch simply titled, *The Anti-Annihilationist*.

45. Banks, "Rise and Growth," 88–89; Dean, "Echoes," 115–17.

46. Dean, "Echoes," 12–26. The *World's Crisis* initially organized to propagate a new "definite time" movement among Adventists. A small band of Adventists that included Miles Grant had begun to advocate 1854 as the year of Christ's return. After the failure of this movement, the publication increasingly became the primary conditionalist publication within Adventism's moderate wing.

47. Dean, "Echoes," 127. Organization did not come without a great deal of struggle. As Dean writes, "Among the Conditionalist Adventists strong opposition to the formation of a denomination was expressed in two forms. Some . . . were opposed to any and all

From 1860 through the end of the nineteenth century, Advent Christians wrestled with how to define themselves both organizationally and theologically. Because most of the Adventist elite had identified with the American Evangelical Adventist Conference,[48] and because of the powerful anti-denominational sentiment among many of the people and congregations that identified with the conditionalist Adventists, the Advent Christian Association experienced a host of organizational and theological difficulties. During the first decade of its existence, three important doctrinal developments occurred. First, after his appointment as editor of the *World's Crisis* in 1861, Rufus Wendell began to advocate the rather unpopular belief that those who died without knowledge of Jesus Christ as Savior and Lord would not be resurrected at the return of Christ, but would simply cease to exist at the time of their physical death. Advocates of this view would establish their own denomination, the Life and Advent Union, in 1863.[49]

Second, Advent Christians gravitated away from premillennialism toward an amillennial understanding of biblical eschatology. For the non-resurrectionist Life and Adventists, the notion of a one-thousand reign of Christ that concluded with a universal judgment that included both the righteous and the wicked demanded reinterpretation. While Advent Christians on the whole rejected the non-resurrectionist arguments, many were receptive to the symbolic interpretation of Revelation 20 that the Life and Adventists offered.[50]

Not only had many Advent Christians shifted their understanding of the millennium, many were wrestling with precisely how to understand

organization. But, most of the opposition came in the form of those who withstood the adoption of an extra-biblical name for any believer, church, or association of believers."

48. A notable exception is Joshua Himes. While Himes originally opposed the conditionalist Adventists and participated in the organization of the American Evangelical Adventist Conference, he shifted his theological position on this issue and by 1864 had identified himself with the Advent Christian Association. Ironically, after a series of conflicts with *World's Crisis* editor Miles Grant, Himes returned to his Episcopal roots and later associated with Seventh-day Adventism.

49. For a concise summary of the issues involved and the formation of the Life and Advent Union, see Banks, "Rise and Growth," 95–100; and Dean, "Echoes," 13–58. The Life and Advent Union rejoined the Advent Christian General Conference in 1964.

50. In the words of Dwight Banks, "It is an entirely unexplainable paradox that the group whose view was so vigorously rejected by the denomination as a whole, should nevertheless, succeed in changing the entire doctrinal trend of the body" toward amillennialism. See, Banks, "Rise and Growth," 99. It should be noted that premillennialism has never disappeared within the Advent Christian Church and that there continues to be a strong historic premillennial faction within the denomination today.

the person of Jesus Christ. While William Miller and the first generation of Adventist leadership had been unabashedly Trinitarian,[51] as a result of the desire to follow "no creed but the Bible," there developed among Advent Christians a hesitancy to embrace language not explicitly used in the Bible itself. That, combined with their suspicion of academic theology and their isolation from the mainstream of Protestant Christianity, led many Advent Christians to question both the word "Trinity" as applied to God and the Trinitarian idea of one God eternally existent in three persons—Father, Son, and Holy Spirit.[52] By the end of the nineteenth century, there were essentially four viewpoints expressed among Advent Christians: the traditional Trinitarian view; a Christian monotheist view that held to both the deity of Christ and the personality of the Holy Spirit but hesitated to use the term "Trinitarian" to describe that belief; a Christian monotheist view that held to the deity of Christ but to the non-personality of the Holy Spirit; and an Arian view that advocated the non-preexistence of Christ.[53]

These theological struggles were difficult for early Advent Christians to deal with because of an interesting paradox that had been present within the denomination since its founding. Unlike the Seventh-day Adventists, who defined themselves primarily through a distinct social identity, Advent Christians in the later nineteenth and early twentieth century saw their distinctiveness not so much in social or cultural contexts but in doctrinal terms. Identity for Advent Christians has traditionally been measured in terms of belief in a distinctive group of doctrines relating to individual and general eschatology. Paradoxically, Advent Christians have throughout their history maintained a non-creedal stance toward defining Christian doctrine.[54] This orientation toward doctrinal definition has meant that

51. *Brief History of William Miller*, 90. See also, Banks, "Rise and Growth," 33. In Miller's words, "I believe in one living and true God, and that there are three persons to the Godhead—as there is in man, the body, soul, and spirit. And if any one will tell me how these exist, I will tell him how the three persons of the Triune God are connected."

52. At this point, the restorationist impulse is again active among Advent Christians. One fascinating area of historical study that deserves more attention than it has received is the early tendency of churches affiliated with restorationist movements to struggle with Trinitarianism.

53. Banks, "Rise and Growth," 100–101, 133.

54. Dean, *Resurrection Hope*, 10–12. "One of the most precious privileges possessed by Advent Christians is that of freedom of conscience to study and follow the teachings of Scripture . . . While strict doctrinal standards have been set for those in the ministry and teaching positions, Advent Christians have granted to one another the freedom and responsibility of believing, studying, and following the Scriptures."

while Advent Christians have defined their distinctiveness in terms of specific doctrines, at the same time they have allowed for a wide range of belief on issues like those just discussed.

While nineteenth-century Advent Christians struggled with several issues of doctrinal and theological identity, they were strongly united on several others. Perhaps the most important was their view of Holy Scripture. In their view, Adventism had been built upon the belief that the Bible was the written Word of God. While they had departed from Miller in several ways theologically, they continued to share his passion for seeing the Bible as the sole authority for all Christian doctrine. They also shared Miller's distrust of academic theology and church tradition, as well as his belief that the Bible could be interpreted by any common person willing to patiently explore its teaching. Because of their isolation from other Protestant churches and denominations, Advent Christians needed to justify their existence through a biblical defense of their distinctive doctrinal beliefs. That necessitated an understanding of the Bible as the written revelation of God.

The late-nineteenth- and early twentieth-century Advent Christian attitude toward the Bible is reflected in two doctrinal statements affirmed by delegates to Advent Christian General Conference meetings in 1881 and 1900.[55] The earlier of the two statements reflects a total unawareness of the brewing controversy between fundamentalist and modernist theologians and biblical scholars and treats the Bible in two ways. First, in Article One, the statement declares that Advent Christians "believe that the Scriptures, consisting of the Old and New Testament, contain the only divine system of religious faith." Then, twelve of the next fifteen doctrinal statements specifically use the phrase "we believe the Bible teaches" or a variation of it.[56] The 1881 statement focuses little attention on how the Bible is inspired and much attention on the role of the Bible in formulating Adventist belief.

Nineteen years later, a new Declaration of Principles would reflect a significant change in the way Advent Christians stated their belief in the Bible. "We believe," according to Article one of the new Declaration, "that

---

55. Advent Christians have been careful not to use the term "creed" to describe either the 1881 or the 1900 doctrinal statements. Instead they are referred to by the term "Declaration of Principles," with use of that term intended to mean that while Advent Christians affirm "no creed but the Bible," these statements represent the things most commonly believed by individuals and congregations associated with the Advent Christian General Conference.

56. For a listing of the 1881 Declaration of Principles, see Appendix Two. This appendix is from Banks, "Rise and Growth," 10–24.

the Bible is the Word of God containing a revelation given to man under Divine supervision and providence; that its historic statements are correct, and that it is the only Divine standard of faith and practice."[57] The emphasis on the function of the Bible within the life of the Advent Christian Church is replaced with an emphasis on the inspiration of Scripture. The Bible is the Word of God. At the same time, it is God's revelation mediated through human authors under divine guidance. When the Scriptures speak to events in human history, they are correct. They provide a standard for Christian faith and living both for individuals and for local congregations. It is clear from the 1900 Declaration of Principles that while Advent Christians theologically parted company from other Protestants in some important areas, they wanted to maintain a strong commitment to the Bible as the foundation for doctrine and theology.[58] Even though their understanding of how Scripture should be interpreted was restorationist, as opposed to reformationist, their understanding of how the Bible was inspired demonstrates at least some continuity with the broader scope of American evangelicalism in the nineteenth century.

The Impact of Miles Grant

Because Advent Christians wanted to distinctively define themselves in doctrinal terms, and because they allowed a wide divergence of opinion on most doctrinal matters, the task of articulating a distinct Advent Christian theological approach was a difficult one. The most significant and important attempt to do that during the first fifty years of Advent Christian history was undertaken by Miles Grant.[59] A Connecticut native, Grant entered the Adventist ministry in 1849 and served as editor of the *World's Crisis* for

---

57. For a copy of the 1900 Declaration of Principles in its original form, see Appendix Three. This appendix is taken from Banks "Rise and Growth," 108–13. Articles one and two of this Declaration were amended in 1964 and article eleven was added in 1972. With the exception of those changes, the 1900 Declaration of Principles continues to serve as the doctrinal statement of the Advent Christian General Conference.

58. The recent shift in the theological direction of the Worldwide Church of God from a heterodox to an orthodox Christian theology in terms of doctrines relating to God, Christ, and salvation demonstrates the importance of this principle. According to Ruth A. Tucker, the reason that the WCOG could make this shift, despite their previously flawed theological perspective was the group's commitment to the Bible as the sole authority for Christian faith and practice. See Tucker, "From the Fringe to the Fold," 26–32.

59. For a biography of Miles Grant, see Piper, *Life and Labor*.

twenty years (1856–1876; with a short absence during 1861–62). Because of his extensive travel, speaking, and writing, Grant was well-known and respected throughout the denomination. He felt a special call to articulate and defend Advent Christian theology.[60]

Grant's prolific writing ministry culminated in *Positive Theology*, his attempt at systematizing Advent Christian doctrine. For Grant, the Advent Christian doctrine of conditional immortality was the starting point for Christian theology.[61] Because of that, Grant's theology has an anthropological focus with a strong emphasis on human freedom.[62] Grant rejects any separation between body and soul in the human constitution. "No amount of immaterial properties, or attributes," according to Grant, "can make a material, personal entity . . . in man, mind and personality are co-extensive. They begin together, and the mental properties never extend, or exist, beyond the life of the physical constitution."[63] Grant's materialist anthropology was designed for apologetic purposes. By asserting that man's immaterial nature cannot exist independently of his material nature, Grant sought to defend the Advent Christian understanding that the intermediate state (the time between death and the return of Christ) is a period when the person is unconscious or "asleep."[64]

Grant was able to arrive at his materialistic view of human nature because of how he understands the role of Scripture. While Grant maintains a belief in the literal interpretation of the Scriptures, he treats the Bible as one of several equally reliable sources of truth. "The theology of the Bible," in Grant's words, "is perfectly harmonious with the eternal

---

60. Dean, "Echoes," 253.

61. Grant, *Positive Theology*, iii.

62. Dean, "Echoes," 270–71.

63. Grant, *Positive Theology*, 302. Dean writes that Grant "embraced a naive scientific materialism in the defense of Conditional Immortality. Man consists of an animated material body; there is no immaterial, or spiritual, substance. Vitality and mentality are only results of the functioning of physical organs, such as heart, lungs, and brain."

64. In that context, Advent Christians have had different understandings of the unconscious intermediate state. For an excellent discussion of the sixteenth-century roots of this doctrine, see Crouse, "Psychopannychism," 40–64. Crouse writes: "Psychopannychism needs some explanation and definitions because it took several forms during the sixteenth century and no single system of terminology has arisen. One form of the doctrine was the belief that the souls of the dead sleep during the intermediate state between earthly life and resurrection . . . Others believed that the soul cannot be separated from the body and think of it as the spark of life. Thus at death each person ceases to exist until God raises everyone at the resurrection."

principles of pure reason, metaphysics, common sense, and the facts of science."[65] In interpreting a passage of Scripture we must ask if our interpretation is "in harmony with the laws of rhetoric, logic, the facts of science, and common sense."[66]

Like many others in his generation, Grant's understanding of truth is shaped by the Scottish Common Sense school of philosophy, but with a different twist than that used by his orthodox Presbyterian Calvinist contemporaries who taught at Princeton Theological Seminary. "Common sense, aided by the Spirit of God, is the ultimate standard of truth and error, right and wrong,"[67] according to Grant. "Common Sense is the result of the normal action of our mental and moral faculties, which are made in the "likeness" of those in our creator. It may be said to be the voice of God in man."[68] As opposed to the Princeton theologians who based their theology on observation of the "facts" of the Bible, in Grant's method the "facts" were not limited to the Bible but covered the expanse of human knowledge.[69] Therefore, reason stands as a judge of the proper interpretation of Scripture.[70] If a particular interpretation of Scripture does not square with all known facts, then that interpretation must be called into question.

---

65. Grant, *Positive Theology*, iii.

66. Ibid., 44. Grant writes, "Before the meaning of a passage of Scripture is fully settled, the following questions should be asked:

　1. What saith the lexicon and grammar about the Scripture?

　2. Does the historical aspect demand any modification?

　3. Is it in harmony with the laws of rhetoric, logic, the facts of science, and common sense?

　4. What meaning best agrees with the context and the general teaching of the Bible?

　5. Is the passage an important part of Scripture?

　6. Is it superseded by any later revelation?

　7. Is it of local and temporary import; or general in its application?

　8. Is the interpretation confirmed by the general agreement of all the plain Scripture relating to the subject?"

67. Ibid., 53.

68. Ibid. Grant writes, "Holiness may be defined as 'sanctified common sense.'"

69. Ibid., 45. In Grant's words, "All intuitive and self-evident propositions must be admitted as facts."

70. Ibid., 49–51. Grant lists thirty-two "ultimate principles which must be assumed as the basis of all reasoning."

For many Advent Christians of the late nineteenth and early twentieth centuries, Grant's theology represented a powerful apologetic for a distinctive Advent Christian theology.[71] Throughout the first half of the twentieth century, *Positive Theology* was used to train Advent Christian pastors, especially the sizable number who did not have opportunity to study at Aurora College or at New England School of Theology.[72] However, Grant's theology included significant doctrinal deviations on important issues like the person of Christ and the nature of the Holy Spirit.[73] Even more significant, "the fact that he permitted other elements besides the Bible to control theological thought contributed to a denominational climate in which 'philosophical theology' threatened to replace 'biblical theology.'"[74]

Through the widespread popularity of Grant's theology, many Advent Christian pastors and laypeople were exposed to a theological method that saw Scripture as only one of several equal sources of revelation. While the Advent Christian doctrinal statements produced during the last twenty years of the nineteenth century featured a strong commitment to the Bible as the only source for Christian theology, in practice, Grant's methodology subtly undermined that commitment. While Grant could by no means be called a modernist, his willingness to see Scripture as only one of several sources of truth would be picked up by several key Advent Christian thinkers during the first half of the twentieth century. Ironically, though Miles Grant no doubt viewed the Scriptures as the written Word of God and maintained an early enlightenment understanding of science, his willingness to consider the Bible as one of several sources of revelation is similar to his late nineteenth-century liberal contemporaries who were attempting to address how Christianity should come to grips with the modernist impulse and its impact on the study of science and history.[75]

71. *Positive Theology* was endorsed by a significant number of Advent Christian leaders. See Banks, "Rise and Growth," 11–45.

72. Grant's theological approach was widely accepted by Advent Christians in the Midwest, in the South, and on the West Coast.

73. Grant was strongly Arminian and militantly non-Trinitarian. He rejected any notion of the Holy Spirit being personal.

74. Dean "Echoes," 262.

75. One of the key dividing points between fundamentalists and modernists was the role of Scripture as a source of revelation. Outside of his interpretive principles, Grant does not articulate a specific understanding of inspiration, but in common with those who followed the modernist impulse, Grant saw the Bible as one of several equal ways that God revealed himself. Moreover, Grant believed that any proper interpretation of Scripture must harmonize with common sense and known science.

The Advent Christian Church, born out of the restorationist impulse that dominated the Second Great Awakening and out of the profound tragedy of Millerism, stood on the edge of twentieth century isolated not only from its Adventist denominational cousins, but from most of Protestant Christianity. While Advent Christians struggled to maintain a biblically based theology, the dominance of Miles Grant had tilted the fledgling denomination toward a dangerously rationalistic path. In the chapters that follow, we will explore how Advent Christians began to move away from their isolationist posture toward both church and society through the establishment of two institutions of higher learning, each with a unique purpose.

As we explore their cautious moves away from isolation, this small Adventist denomination would find a much different American Protestant context than forty years earlier when their isolationist path was chosen. That leads us first to an exploration of the Protestant conservative reaction to the rise of the modernist impulse within American Christianity.

CHAPTER TWO

Setting the Stage

The Conflict Between
Fundamentalists and Modernists

WHILE ADVENT CHRISTIANS STRUGGLED during the last two decades of the nineteenth century both to define and defend their unique doctrines and relate them to the whole of Christian faith, modernist theological ideals began to have significant impact within the major denominations and their educational and missions agencies. Of special interest for our study is the growth of theological liberalism within key colleges and seminaries during the late nineteenth and early twentieth centuries, and conservative responses to that. This coincides with a dramatic change in the nature of American higher education following the Civil War, a change that would impact the two Advent Christian related colleges that would be established in the 1890s.[1]

Before the war, higher education was primarily the domain of private church-related colleges. Education focused on the development of moral character and exposure to the broad scope of human learning. Clergy served as college presidents and on the boards of directors. After the war, state governments began active involvement in higher education. Land grant colleges were established. The focus of education shifted from the British ideals of character and broad exposure to human learning to the German ideals of research and specialization in a particular field of study. Even at historically church-related colleges, clergy were moved aside for

---

1. Marsden, *The Soul of the American University,* offers a discussion of the themes surrounding these changes in American education.

administrators and board members who possessed savvy in fund-raising and institutional management.

The changes within American colleges and universities were not only external, but internal as well. Beginning in the 1880s, an intellectual revolution took place within American higher education. The scope of that revolution was well summarized by the words of Charles Eliot, then president of Harvard University: "A new method, or spirit, of inquiry has been gradually developed, which is characterized by an absolute freedom on the part of the inquirer from the influence of prepossessions or desires as to results."[2] No external authority or theological tradition would be allowed to limit the boundaries of academic inquiry. Through the influence of historicism, the emphasis in academic inquiry shifted from the quest for timeless truths to explaining how human belief changes and progresses.[3]

The Chicago School of Theology

Not only was there dramatic administrative and intellectual change in American higher education during the late 1800s, there was major expansion as a host of public and private colleges were established. One of the most significant was the University of Chicago, established in 1892. Chicago was one of several colleges and universities established by wealthy industrialists who sought to use at least some of their assets for what they considered the betterment of society. Its establishment was substantially financed by John D. Rockefeller, and Chicago provided a foretaste of what the bureaucratic university of the twentieth century would look like.[4] Chicago was the foremost home of the burgeoning academic discipline of sociology,[5] and in the view of its first president, William Rainey Harper, universities like Chicago existed to foster the values necessary for the strengthening of American democracy.[6]

2. Eliot, *Educational Reform*, 69–70. Eliot adds, "This spirit seeks only the fact, without the slightest regard to consequences; any twisting or obscuring of the fact to accommodate it to a preconceived theory, hope, or wish, any tampering with the actual result of investigation, is the unpardonable sin."

3. Marsden, *Soul of the American University*, 20–67.

4. Ibid., 239.

5. Ibid., 251.

6. Ibid. "[John] Dewey and [William Rainey] Harper both believed in the redemptive functions of education. Dewey viewed the public schools as virtually the new established church, teaching the values of American democracy. Though Dewey had worked out the

Harper, a recognized Old Testament scholar, believed that scientific inquiry provided the foundation for the academic enterprise. Echoing the words of Eliot, Harper declared that "the three birth-marks of a university are . . . self-government, freedom from ecclesiastical control, and the right of free utterance."[7] He applied this not only to his administrative work as president, but to his work with the Bible. Traditional approaches to Bible teaching and interpretation were an embarrassment. "The friends of the Bible have been its worst enemies. A faith in the Bible constructed on a scientific basis will be acceptable to everyone who takes pains to look at it."[8]

As president, Harper set the tone not only for the university as a whole but for its biblical studies and theological departments. Historian Sydney Ahlstrom describes the theology that developed at Chicago as "Modernistic Liberalism,"[9] characterized by,

> a much smaller group of more radical theologians. Men who took scientific method, scholarly discipline, empirical fact and prevailing forms of contemporary philosophy as their point of departure. From this perspective, they approached religion as a human phenomenon, the Bible as one great religious document among others, and the Christian faith as one major religio-ethical tradition among others.[10]

Successive generations of Chicago theologians sought to develop the implications of this framework in every branch of the divinity school curriculum.[11] From 1892 until the mid-1920s, the Chicago school of theology was characterized by use of the historical-critical method of biblical interpretation, an orientation that viewed Christianity as a social movement to be studied by secular historical and sociological methods, and a

---

theory further than Harper, each believed that science was the key to finding unifying communitarian values, because only through science could one eliminate superstitions and sectarian differences and thus build an inclusivist 'community of truth.' Dewey's talk, presented to the students at Michigan, 'Christianity and Democracy,' and Harper's 'Democracy and the University,' despite some obvious differences, were two of a kind."

7. Ibid., 249.

8. Ibid., 242.

9. Ahlstrom, *Religious History*, 782. In Marsden's words, "The (Baptist) Divinity School at the University of Chicago became after the 1890s the leading center for aggressive theological liberalism." See Marsden, *Fundamentalism and American Culture*, 105.

10. Ahlstrom, *Religious History*, 783.

11. Ibid.

commitment to pragmatism that focused on the practical aspects of religion.[12] That would later be supplemented by what would come to be known as Process Theology, a theological movement which viewed God as Cosmic Process, not the supernatural and timeless creator of historic Christian orthodoxy.[13]

While the Chicago theologians were probably more aggressive in propagating their brand of theological liberalism than others within that broad movement, it provoked dramatic response from many who felt that the new theological trends represented a serious challenge to the validity of the Christian faith. Before we survey those responses, it is important to briefly sketch one aspect of the thought of one prominent theologian whose work began to galvanize opinion especially within the Presbyterian Church.

At Union Theological Seminary, a Northern Presbyterian sponsored school in New York City, professor Charles Briggs expounded a view of biblical inspiration and interpretation that theological conservatives deemed heretical. While Briggs retained orthodox views regarding the deity of Christ,[14] he thought that any notion of verbal/plenary inspiration was not only unscientific but heretical. For Briggs,

> Christian theology must be constructed by the induction of divine truth from all spheres of information . . . . God reveals truth in several spheres; in universal nature, in the constitution of mankind, in the history of our race, and in the sacred scriptures, but above all in the person of Jesus Christ our Lord.[15]

The Scriptures are not the sole source of Christian theology and "do not decide for us all questions of orthodoxy."[16] One who refuses to accept the new discoveries of science and historical studies on the basis that it conflicts with traditional standards of orthodoxy "has become unfaithful to the calling and aims of the Christian disciple, has left the companionship of Jesus and His apostles and has joined the Pharisees."[17]

---

12. *Dictionary of Christianity in America*, 1st ed., s.v. "Chicago School of Theology," by S. T. Franklin.

13. Ibid. Process thought was introduced to the University of Chicago Divinity School via Henry Nelson Wieman, Bernard M. Loomer, and Charles Hartshorne.

14. Briggs, "Orthodoxy," in *American Protestant* Thought, 27–36.

15. Ibid., 33, 28.

16. Ibid., 31.

17. Ibid., 30.

While Briggs' opponents may have done that in his view, in their view Briggs had left Presbyterian orthodoxy and therefore should be censured. Presbyterian conservatives attempted to block Briggs appointment to the Robinson Chair of Biblical Theology at Union Seminary, and they did manage to exclude him from ordained ministry within the Presbyterian Church. The Seminary stood behind him however, and in 1898 Briggs was received into the Episcopal Church.[18]

Conservative Responses

The Briggs episode illustrates the growing fragmentation of response within American Christianity to the intellectual and social changes of the late 1800s and early 1900s. Before 1870, most Christians assumed two fundamental premises in their understanding of culture. First, God's truth was a single unified order. Second, all persons of common sense were capable of knowing that truth.[19] By the turn of the century, those premises were being severely tested and any notion of a Christian cultural consensus was breaking down. Those who wished to maintain traditional Christian understandings of doctrine, theology, and practice responded in several distinct and important ways.[20]

Not all colleges and seminaries embraced the liberal/ modernist paradigm. Wheaton College in Wheaton, Ill. successfully maintained a conservative theological position. However, for many theological conservatives, Princeton (NJ) Theological Seminary became the focal point not only for a theologically conservative engagement with changing American culture but for the defense of Christian orthodoxy against what they perceived as the threat of modernism.

What came to be called the "Princeton Theology" emerged through a line of theologians that included Charles Hodge, Benjamin Warfield, and finally John Gresham Machen. Unlike other movements within the

---

18. Ibid., 27.

19. Marsden, *Fundamentalism*, 14.

20. As with all movements, what came to be called Fundamentalism was not monolithic. Within the orbit of theological conservatism, there were several theological submovements including the Princeton theology, Dispensational-premillennialism, Keswick holiness, and Pentecostalism. Within the broad umbrella of the movement, there was dispute concerning who was part of the coalition and who was not. See Dayton, and Johnston, eds. *Variety of American Evangelicalism*; and George Marsden, *Understanding Fundamentalism* for background.

emerging fundamentalist coalition, the Princeton theologians were not anti-intellectual. In their view, the Bible and science were two sources of revelation that could be reconciled.[21] In a climate of authentic free inquiry, they believed that the authority and reliability of the Bible could be maintained and defended. For that type of inquiry to take place, in the words of Francis Patton, "it will be insisted that on the one side that the critic shall not assume the impossibility of miracles, and with equal fairness, it will be demanded on the other side that evangelical critics will not postulate plenary Inspiration."[22] Based on that, the Bible's reliability would be settled via inductive investigation that takes into account "all the facts."[23]

That phrase gets at the heart of the philosophical assumptions not only behind the Princeton theology but behind much of Dispensational-premillennialism. In 1822, the orthodox Congregationalist Leonard Woods Jr. wrote that the best strategy for interpreting the Bible was "that which is pursued in the science of physics" and governed "by the maxims of Bacon and Newton." In his view, Newtonian method "is as applicable to the science of theology as to the science of physics." In each science the process of reasoning is the same. "We first inquire for the facts; and by reasoning from facts, we arrive at general truths."[24] Woods provides a picture of how aspects of the Enlightenment impacted much of Christian theology in the nineteenth century, including the Princeton theology articulated by Hodge, Warfield, and later Machen.[25] The most significant aspect of Enlightenment influence is through what historian Mark Noll terms the "didactic enlightenment,"[26] the Common Sense philosophy articulated by the Scottish philosopher Thomas Reid (1710–1796).

21. Marsden, *Soul of the American University*, 205.

22. Patton, "Dogmatic Aspect."

23. Ibid.

24. Woods, *Works of Leonard Woods*, 20–21.

25. The case for linkage between the early enlightenment and nineteenth-century Princeton theology has been forcefully argued by George Marsden, Mark Noll, and others. For an opposing view, see Fuller and Gardiner, "Reformed Theology at Princeton," 89–117. Fuller and Gardiner assert that "while Old Princeton maintained and championed a pre-Kantian theological method, the Dutch Neo-Calvinist theologians reshaped Reformed theology to fit the mold of the Kantian worldview and a distinctively modern philosophy."

26. Noll asserts "that eighteenth-century Americans perceived several Enlightenments, rather than just one. Americans in general held in high regard, but from afar, what [Henry] May calls the moderate Enlightenment exemplified by Isaac Newton and John Locke. By contrast, evangelicals in America came to repudiate two other forms of

Contrary to those who followed John Locke in the belief that "ideas," and not external realities are the objects of our thought, the Common Sense school taught that we can know the real world directly through our senses.[27] The existence of an objective world governed by moral principles could be known by anyone in his/her right mind. Moreover, truth is a unified single entity. It is absolute, permanent, and discoverable by all people in all times. Truth is discovered through inductive scientific method—observing the "facts" perceptible to common sense and then classifying them.

The Princeton theologians applied Common Sense philosophy to their theology, but in a significantly different way than did the Adventist Miles Grant. For the Princeton theologians, theology could be articulated by applying the same scientific method used in physics, mathematics, and other disciplines. At the beginning of his *Systematic Theology*, Charles Hodge argues that "theology is concerned with the facts and principles of the Bible." The theologian's task is to "systematize the facts of the Bible, and ascertain the principles or general truths which those facts involve."[28] Unlike Grant, for whom the study of theology involved Common Sense applied to the Bible, human reason, human experience, and the discoveries of modern science, the Princeton theologians viewed the Bible as the sole sourcebook for Christian theology and applied the Common Sense method of induction to that source. For the Princeton theologians, religious experience could not be the foundation for Christian thinking because for it to be authentic, experience must grow out of right ideas which in turn could only be expressed in words.[29] Authentic faith grows out of right reason.

The Common Sense view of unified, timeless truth was articulated in how the Princeton theologians understood the inspiration of the Bible. The written word of God was the surest arbiter of truth. Experience, ritual, and tradition are transitory but the Bible is permanent. In it, the theologian finds his storehouse of facts.[30] The Bible not only contains God's word, it

---

European Enlightenment—skeptical, as defined by Voltaire and David Hume; and revolutionary, as in the work of Rousseau, William Godwin, and (after 1780) Tom Paine. A fourth variety of Enlightenment, however, received a very different reception in Protestant America. This didactic Enlightenment, which has recently been the subject of fresh scholarly attention, was largely a product of Scotland." See Noll, *Scandal*, 84.

27. Longfield, *Presbyterian Controversy*, 34. The summary of Scottish Common Sense philosophy that follows is based on Longfield's summary beginning on p. 34.

28. Hodge, *Systematic Theology*, 1:18.

29. Marsden, *Fundamentalism*, 112.

30. Ibid., 113.

is God's word and is errorless in all its affirmations. Inspiration applies not only to thoughts, but to the words of Scripture.[31]

In their work with Scripture, the Princeton theologians minimized any notion of the text as representative of the point of view of the author. Truth was an objective statement of fact with little or no subjectivity.[32] This Common Sense view placed them in growing conflict with the historicist notion that all observers are caught up in historical processes.[33] With growing acceptance of the historicist paradigm within academic circles, the Princeton theology was seen as archaic by many, even heretical by some like Briggs. As the conflict deepened, Princeton theologians began to argue that theological liberalism was the antithesis of authentic Christianity.

While the Princeton theologians were determined to foster an intellectual engagement of Christian faith based on the Common Sense philosophy of the early American Enlightenment, another large subgroup within the emerging Fundamentalism began to take shape around a new form of premillennialism, a form significantly different from the historic premillennialism advocated by William Miller and many of his Adventist colleagues. While Adventism was the first major American Christian movement to challenge the postmillennial eschatology embraced by most evangelical Christians during the nineteenth century, events surrounding the 1844 Great Disappointment had in the eyes of many evangelicals, discredited the historic premillennialism advocated especially by Adventism's so-called moderate wing.

In Timothy Weber's words, "Christian millennialism is the belief that there will be a long period of unprecedented peace and righteousness closely associated with the second coming of Christ."[34] Before 1844, the general consensus within American Christianity was postmillennial, the belief that the return of Jesus Christ would follow a long period of peace and prosperity ushered in by Christian teaching and preaching.[35] During this time, the influence of evil would be greatly reduced and through Christian influence most major economic and social problems would be solved.

Postmillennialism fit well with the climate of pre-Civil War America. A spirit of optimism pervaded the country. In a nation with vast untapped

31. Hodge, and Warfield, *Inspiration*, 22–23.

32. Marsden, *Fundamentalism*, 114.

33. Longfield, *Presbyterian Controversy*, 89.

34. Weber, *Living in the Shadow*, 9.

35. *Dictionary of Christianity in America*, 1st ed., s.v. "Postmillennialism," by Clouse.

natural resources and unlimited opportunities and freedom for its people, many Christians in the United States developed a strong sense that God had given their nation a special place in his purposes. America would be the vehicle by which God would build his kingdom on earth.[36] After 1840, that mood began to change. The young nation was unable to peacefully resolve the conflict that had developed over enslavement of African-Americans in the American south. That conflict not only brought ecclesiastical division to Methodists, Baptists, and Presbyterians; but a Civil War that divided the United States and brought untold bloodshed to its people. In the aftermath of that conflict, a host of new economic and social problems began to shape American life and the optimistic mood that permeated the nation before 1840 was giving way to pessimism. Protestant Americans began to sense that the evangelical consensus that had dominated American religious and cultural experience was breaking down.

The premillennialism that emerged among American evangelicals after 1870 was similar in several key ways to the pre-Civil War premillennialism advocated by William Miller and many early Adventists. The new premillennialists agreed with Miller that, interpreted properly, Revelation 20:1–6 teaches that Jesus Christ will return and then rule as king during a 1,000 year millennial period. Before his return, things would get worse, not better. The millennium would come not via Christianization of the world through the work of the visible church, but through God's swift and decisive intervention in the soon return of Jesus Christ.[37] However, the premillennialism that emerged in the United States after 1870 had its roots in Great Britain. A British premillennial movement had developed during the early 1800s with four strong tenets: 1. The authority of Scripture meant the literal fulfillment of biblical prophecy; 2. The world was becoming corrupt and rushing toward divine judgment; 3. The Jewish people would be restored to Palestine before the visible return of Jesus Christ to usher in the millennium; 4. The prophecies of Scripture foretold the events leading to Christ's return.[38]

---

36. For development of this theme see, Dyrness, *How Does America?*, 61–81.

37. Sandeen, *Roots of Fundamentalism*. Sandeen wrote, "Thus belief in the pre- rather than the postmillennial return of Christ involved much more than a question of the timing of the second advent. Converts to premillennialism abandoned confidence in man's ability to bring about significant and lasting social progress and in the church's ability to stem the tide of evil, convert mankind to Christianity, or even prevent its own corruption."

38. Ibid., 39.

During the middle 1800s, John Nelson Darby emerged as perhaps the major figure among premillennialists in the British Isles. Darby had broken with the Church of Ireland, established his own separatistic sect, the Plymouth Brethren, and developed the prophetic principles that shaped dispensational-premillennialism.[39] He traveled extensively in the United States during the late 1860s and early 1870s and found acceptance for his prophetic interpretation.[40] Darby's dispensationalism built on the four tenets of the earlier British premillennialism and added several important prophetic principles. Dispensationalists believed that world history was divided into seven periods of time and in each period of time, God dealt with humanity in a unique way.[41] Moreover, God had two distinct peoples, Israel and the Church, and a distinct program for each. Because Israel had rejected the messiahship of Jesus Christ, God's current activity in the world is being accomplished through the church. In addition, because God's purposes for Israel were not yet complete, the church will be removed by what dispensationalists termed the secret, pre-tribulational rapture of the church. After that, God will complete his program during a seven-year Great Tribulation that will be marked by the reign of Antichrist.

The foundations of the dispensationalist interpretative scheme are built on a complex interpretation of Daniel 9.[42] The "seventy weeks" (or "seventy sevens") are interpreted as meaning 490 years. However, the seventieth week does not immediately follow the first sixty-nine and in the dispensationalist scheme, the entire church age lies between the sixty-ninth and seventieth weeks. That leaves a number of biblical prophecies to be fulfilled during the seven years between the secret rapture of the church and the visible return of Jesus Christ to usher in the millennium.

Their complex eschatology led dispensationalists to a unique understanding of the Christian church, one that built upon the earlier Restorationism of the Second Great Awakening. It was an understanding

39. Longfield, *Presbyterian Controversy*, 20. Darby was a strong opponent of the historicist variety of premillennialism advocated by William Miller and his Adventist successors.

40. Sandeen, *Roots of Fundamentalism*, 75–77. Darby was frustrated that although many Christians accepted his prophetic methodology, they did not accept his separatistic views regarding the church.

41. The following summary of dispensationalism is drawn from Marsden, *Fundamentalism*; Sandeen, *Roots of Fundamentalism*; Weber, *Living in the Shadow*; and Longfield, *Presbyterian Controversy*.

42. Marsden, *Fundamentalism*, 52.

surprisingly similar to the views that developed within the various Adventist movements. The visible church, as represented by Roman Catholicism, Eastern Orthodoxy, and the major Protestant denominations, was rapidly becoming worldly and apostate. The true church is a faithful and holy remnant of saints who are separate from the world. In the interim age between the sixty-ninth and seventieth week of Daniel's prophecy, God's work would be accomplished through the Holy Spirit in a non-institutional context.[43] This understanding of the church would come to predominate within the fundamentalist movement and in many instances translate into withdrawal from the mainline denominations and formation of independent congregations and para-church agencies.

Dispensational premillennialism spread rapidly through a series of Bible conferences, camp-meetings, and independent mission and para-church agencies. Two projects are worth special mention for our purposes. In 1876, A.J. Gordon, Nathaniel West, William J. Erdman, and others organized what would later become the Niagara Bible Conference. This annual event lasted for twenty-five years and became a model for a host of other conferences.[44] The conference adopted a statement of faith that was moderately Calvinistic and strongly premillennial in tone.[45]

Premillennialists also organized a new type of educational agency—the Bible institute. Chief among these was Moody Bible Institute founded in 1889. Moody was prominent not only because of its ties to the most

---

43. Ibid., 54. While Adventists and dispensationalists share essentially the same understanding of the church, their reasons for coming to a similar conclusion were different. For dispensationalists, the institutional church was becoming apostate because of doctrinal compromise. For Adventists, those churches were guilty of apostasy first for the refusal to embrace the second advent message and later, for their refusal to recognize the biblical nature of Adventist distinctive doctrines like conditional immortality.

44. Ibid., 46.

45. Sandeen, *Roots of Fundamentalism*, Appendix A. The statement of faith was drawn up in response to controversy over the Advent Christian doctrine of conditional immortality. Phillips Brookes published the creed with the following admonition to those who believed in conditional immortality, "If they do not stand upon it, and yet choose to attend, they are expected to keep silent. We do not deny the right of those who hold that what are known as 'annihilation views,' to assemble when and where they please." Five years later, Brookes remarked, "no countenance whatever has been given to the unscriptural and mischievous notions, now so widely spread, of annihilation, soul-sleeping, restoration of the wicked, and perfectionism in the flesh." See Sandeen, *Roots of Fundamentalism*, 140–41. The action would lead to ongoing conflict between dispensational-premillennialists and Adventists and would have implications for how Advent Christians perceived Fundamentalism and Evangelicalism in the twentieth century.

prominent evangelist of the time, Dwight L. Moody; but because of two important dispensational-premillennialists, Reuben A. Torrey and James M. Gray, who led the college during its first half-century. Bible institutes like Moody provided a sense of unity among dispensationalists and focused on training Christian workers for evangelistic and missionary service.[46] Moody's curriculum focused on Bible study, missions, and practical Christian and evangelistic work.[47] Instruction in dispensational-premillennialism was meshed with an emphasis upon separation from what the Moody faculty and administration viewed as worldly culture.

The emphasis upon this form of separation grew out of a related movement within the emerging fundamentalist coalition called Keswick holiness. Darby and other premillennialists reacted strongly against the Wesleyan doctrine of perfectionism[48] (sometimes called "entire sanctification") and Keswick holiness offered a somewhat Calvinistic alternative with many of the same practical implications as the Wesleyan and Methodist varieties.[49] Like the dispensational variety of premillennialism, Keswick originated in Great Britain and stressed the empowerment of the Holy Spirit for an effective life of Christian service.[50] Keswick rejected the Wesleyan notion that a person could be totally without sin in favor of a notion that if Christ dwelt in a person's heart, that person could become free of committing any known sin by definitive acts of consecration.[51] Through these actions, a Christian would move from a "carnal" to a "spiritual" state and be effectively empowered for Christian service. Keswick teachings were integrated into what was probably the most influential book among dispensational-premillennialists, the *Scofield Reference Bible*.[52]

46. Marsden, *Fundamentalism*, 128. For an institutional history of Moody Bible Institute written by a graduate of the school, see Getz, *Moody Bible Institute*.

47. Ibid., 129.

48. Sandeen, *Roots of Fundamentalism*, 77–78.

49. Marsden, *Fundamentalism*, 78.

50. Longfield, *Presbyterian Controversy*, 139.

51. Marsden, *Fundamentalism*, 78. The terms used to describe this action are "absolute surrender" and "yielding."

52. Ibid., 79.

The Establishment of Advent
Christian Higher Education

The last decade of the nineteenth century was a time of growing theological polarization within the mainstream of American Protestant Christianity. Fault lines were beginning to emerge within the Northern Baptist and Northern Presbyterian denominations between emerging coalitions of fundamentalists and modernists, especially in the seminaries that trained many of their ministerial candidates. Even among those who would identify as fundamentalist, different theological families were emerging. While this was happening in American Protestantism, some Advent Christians had become uncomfortable with the isolationist posture of their denomination in terms of church and society. For them, the time had come to establish institutions of higher learning to preserve the denomination's theological message. Since the founding of the denomination in 1860, a number of Advent Christians had advocated establishing a college or Bible institute to train Advent Christian pastors. In the words of A.A. Phelps, "The constant expectancy of the Lord's return has had a natural tendency to keep us from founding permanent institutions, or pursuing extensive courses of study."[53] That tendency was exemplified by Miles Grant who concluded that it was sinful to plan more than six months in the future.[54] The Advent Christians who founded Mendota College[55] (later Aurora College) in 1893 and the Boston Bible School (later the New England School of Theology) in 1897[56] discovered that this bias against organization and planning would become a major barrier to the fulfillment of their goals.

From its beginning, Mendota College pursued a broad educational purpose oriented toward the liberal arts. The college desired to give students "a liberal education and to prepare them for usefulness in the different avocations of life."[57] The board and administration hoped that the

53. A. A. Phelps quoted from Fillinger, "Berkshire Christian College," 45.

54. Dean, "Echoes," 267. This attitude toward organization and planning has affected Advent Christian organizations throughout the nineteenth and twentieth centuries. For its impact on Berkshire Christian College, note Fillinger, "Berkshire Christian College," 83–87.

55. Arthur, "Aurora College: Past and Present," 1. The school was originally named Mendota Seminary. But seven months after classes began, the school name was changed to Mendota College.

56. Fillinger, "Berkshire Christian College," 28–29.

57. Arthur, "Aurora College," 7. Arthur quotes from the Mendota College catalog of

college would foster a distinctively Christian approach to liberal arts education that would qualify graduates for "the varied duties of life and make them a benefit to their fellow man."[58] Because the vision of the founders was oriented toward liberal arts and because Advent Christian financial support for the college was sporadic at best, Mendota College was never narrowly denominational.[59] By the time the college moved to Aurora in 1912, its liberal arts direction was becoming well established. Its purpose was articulated well by its new president Orrin Roe Jenks. "The work of every institution of higher education," in Jenks words, "is in a measure a missionary movement for the betterment of humanity at large. Aurora College is no exception to this rule. Our educational field is world-wide, and the benefits accrue to no particular class."[60]

As the Mendota College administration and board focused their efforts on liberal arts education, Advent Christians in New England saw the necessity for a school in their region. While part of the justification was pragmatic,[61] these Advent Christians intended to establish a Bible school to train young people for Christian vocational service as pastors, missionaries, and church workers.[62] To do that, the school would "promulgate Bible Christianity; including its doctrines, experiences, and practice."[63] It would present Advent Christian distinctive theology to use the words of A. A. Phelps "in the most attractive and convincing manner."[64] Unlike its Midwest counterpart, Boston Bible School was created as a Bible institute (on the pattern of Moody Bible Institute) designed to promote the training of Advent Christian workers and the propagation of a distinctive Advent Christian doctrinal approach. However, like Mendota College, the early years of Boston Bible School were unstable and financial support from Advent Christian people and churches was erratic.[65] These two realities—dif-

---

1894–95. The theological school was an important part if not the major function of the college in these early years.

58. Ibid., 7.

59. Ibid.

60. Ibid.

61. Fillinger, "Berkshire Christian College," 33. Fillinger quotes from the January 13, 1897 issue of the *World's Crisis*: "But it cannot be expected that eastern students will go west for educational facilities."

62. Ibid., 33.

63. Phelps quoted by Fillinger, "Berkshire Christian College," 34.

64. Ibid.

65. Ibid., 35.

fering educational philosophies and common financial struggles— would become more pronounced during the first half of the twentieth century. Both schools would face an important if discouraging reality: the theological direction of the Advent Christian Church during the time between 1890 and 1930 was being shaped not by them, but by the work of Miles Grant, an individual who was sharply opposed to what they hoped to accomplish.

During this same time frame, both schools would begin to diverge theologically. At Aurora, Orrin Roe Jenks and his theological successor Clarence Hewitt would be influenced by theological focus of William Rainey Harper and other University of Chicago theologians, especially in terms of their understanding of Scripture and the role it played in the life of the church. At the New England School of Theology, a fundamentally different understanding of Scripture would emerge more slowly, an understanding shaped by theologians like Cornelius van Till and like-minded theologians at Westminster Theological Seminary in Philadelphia and Gordon-Divinity School in Boston. To understand these increasingly divergent directions, we must survey the larger developments in early twentieth-century American Protestantism—developments that led to the fracturing of American Protestantism into two broad coalitions represented by schools like the divinity school at the University of Chicago and Westminster Theological Seminary.

Conflicts Between Fundamentalists and Modernists

As Aurora College and the New England School of Theology struggled during the first quarter of the twentieth century with organizational identity and financial survival, the conflict between the emerging progressive and traditionalist parties within mainstream American Protestantism exploded. While historians often speak of the Fundamentalist-Modernist "controversy," it is important to think in terms of a series of theological and organizational controversies that began as early as 1874 and lasted until the mid-1930s. Our focus is on two of those controversies that would directly affect the two Advent Christian institutions of higher learning and through them, the Advent Christian Church.

The first would take place in Chicago as two educational institutions which had done so much to shape the fundamentalist and modernist parties. Moody Bible Institute and the University of Chicago Divinity School, would square off over a surprising issue. As alluded to earlier, the University of Chicago Divinity School pursued its Modernist vision in a unique way. While the Chicago theologians shared with their liberal/modernist counterparts an appreciation for the role of experience, they did not follow the eighteenth-century German theologian Frederich Schleiermacher by focusing on personal religious experience. Instead, they focused on the broader scope of common experience found in society at large.[66] Religion must be studied as a social movement within the broad scope of a given culture. Its focus is not divine behavior, but human behavior. Therefore, the study of religion draws on the scope of common human experience, not on analysis of rigid, abstract bodies of doctrine.[67]

During the first quarter of the twentieth century, the Chicago Divinity School became the leader in propagating an aggressive theological liberalism.[68] For the Chicago theologians, Dispensational-premillennialism in general and Moody Bible Institute in particular represented everything they abhorred intellectually. In 1917, they attacked their Moody counterparts in a surprising way. American involvement in World War I was growing more likely with each passing day and many within the liberal/modernist camp viewed the war as a struggle for democratic civilization and ultimately world peace.[69] Patriotism was an integral part of the ethos at Chicago and in the view of two important Chicago theologians, Shailer Mathews and Shirley Jackson Case, premillennialism was not only theologically unsound, it was unpatriotic as well.

Mathews led the attack by publishing a widely distributed pamphlet titled, "Will Jesus Come Again?" Mathews attributed the apocalyptic sections of the Bible to mistakes on the part of the early Christians[70] and argued that the premillennialist understanding of inspiration meant acceptance of slavery, a flat earth, and submission to dictators.[71] Case inflamed the rhetoric to white-hot levels with his January 1918 charge that the rise of Dispensational-premillennialism was a sinister conspiracy. He alleged

66. Axel, "God or Man at Chicago," 73.

67. Ibid.," 73–74. In Axel's words, "The Chicago methodology represented an awareness that theological traditions evolve, according to Shirley Jackson Case, 'ever making new adjustments and manifesting new features in accordance with changing environments and the new demands of varying situations.'"

68. Marsden, *Fundamentalism*, 105.

69. Ibid., 146.

70. Weber, *Living in the Shadow*, 118.

71. Ibid., 117–18.

that "two thousand dollars a week is being spent to spread this doctrine" and called for an investigation to determine whether or not that money was coming from German sources.[72] Later in 1918, Case alleged that premillennialists were enemies of democracy and sympathetic both to the communist propaganda of the I.W.W. (International Workers of the World) and to a German War Victory.[73]

The attacks not only elicited a response, particularly from those connected with Moody Bible Institute; they led to two important shifts within the emerging fundamentalist coalition. In the emotional atmosphere surrounding American involvement in the war, the charges leveled by Case and others demanded a response. Although Case's charges were on the whole outrageous, premillennialism before World War I did contain some strong pacifist sentiments which grew out of their anti-modernist and apocalyptic assumptions.[74] The response to the attacks of Mathews, Case, and others had the effect of creating an interesting paradox within successive generations of fundamentalists—a passionate patriotism combined with a reluctant stance towards political and social involvement.[75]

James Gray, president of Moody Bible Institute, was one of the first to respond. According to Gray, the school supported the American war cause by opening its doors for the sale of Liberty bonds and raising support for the Red Cross. Many Moody students joined the army and a number of them were killed in action.[76] Reuben Torrey not only termed the charges made by Case ridiculous, but turned the heat up another notch by declaring that

72. Marsden, *Fundamentalism*, 146–47.

73. Ibid., 147; Weber, *Living in the Shadow*, 119–20.

74. Both Marsden and Weber discuss the pacifist sentiments of pre-World War I premillennialism. See Marsden, *Fundamentalism*, 14–15; 149–51; Weber *Living in the Shadow*, 121. Weber writes, "Given Gray and Torrey's defense notwithstanding, the liberals were correct in saying that premillennialists could not give unflinching support to America's ideological war aims."

75. There is little doubt that a strong patriotism was advocated by predecessors to the fundamentalist movement, for example Billy Sunday. However, from the 1920s onward, most fundamentalists would maintain a patriotic stance. Much has been written about why fundamentalists saw social concern as a threat to the gospel. But an overlooked factor in those discussions has been the degree to which the liberal attacks of 1917–19 created tension among fundamentalists over their attitude toward their citizenship responsibilities. From the 1920s onward, Fundamentalism winds up with an interesting paradox: a patriotic loyalty combined with a hands-off attitude towards government and political life.

76. Weber, *Living in the Shadow*, 121.

"the destructive criticism that rules in Chicago University emanates from German sources is undeniable."[77] Dispensationalist writer Arno Gaebelein expanded on that theme by equating German militarism with German theology. Liberal theology leads to barbarism.[78] Leaders within the emerging Fundamentalist coalition began to believe that if the growth of liberalism were not checked, all of civilization would be threatened.

The skirmish between Chicago and Moody had far-reaching implications. Not only did attacks from the Chicago theologians drive the emerging fundamentalist coalition toward an embrace of patriotism, they helped create a sense that the differences between liberals and fundamentalists were no longer merely a matter of theological debate. Now they were about the future of civilization, especially American civilization. A crossroads had been reached. Would America succumb to the barbaric philosophy of Darwinism and German rationalism? Or would Americans see that the only hope for society rested in a return to traditional Christian principles? An emerging theological movement had been radicalized. Fundamentalist leaders were now willing to fight in both church and society for what they saw as the survival of civilization.[79]

The conflict between the University of Chicago Divinity School and Moody Bible Institute led to a powerful polarization between fundamentalist and modernist Protestants in Chicago and the surrounding area, a polarization that is still apparent today. It also led to major conflict within the Northern Baptist Convention. Ironically, it was a Northern Baptist clergyman serving a Presbyterian congregation in New York City who fired what many considered the first verbal shot in a fourteen-year battle between Northern Presbyterian fundamentalists and modernists. Harry Emerson Fosdick's presence at the 1919 Northern Baptist annual convention in Denver, CO was one of the events that caused Northern Baptist conservatives to

---

77. Ibid. Marsden, *Fundamentalism*, 148.

78. Marsden, *Fundamentalism*, 148.

79. Ibid., 159. As an example of this sentiment, Marsden cites David S. Kennedy, editor of the *Presbyterian*, "There has been some weakening of this moral standard in the thought and life of America. This is the result of an age of luxury within and freedom from conflict from without. There is but one remedy: the nation must return to her standard of the Word of God. She must believe, love, and live her Bible. This will require the counteraction of that German destructive criticism which has found its way into the religious and moral thought of our people . . . The Bible and the God of the Bible is our only hope."

organize.[80] Three years later, the gifted liberal pulpiteer preached his most famous and controversial sermon, "Shall the Fundamentalists Win?" Fosdick saw his sermon as a plea for "magnanimity and tolerance of spirit."[81] He did not object to the right of theological conservatives to maintain their personal belief in the inerrancy of Scripture, substitutionary atonement, or the premillennial return of Jesus Christ. "The question is," in Fosdick's words, "has anybody a right to deny the Christian name to those who differ with him on such points and to shut against them the doors of the Christian fellowship?"[82]

Liberals, in Fosdick's view were evangelical Christians who were attempting to come to grips with new knowledge about the physical universe and about other religions. For the sake of intellectual and spiritual integrity, liberal Christians were seeking to love God not only with their hearts but "with all their mind, they have been trying to see this new knowledge in terms of the Christian faith and to see the Christian faith in terms of this new knowledge."[83] The church has always faced the task of thinking through the Christian faith in modern terms, and vice versa. That is what liberal Christians, in Fosdick's view, were attempting to accomplish.

Fosdick's sermon focused on three theological issues dividing liberal and Fundamentalist Christians.[84] He argued that while liberal Christians like himself did not accept the virgin birth of Christ, they saw it as reflecting the fact that the first disciples adored Jesus and saw his coming as a special part of God's purpose. "This adoration and conviction they associated with God's special influence . . . but they phrased it in terms of a biological miracle that our modern minds cannot use."[85] Fosdick's treatment of the virgin birth provides important insight for how he and other theological liberals understood the task of relating Christian teaching to modern thought. For them the blending of the old faith with the new knowledge meant that in most cases where the two conflicted, intellectual integrity demanded that the old faith be revised in a way that harmonized with the new knowledge.

---

80. Weber, *Living in the Shadow*, 163.

81. Fosdick, "Shall the Fundamentalists Win?," in *American Protestant Thought*, 170–82.

82. Ibid., 173.

83. Ibid., 172.

84. Fosdick's sermon focused on the issues of the Virgin Birth of Christ, the inspiration of Holy Scripture, and the return of Jesus Christ.

85. Hutchison, *American Protestant Thought*, 175.

Fosdick's treatment of the second advent of Jesus Christ further illustrates this. When liberal Christians speak of Christ's return, "they are not thinking of an external arrival on the clouds," but of God at work through historical process.[86] When liberals speak of Christ's return, according to Fosdick, they mean that "slowly it may be, but surely, His will and principles will be worked out by God's grace in human life and institutions" until the goal of a society based on Christian principles will be realized.[87]

While his views of the virgin birth and the return of Christ were enough to alarm many conservatives,[88] Fosdick's understanding of inspiration gets at the core of the dispute between fundamentalists and modernists. In Fosdick's view, the idea of biblical inerrancy leaves no room for the progressive unfolding of God's revelatory purpose for humanity.[89] The Fundamentalists believe that the Scriptures "were inerrantly dictated; everything there—scientific opinions, medical theories, historical judgments, as well as spiritual insight— is infallible."[90] He likens this understanding of Scripture to Islam's static view of the Koran as having "been infallibly written in heaven before it came to earth."[91] For Fosdick, God's revelation progresses beyond the Bible. For example, "slavery, never explicitly condemned before the New Testament closes, is nevertheless being undermined by ideas that in the end, like dynamite, will blast its foundations to pieces."[92] Embracing a mechanical, static understanding of inspiration, in Fosdick's view, denied the essence of God's character and purpose, and would drive educated people away from the Christian faith.[93] What the church needed in this time was a spirit of tolerance and liberty, combined with clear insight into the main issues faced by Christianity in its relationship with the modern world.[94]

While Fosdick saw his sermon as a plea for mutual tolerance and Christian unity, his opponents saw it as a direct attack on the core of traditional Christian faith. Like their Northern Baptist counterparts, fundamentalists

86. Ibid., 178.
87. Ibid.
88. For example, see Fountain, *Case against Dr. Fosdick.*
89. Hutchison, *American Protestant Thought,* 176.
90. Ibid., 175.
91. Ibid., 176.
92. Ibid., 175.
93. Ibid., 176–77.
94. Ibid., 179–80.

in the Presbyterian Church now saw their work in the larger context of preserving both church and society from the influence of a barbaric paganism. As they organized, two men, one a pastor and one a Princeton Seminary professor, stood out as visible leaders of the emerging Presbyterian fundamentalist coalition. Clarence Macartney and John Gresham Machen would work as allies. Each would ultimately choose a different path as the Presbyterian controversy drew to a close in 1936.

Even before Fosdick's controversial sermon, Clarence Macartney had tangled with him over Fosdick's 1919 warning that American soldiers returning home from World War I, "having experienced the ravages of war, would never accept the traditional doctrines and mores of yesterday's Christianity. The church therefore needs to adjust its doctrines to the spirit of the age."[95] Macartney responded that when people like Dr. Fosdick, "call upon the church to reform herself by abandoning all that is distinctively Christian in her teaching," it is the duty of those loyal to Jesus Christ to respond.[96]

While Macartney's career focused on his service in three Northern Presbyterian pastorates,[97] he was theologically articulate and a staunch defender of the Presbyterian orthodoxy taught by Princeton Seminary.[98] Christian truth, for Macartney, was true in all ages and not subject to adaptation. The Bible, as God's inerrant word, was the repository for Christian truth and the ultimate religious authority. Macartney combined his orthodox Presbyterianism with a passion not only for moral reform but for the preservation of Christian civilization in America against what he saw as a growing secular onslaught.[99] Christianity was more than doctrine, it was a religion with personal and societal implications. While Macartney was concerned with the threat of liberal theology to the historic witness of the

95. Longfield, *Presbyterian Controversy*, 113. The quotation is Longfield's summary of Fosdick's 1919 argument.

96. Ibid., 113–14.

97. Longfield, "Macartney," 680–81.

98. Longfield, *Presbyterian Controversy*, 114. In Longfield's words, "Like Machen, Macartney, in adopting the Princeton tradition, accepted not simply the theology of the Westminster divines but the epistemology of Scottish Common Sense Realism and the Baconian method as well. Truth, according to Macartney, was concrete and eternal."

99. Ibid., 116. Macartney's passion for social reform and Christian civilization was grounded in his Reformed Presbyterian heritage. That heritage was part of the Northern evangelical tradition, which emphasized those themes.

church, his actions were motivated as well by concern to preserve Christian civilization through evangelism and social reform.

"Shall Unbelief Win?" That was the title of Macartney's point-by-point response to Fosdick's 1922 sermon.[100] In essence, he declared that Fosdick's liberal views were out of line with the doctrinal standards of the Presbyterian Church and would result in "a Christianity without worship, without God, and without Jesus Christ."[101] Motivated by Macartney, the Presbytery of Philadelphia asked the General Assembly to give the New York City Presbytery a specific directive— assure that what was taught at First Presbyterian Church in New York City conformed to Presbyterian doctrine as taught by the Confession of Faith.

The strongest response to Fosdick came from Macartney's Princeton Seminary ally John Gresham Machen. Unlike most of his colleagues among Presbyterian conservatives, Machen's Presbyterian roots were Southern, not Northern; and while sharing their alarm over the inroads made by liberalism, his perspectives on moral reform and the role of doctrine were markedly different.[102] Machen had also studied directly under Johannes Weiss, Wilhelm Herrmann, and other critical biblical scholars during a year of graduate studies in Germany. Herrmann asserted that the domains of modern science and faith were completely separate, something radically different from the Old School Presbyterian tradition Machen had assimilated. All of this exacerbated the intellectual and theological struggle Machen had started to experience before his year in Germany.[103]

The conclusions Machen adopted in resolving his struggle would be important for the role he played in the controversy between Presbyterian fundamentalists and modernists. He returned to Princeton and would eventually make that tradition his own. Benjamin Warfield, the veteran Princeton scholar, especially influenced Machen's understandings of apologetics, the doctrine of Scripture, and the relationship between Christianity and

---

100. Macartney, *Shall Unbelief Win?* The year, 1923, is handwritten on the copy.

101. Ibid., 23.

102. Longfield, *Presbyterian Controversy*, 31–38. Machen's Southern Presbyterian heritage included the notion of the "spirituality of the church." Church and state were distinct bodies with distinct spheres of influence. Neither had the right to usurp each other's authority. Individual Christians had a duty to impact cultural life, but the church, as a spiritual institution, had no role to play in social matters.

103. Ibid., 41–43. Longfield describes Machen's year in Germany and its impact on his life and thought.

culture.[104] Contra Wilhelm Herrmann, Machen would argue that history and faith cannot be divorced. Christian doctrine is grounded in historical fact, not in religious experience, and to give up history would mean giving up the gospel.[105] Machen would follow Warfield by insisting that Christianity influenced culture primarily by the furtherance of right doctrine through intellectual rigor.[106] Christianity's influence on American culture would not ultimately be determined in the pulpit, but in the academy.

For Machen, liberalism was more than an attack on the fundamentals of Christian doctrine, it was another religion.[107] In rejecting God's transcendence, "liberalism has lost sight of the very centre and core of the Christian teaching."[108] Liberals, in Machen's view, minimized human sinfulness,[109] rejected the substitutionary atonement of Christ,[110] and maintained a radically different view of the person and work of Christ. "Liberalism regards Jesus as the fairest flower of humanity; Christianity regards Him as a supernatural person."[111] In opposition to the Christian view that in the Bible, we find "the very word of God"[112] and the final authority for Christian thinking, "the real authority for liberalism, can only be 'the Christian consciousness' or 'Christian experience.'"[113]

"It is no wonder," in Machen's words, "that liberalism is totally different from Christianity, for the foundation is different. Christianity is founded upon the Bible . . . Liberalism on the other hand is founded upon the shifting emotions of sinful men."[114] Because Christianity and liberalism

---

104. Ibid., 44.

105. Machen, *Christianity and Liberalism*, 27. Machen writes, "From the beginning, the Christian gospel . . . consisted in an account of something that had happened. And from the beginning, the meaning of the happening was set forth; and when the meaning of the happening was set forth then there was Christian doctrine. 'Christ died'— that is history. 'Christ died for our sins'— that is doctrine. Without these two elements, joined in an absolutely indissoluble union, there is no Christianity."

106. Ibid., 47–48. For a contemporary application of this line of thought, see Wells, *No Place for Truth*.

107. Machen, *Christianity and Liberalism*, 15–16; 17.

108. Ibid., 62.

109. Ibid., 64.

110. Ibid., 117–19.

111. Ibid., 96.

112. Ibid., 78.

113. Ibid.

114. Ibid., 79.

were two separate religions, it is undesirable for the two to be propagated within the same organization. Therefore, Christians should not be afraid of conflict with the liberal party because "a separation between the two parties is the crying need of the hour."[115] If the liberal party gains control of the Presbyterian Church, "evangelical Christians must be prepared to withdraw no matter what it costs."[116] However, if liberals want to demonstrate their intellectual honesty, they should take the initiative and withdraw.[117]

Ironically, it would be Machen and his followers who would eventually withdraw first from Princeton Theological Seminary, and then from the Presbyterian Church. John Gresham Machen has been described as a lone Southern Presbyterian in a Yankee church.[118] The significance of this is found not only in Machen's lack of interest in the social issues that animated many northern Presbyterian evangelicals, but in his understanding that the essence of Christian orthodoxy is grounded in Christian doctrine. According to Machen, "Christian doctrine . . . is not merely connected with the gospel, but it is identical with the gospel."[119] As one with a Southern disposition, Machen was more inclined than his Northern allies to see separation as a proper strategy for maintaining theological and organizational purity and confronting doctrinal laxity.[120] On the surface, while the impact of the Princeton reorganization would seem to have had little immediate effect on the Old School Presbyterianism that characterized a sizable portion of the faculty, Machen saw it as a large first step in what would become Princeton's inevitable decline. By July 1929, a sizable contingent of students, faculty, and directors were committed to withdrawal from Princeton and the establishment of a new school based on "unswerving loyalty to the word of God and to the Westminster Standards."[121] That school, Westminster Theological Seminary, would for Machen and others carry the torch that Princeton had abandoned—a scholarly evangelical Presbyterianism standing in

---

115. Ibid., 160.

116. Ibid., 166.

117. Ibid., 167.

118. Longfield, *Presbyterian Controversy*, 227. For a detailed description of events related to the nuances of the conflicts within the northern Presbyterian Church and Princeton Seminary from 1924–1936, Longfield's work is the best source.

119. Machen, "Dr. Machen Replies to Dr. Erdman," 20–21.

120. Ibid., 173.

121. Stonehouse, *J. Gresham Machen*, 448.

opposition to the secular intellectual tendencies that were tightening their grip on the academy, the church, and society.

Westminster Theological Seminary would hold its first day of classes on September 25, 1929, just two weeks prior to the financial collapse on Wall Street that would lead to the Great Depression. Oswald Aulis, Robert Wilson, and Cornelius Van Til would join Machen in leaving the Princeton faculty for the new school. It would be Van Til who would have a powerful influence on the growing theological divide between the two Advent Christian-related colleges.

Understanding the Fundamentalist-Modernist Controversy

Until recently, the Fundamentalist-Modernist controversy has been understood in somewhat simplistic, polarized ways. Among liberals with a modernist, progressive spirit, the events were seen as a victory for modernity and tolerance over a narrow-minded anti-intellectualism. For fundamentalists, the events represented the triumph of compromise and apostasy within the mainline denominations. For most of the intellectual elite within America, the events painted Fundamentalism as the relic of an earlier age and its adherents as ignorant.

Those popular understandings ignore several significant underlying issues that divided the two parties. At the heart of the controversy, both parties operated with incompatible views of history. Fundamentalists held to an understanding of history based on Baconian induction and Scottish Common Sense philosophy. History could be reconstructed by identifying, compiling, and organizing facts. Modernists understood history as a process shaped by human and natural events. Moreover, God's work was evidenced primarily through historical process. These conflicting understandings of history spilled over into how both parties understood and interpreted the Bible. For most fundamentalists, Scripture was God's revelation and its message could be grasped by the process of induction.[122] While it is unfair to claim that fundamentalists believed in dictation, this interpretative method dramatically reduced any notion that the human

---

122. This understanding cuts across the various parties within the fundamentalist coalition. See Noll, *Scandal of the Evangelical Mind*, 133–34.

experience of the biblical writers could play a significant role in the formation and interpretation of the Scriptures.[123]

Modernists developed a dramatically different understanding of
Scripture and its role. If God primarily revealed himself through historical
process, then the Bible, although a very good source, was simply one way
that God had revealed himself in history. So the Bible was not immune
from the same critical analysis we would apply to any book. Moreover, God
could reveal himself through other religions outside of Christianity. Christian theology must take into account the progressive nature of God's revelation through historical process and come to grips with modern knowledge.
That means that our traditional understandings of doctrine will need to be
revised where necessary.

Their radically different understandings of history also impacted the
ways the two parties understood the relationship between Christianity and
culture. Because the modernist impulse generally affirmed that God primarily revealed himself in the progression of history, liberals in the period
between the Civil War and World War I were on the whole optimistic about
humanity and human ability to solve the most perplexing local, national,
and world problems. Fundamentalists, on the other hand, saw a deeply
anti-Christian impulse in modern culture. The modern notions of evolutionary and historical process were destroying the Christian foundations
of the United States and replacing them with a secular barbarity. And for
the large segment of fundamentalists who subscribed to the dispensational
version of premillennialism, this was seen as part of God's plan leading to
the visible return of Jesus Christ and the establishment of God's kingdom.
For liberals, the church was to affirm God's work in historical process by
working with others to alleviate society's great social problems. Through
that process, God's kingdom would be inaugurated. For fundamentalists,
society was hopeless and the task of the church was to announce the gospel
as the only way to face the impending judgment of God upon the world.

Progressives and traditionalists were divided not only on how to
use the Bible to formulate Christian doctrine, but on the mission of the
church in the modern world. The conflict between these two parties would
begin to be felt in denominations like the Advent Christian Church, that
were emerging from isolation as the twentieth century moved beyond the
Second World War. As early as the 1920s, the Fundamentalist-Modernist
debates were influencing the two Advent Christian schools committed to

123. Ibid., 133.

training an educated clergy. Two of the institutions mentioned in this chapter, the University of Chicago Divinity School and Westminster Theological Seminary, would have significant impact upon Advent Christian teachers and educators. Through Aurora College and the New England School of Theology, those Advent Christian educators and theologians would approach these issues in very different ways. That will be the subject of our next chapter.

CHAPTER THREE

Advent Christian Responses to the Fundamentalist-Modernist Controversy

IN CONSIDERING HOW THE Fundamentalist-Modernist controversy influenced the Advent Christian Church, it is important to measure the response in denominational pulpits and publications as well as within the New England School of Theology and Aurora College—the two Advent Christian-related institutions of higher learning from which the majority of Advent Christian clergy with post-high school education graduated. Most Advent Christian clergy and laypeople, with little variation, believed in some form of verbal inspiration of the Bible combined with the need for literal interpretation.[1] That conviction was reflected on the pages of Advent Christian periodicals during the early 1900s, of which the largest and most influential was the *World's Crisis*. The *Crisis* was the voice of eastern Adventism, although it was read and respected beyond New England as well. While it primarily focused on matters relating to the return of Christ, distinctive Advent Christian doctrines like conditional immortality, and denominational work, its editors did reflect an awareness of the controversy between Northern Baptist and Northern Presbyterian fundamentalists and modernists.

As early as 1905, the *Crisis* ran an article by I. M. Blanchard arguing that the New Theology was dangerous because by weakening the authority

---

1. Bailey, "Various Theories," 24–25.

of Scripture, it replaced the personal God of Christian faith with the notion of God as eternal principle.[2] The New Theology, according to Blanchard, also minimized the nature and impact of sin, emphasized pantheism, rendered the atonement of Christ superfluous, and nullified traditional Christian understandings of redemption, forgiveness, sanctification, glorification, and other doctrines. In Blanchard's words, "It canonizes scientists, historians, poets, and novelists, and brands New Testament writers with ignorance and superstition."[3]

With the Fundamentalist-Modernist controversy at its peak among Northern Baptists and breaking out among Northern Presbyterians during 1922, several *Crisis* issues featured articles touching on some aspects of the controversy. Most significant was a prominent four-part series titled "Destructive Criticism" by George L. Young with the first installment running on May 17, 1922, only six days before the infamous Harry Emerson Fosdick sermon.[4] After declaring that the Bible presents a wonderful unity despite its diverse authorship and that "Everything—history, prophecy, psalmody, wisdom, literature—falls harmoniously into line,"[5] Young summarized the basics of the Graf-Wellhausen documentary hypothesis of Pentateuchal origins along with other higher-critical assumptions relating to the Old Testament.

The remainder of the four-part series describes what Young saw as the destructive efforts of higher criticism. Higher criticism "is destructive of the miraculous element of the Bible."[6] For Young, higher criticism replaces the "real and objective" revelation of God through Scripture with "an internal or subjective illumination. That is, God did not speak to men, nor in any way give to them direct communication of truth. Instead, men grew into a knowledge of God and of divine things through the workings of their own minds."[7] Higher criticism destroys authentic Christian faith by grossly distorting the nature and character of God. "The god of the critics," in Young's words, "is wholly a manufactured article, as much so as if

---

2. Blanchard, "New Theology."

3. Ibid., 1.

4. Young, "Destructive Criticism." For a brief biographical sketch and summary of Young's understanding of inspiration and his theological and apologetic work, see Dean, "Echoes," 318–59.

5. Young, "Destructive Criticism," May 17, 1922, 6.

6. Young, "Destructive Criticism," May 24, 1922, 6.

7. *World's Crisis*, May 31, 1922, 6.

carved out of wood or stone."[8] Higher criticism destroys the fundamental doctrines of Christianity and "destroys the foundations of all true human hopes."[9] Young's analysis was perceptive and demonstrates not only a confidence in the Bible as the written word of God but an understanding of the important theological issues of his time and their implications for Advent Christians.

Several other articles that appeared in the *World's Crisis* during 1922 reflected an awareness of the debates between Modernists and Fundamentalists. They point to an interesting tension that Advent Christians felt in their relationship with other Protestants. On the front page of the July 19, 1922, issue, an excerpt from William Jennings Bryan's address before the 1922 Northern Baptist Convention in Indianapolis was featured.[10] Several issues included an advertisement for *In His Image*, the book form of Bryan's James Sprint Lectures of 1921.[11] The *Crisis* also published Robert Dick Wilson's *Sunday School Times* article, "Have the Critics Hurt Daniel?"[12] and featured an address by A.Z. Conrad, then pastor of Park Street Church in Boston, titled "The Mistakes of Modernism."[13] The editors leave little room to doubt their sympathy with the theological and social concerns of Northern Baptist and Northern Presbyterian fundamentalists, especially concerning the inspiration of Scripture.

At the same time, Advent Christian uneasiness with parts of the fundamentalist agenda is reflected on these pages as well. In the issue dated May 3, 1922, I.G. Eagen presumes that "there is not a single body of Christian people that does not have error and apostasy to some extent."[14] For Eagen, the Advent Christian way of extending fellowship via Christian character, not doctrinal precision is far better than the intolerant attitude "of the orthodox churches (so-called) toward those who teach Bible Truths."[15] Opposition to dispensationalist-premillennialist eschatology is

---

8. *World's Crisis*, May 31, 1922, 6.

9. *World's Crisis*, June 7, 1922, 6.

10. *World's Crisis*, July 19, 1922, 1.

11. For example, see *World's Crisis*, December 6, 1922, 16. The advertisement billed the book as "the Greatest Rebuttal since 'Darwinism' attacked the Evidence of the Bible."

12. *World's Crisis*, July 26, 1922, 6.

13. *World's Crisis*, September 6, 1922, 6.

14. *World's Crisis*, May 3, 1922, 89.

15. Ibid., 8–9. Many Advent Christians have referred to the doctrinal distinctives of their denomination as "Bible Truths."

reflected in C.V. Tenney's, "Daniel's Seventieth Week: Past, Not Future."[16] In regard to the dispensational doctrine of the secret rapture, Tenney declares, "This theory ought to be refuted every time it is put forth."[17] The tension between dispensationalists and Advent Christians is also illustrated by Horace E. Thompson's strong refutation of an anti-Adventist booklet that appears to have originated within dispensationalist circles.[18] These articles reflect that while most Advent Christians in the east were in harmony with fundamentalists on questions relating to the authority of Scripture and on many questions relating to public morality, they still felt the need to establish their own doctrinal and prophetic identity distinct from that of a futurist oriented dispensational-premillennialism.[19]

The interest in the controversy between fundamentalists and modernists reflected in the pages of the *World's Crisis* was not necessarily shared by other Advent Christian periodicals published in other regions of the United States. While the *Crisis* was the oldest and largest Advent Christian periodical published during the first quarter of the twentieth century, at least three other Advent Christian papers were published in other regions of the country. They reflected an even more parochial character than did the *Crisis*. While it reflects a conservative view of the Bible's inspiration and a strongly anti-Darwinist tone, one must look hard to find any significant references to the controversies between fundamentalists and modernists in the pages of *Our Hope and Life in Christ*, published in Mendota, Illinois, by Advent Christians in the Midwest. The Presbyterian controversy is not mentioned at all although fundamentalists in the Northern Baptist Convention receive an approving response from *Our Hope* editor Fim Murra, "While it is true that we do not endorse all of the

16. *World's Crisis*, May 31, 1922, 7.

17. Ibid., 7.

18. Thompson, "Measuring Adventism," 4.

19. *World's Crisis*, September 13, 1922, 2. Delegates to the 1922 Advent Christian General Conference, held June 22–25 in Plainville, CT, passed the following resolution: "While this Conference is not concerned with the contention of premillennialists, and view with considerable distrust the program of so-called Futurists generally, it is cognizant of a wide movement today that must result in a lessening regard for the old fundamentals of the faith. This Conference stands for an unwavering recognition of the inspired Word of God as the Court of appeal in determining Christian faith and doctrine. It also urges its ministry that its stand should be with the defenders of the Book, and that in that system of doctrine as taught in the New Testament and held by the churches, the doctrine of the Second Advent and of the resurrection of the dead must ever be given a large place."

teachings of the Fundamentalists, yet we may well rejoice that the great truth of the Second Coming of Christ . . . is receiving such prominence by some of the greatest religious leaders of the day."[20]

The focus of *Our Hope* in the early 1920s was strongly oriented in two directions: the apologetic articulation and defense of distinctive Advent Christian doctrines and promotion of the Advent Christian Forward Movement, an attempt at a unified budgeting and fund-raising approach for all Advent Christian-related institutions and ministries.[21] "There should be," in the words of the editor, "an intelligent presentation . . . of those fundamental doctrines as we see them, regarding the atonement, Conditional Immortality, the Second Coming of Christ, the Kingdom of God, and related themes. Too many are growing up in our own churches and Sunday schools without a clear and definite understanding of these great truths, and this is especially true in regard to prophecy."[22] As editor of *Our Hope*, Fim Murra was determined to see that those distinctive doctrinal themes were featured prominently on the pages of his publication.

Two minor but fascinating articles appeared on the pages of *Our Hope* during 1922. The first appeared amidst a flood of positive reporting on the Forward Movement that characterized the paper during that year, and points to a subtle yet important undercurrent within the denomination. "Our independent sectoral growth of the past," according to J.H. Crouse, "has developed too great a burden for the denomination to shoulder. We

20. *Our Hope*, July 12, 1922. Murra describes how Northern Baptist progressives fought off an attempt by Fundamentalists to make the New Hampshire Confession of Faith the official creed of the Northern Baptist Convention. For the progressives to argue that the New Testament is sufficient as a rule for faith and order and subsequently deny the return of Christ and the bodily resurrection of the dead demonstrates why "the issue is so sharp between the Fundamentalists and the Liberals among the Baptists."

21. For a description of the Forward Movement, see Hewitt, *Devotion and Development*, 209–66. This movement represented the first attempt at organizational unity within the Advent Christian Church. In Hewitt's view, the Forward Movement ultimately failed and that failure established an unfortunate precedent for later attempts at budgetary and structural unity. For another study of the Forward Movement, see D. E. Dean, "Forward Movement," 11–29.

22. Murra, "Encouraging Tokens," 2–3. Murra argues that the proclamation of these distinctives must also be done in the context of a clear, compassionate presentation of the gospel of Christ. And that work can involve cooperation with other Christian congregations in the community. "This can be done in the best of fellowship, and, even cooperation of sister churches in the community. The need is so great that there is plenty of work for all, and if we go forth in love and compassion for lost men, God will honor and bless the efforts."

have grown up almost as four distinct denominations with only an occasional exchange of fraternal delegates. Each section has its paper and other expenditures which mean an overlapping or double expenditure which is wasteful."[23] The author boldly discusses an issue that many Advent Christians, especially those in denominational leadership, tried to ignore—the strong regionalism that had emerged within the denomination since its founding in 1860 and that would continue to be a major force within the Advent Christian Church well into the latter part of the twentieth century. That regionalism would impact the doctrinal controversies which would emerge a quarter of a century later.[24]

The second article is a reprint of an unsigned editorial from a publication called *Homiletical Review*. Conservatives and progressives can fellowship together, asserts the unidentified writer, if they base their community not on doctrine but on Christ. "True fundamentalism founds faith upon Christ and not upon any doctrines or theories about him . . . . Unless we can adhere to this essential unity in Christ— united in him and agreeing to differ in our doctrinal interpretations and ideas—we shall be untrue to our common faith; and the result will be reproach to ourselves, and disaster to our cause."[25] Here is a theme reflected by a large number of moderates, even some progressives—a theme that by the 1940s would be articulated by Advent Christian theologians at Aurora University and embraced among Advent Christian graduates from that institution.

Like the *World's Crisis*, its eastern counterpart, the editor of *Our Hope* focused on distinctive Advent Christian doctrines. Unlike his New England colleagues, Murra devoted less space to events and controversies outside of the denomination. On the surface, an Advent Christian reader of both publications would probably see little difference between them. However, as evidenced from our discussion above, one can see glimpses of emerging fissures between Eastern and Midwestern Advent Christian thinking. Eastern Adventism, as represented by the *World's Crisis*, offers a more nuanced understanding of the Bible's inspiration and reflects a greater interest

---

23. Crouse, "An Expression," 78.

24. Ibid. In his discussion of overlapping programs, Crouse suggests that Advent Christians in New England "surrender [their] school toward making a theological department worth while at Aurora." His statement provides evidence that the rivalry between the New England School of Theology and Aurora College was already being felt within the denomination and was most likely contributing to the growing regional divisions between Advent Christians in different parts of the United States.

25. "Can We Fellowship?," 8.

for events within the wider scope of American Christianity. Midwestern Adventism, as seen in *Our Hope*, is focused more exclusively on Advent Christian doctrine and church life. While it is easy to conclude that Murra and the bulk of *Our Hope* authors understood the Bible as the inspired Word of God, they were more concerned to use it to articulate and defend distinctive Advent Christian doctrines. Advent Christians in the 1920s were strongly sectarian and it appears that Midwestern Advent Christians were more strongly so than their counterparts in the east.

That sectarian spirit was reflected even more strongly on the pages of the *Messiah's Advocate*, published in Oakland, California, by Advent Christians on the Pacific Coast. The first Advent Christian congregation on the West Coast was organized in Vallejo, California, in 1871. From there, Advent Christians were able to organize a sizable number of congregations in California, Oregon, Washington, and Idaho.[26] Ten years later, West Coast Advent Christians had established their own periodical, to function, in the words of its first editor, Henry F. Carpenter, "as a medium of communication between those 'waiting for God's Son from Heaven' on this coast."[27]

The content of *Messiah's Advocate* during the year 1922, reflected a strong emphasis on the interpretation of biblical prophecy. In the view of editor J.J. Schaumberg, Advent Christians needed to turn from sinful practices and from focusing on building successful enterprises and recapture the passion of the early Adventists for proclaiming the message of Christ's soon return. "But in the early days of our message," according to Schaumberg, "men did not stress the material and commercial things."[28] Advent Christians, in the editor's view, must reject sinful practices (belonging to lodges, attending places of amusement, using tobacco products). Advent Christian ministers must recognize that it is wrong to "play politics, or to turn higher critic, and deny any portion of Old Testament history, or to marry couples who have been divorced for no reason other than modern reason." What does God expect of Advent Christians? He expects them to emphasize "Jesus' coming soon, preparation to meet him, lamps filled with oil, wicks trimmed, and everything ready for such a trip to the city above."

---

26. For a discussion of Advent Christian organization and expansion on the Pacific Coast, see Hewitt, *Devotion and Development*, 42–66.

27. *Pacific Missionary Advocate and Herald of the Advent*, January 1881; reprinted in Johnson, *Advent Christian History*, 375. For a history of the *Messiah's Advocate*, from its establishment in 1881 to its end in 1952, see Hewitt, *Responsibility and Response*.

28. Schaumberg, "Adventism," 60–61.

Advent Christians have but one message: "Jesus is at the door! Seek God! Get Ready!"

Advent Christian distinctive doctrines were emphasized but more in the context of how to properly understand biblical prophecy and the soon return of Jesus Christ. Under Schaumberg's editorship, the content of *Messiah's Advocate* reflected strong anti-Catholic,[29] anti-Darwinist, and anti-dispensationalist views. In terms of the larger controversy between fundamentalists and modernists, while the paper is largely silent about the battles raging within Northern Baptist and Northern Presbyterian circles, the editor does demonstrate awareness of the larger issues. "Any one who thinks," in the words of Schaumberg, "that the evils of the modern "New Theology" are but slight, and will soon be dead, has another guess coming."[30] This theology, in the editor's view, emasculates the gospel and damages the cause of world missions. Therefore, Advent Christian ministers and schools, "must stand on the Old Jerusalem gospel built on an inspired Bible." Moreover, "a man . . . who has no real convictions concerning the Book, is not qualified to act as a teacher or preacher of the Word. God help us as Adventists to see this before it is too late."

What can we conclude from our survey of 1922 issues of these three publications? Despite the large controversies that had gripped the major denominations of American Protestantism, Advent Christians were focused more on attempting to articulate what they saw as their distinctive identity. What was that unique identity? While the content of the three papers overlaps significantly, we discover that each poses a slightly different understanding of Advent Christian identity. In the east, the editors of the *World's Crisis* imply that a unique Advent Christian identity, while grounded in doctrinal distinctives, must take into consideration the context of events in the larger world of American Protestantism. In the Midwest, that identity appears more dependent upon the articulate presentation of a distinctive Advent Christian doctrinal approach that emphasizes conditional immortality and the unique Advent Christian teaching on the nature of humanity. On the West Coast, that identity focuses primarily on recapturing the early Advent Christian emphasis on biblical prophecy and the imminent return of Jesus Christ.

29. Schaumberg, "The Church of Rome Today," 108. "Brethren, keep your eyes on Rome! The Church of Rome represents the very last part of the great image of Daniel two. The crash and smiting must soon come. Mistic [sic] Babylon goes down and the Kingdom of God comes up! Hallelujah!"

30. Schaumberg, "Missions and Modernism," 156–57.

These differences are subtle but real. They point us to subtle but real regional differences within the Advent Christian church as a whole. They also help us see that while most Advent Christians believed that the Bible was the inspired Word of God, how they understood the doctrine of inspiration and how they understood the controversies over inspiration within American Protestantism during the 1920s were shaped in part by how they understood the unique identity of the Advent Christian Church. Advent Christians were overwhelmingly traditional and conservative in their approach to the inspiration of the Bible, although for most of them, the denomination had a far more important task—emphasizing and communicating their unique doctrinal truths and message first to people who attended their congregations, and second to the outside world. That was far more important than worrying about theological conflicts within other denominations, especially when the combatants seemed hostile to Advent Christian doctrine.

Aurora College and "Dynamic Inspiration"

While the various Advent Christian publications viewed the controversy between fundamentalists and modernists with differing degrees of interest, its impact was felt in significant ways at both Aurora College and the New England School of Theology. In the Midwest, with the move of Mendota College to Aurora, Illinois, a growing community approximately forty miles west of Chicago, Orrin Roe Jenks began his twenty-two-year tenure as president of the fledgling institution. Jenks would become widely influential among Advent Christians during the first half of the twentieth century. A gifted theologian, author, speaker, and administrator; his service to the Advent Christian Church in addition to his Aurora College presidency included pastoral ministry, and several denominational positions including the presidency of the Advent Christian General Conference.[31]

Jenks was converted to the Christian faith in July, 1884. One year later he was ordained into the ministry of the Church of God (Abrahamic Faith), a denomination that emerged from the Joseph Marsh wing of the Millerite Movement.[32] His service with the Advent Christian Church began in 1888

31. For biographies of Orrin Roe Jenks, see Anderson, *Upon a Rock*, 21–24; and Dean, "Echoes," 359–60. Dean provides a discussion of Jenks's understanding of inspiration and his theological method on pp. 359–400.

32. The Church of God (Abrahamic Faith) was the last Adventist grouping to

with a succession of three pastorates in the upper Midwest and editorship of an independent Advent Christian paper, *Gleams of the Morning*. Throughout the 1890s, Jenks was a strong advocate of distinctive Advent Christian doctrines, an apologist for understanding the Bible as the written Word of God, and an opponent of the higher criticism of Scripture.[33]

In 1900, Jenks moved to Chicago to begin a ten-year pastorate of the Advent Christian Church in that city. While there, he began to teach Bible at Mendota College and pursue graduate study in Old Testament at the University of Chicago Divinity School. His mimeographed lecture notes and classroom syllabi reflected not only his ongoing studies at the University of Chicago but his growing acceptance of higher critical categories and conclusions.[34] By 1909, Jenks had published two sets of classroom syllabi in pamphlet form. The first focused on Amos and Isaiah and concluded with these words, "Thus, in bare outline, we have studied the life of Isaiah, viz., chapters 1–39. The second part of the book, 40–66, must be reserved for another period."[35] While those words could have been interpreted in several ways, with publication a year later of *The Last Prophets of Israel*,[36] Jenks affirmed his belief that Isaiah 40–66 represents "not the production of the prophet Isaiah, but of a later prophet, or even of several prophets."[37] Jenks referred to Isaiah 40–66 as Second Isaiah and remarked that "the historical situation is not that of the eighth century, the time when Isaiah lived, but that of the sixth century when Israel was in captivity in Babylon."[38] In the preface to his pamphlet on Amos and Isaiah, Jenks

---

formally organize, waiting until 1921 to do so. This Adventist body descended from the "Age to Come" Adventism of Joseph Marsh. Marsh and his followers taught that the Jewish people would return to Israel and that individuals would have a second chance to be saved during the Age to Come. In Clyde Hewitt's words, they "were so infused with a belief that any ecclesiastical organization beyond the local church level was unscriptural that it was not until the later part of the nineteenth century that serious efforts looking toward a denomination began to be made." Hewitt, *Midnight and Morning*, 272–75. See also, Knight, *Millennial Fever*, 289.

33. Dean, "Echoes," 263. Jenks urged his readers to "grasp anew the Protestant faith: that the Supreme authority of the Christian religion is the Word of God." Jenks quoted by Dean from an undated sermon in O. R. Jenks's papers at Aurora University.

34. Dean, "Echoes," 380–81. Jenks moved from outright rejection to acceptance of the GrafWellhausen documentary hypothesis of Pentateuchal origins.

35. Jenks, *Life and Times*, 35.

36. Jenks, *Last Prophets*, 2, 17.

37. Ibid., 17.

38. Ibid.

expresses appreciation for the valuable help he received from the lectures of Dr. Ira M. Price.[39] Price was a recognized scholar in biblical languages who focused on Old Testament studies. For Price, the Old Testament writers were holy but fallible men who wrote to emphasize some particular thought on their mind.[40] Not only were the Old Testament writings never intended to teach science, in Price's view, they were dependent upon much older sources and traditions.[41]

As Jenks continued to use higher critical tools in his work, his view of predictive prophecy and the inspiration of Scripture underwent transformation. While he retained his belief in the visible return of Jesus Christ, the focus of Bible prophecy for Jenks was not primarily predictive but moral.[42] In his view of Scripture, he followed his mentor, Ira Price. Jenks had adopted the view that the creation narrative of Genesis was not in agreement with modern science.[43] So for Jenks, "the Old Testament writer always has the religious purpose in view. One must remember that he is not concerned primarily with history, chronology, sociology, science, psychology, etc."[44] The Bible, for Jenks, focused primarily on man's conduct and his relationships with God and others.[45]

Orrin Roe Jenks was a man of considerable intellectual and administrative skill. Without him, Aurora College probably would not have succeeded. His views created controversy within the denomination and accusations of heresy would raise Jenks' ire.[46] His identification with the University of Chicago likely created tension between the college and the evangelical institutions of higher learning in the area, especially Moody

---

39. Jenks, *Life and Times*, 2. In both pamphlets, the bibliographies list works by Price and other University of Chicago Divinity School professors.

40. Axel, "God or Man at Chicago," 146.

41. Ibid.

42. Anderson, *Upon a Rock*, 44. Anderson and Dean point out that Jenks received several challenges from within the Advent Christian Church regarding his higher critical views. Anderson remarks that Jenks sought to "find meanings in the prophetic writings that concerned the days in which they were written, rather than using them to sustain current Adventual doctrinal and prophetic interpretations."

43. Dean, "Echoes," 390.

44. Jenks, "The Poetry of the Old Testament," 2. I appreciate David A. Dean calling my attention to this source.

45. Ibid.

46. Anderson, *Upon a Rock*, 44–60; Dean, "Echoes," 383.

Bible Institute.[47] Moody, Wheaton College, and other fundamentalist institutions in the greater Chicago area were strongly dispensational and opposed to the historicist prophetic interpretations characteristic of Adventism. The adoption of higher-critical views by the president of an Advent Christian-related college would only increase the mutual tension between Aurora College and fundamentalist leaders in the Chicago area.[48]

While Orrin Roe Jenks' influence was still at its height, one of his students would begin a rise to prominence both at Aurora College and within the denomination. Like his mentor, Clarence Horace Hewitt would make his mark as a pastor, teacher, administrator, theologian, and author. He graduated from Aurora College (B.Th., 1926); the University of New Hampshire (M.A. in Psychology, 1927); and studied at the University of Chicago Divinity School. During his career, Hewitt served several Advent Christian congregations as pastor, taught as a member of the Aurora College faculty for twenty years (1927–1947), and served full-time as Executive Secretary for the denomination from 1942 through 1947.[49] Hewitt was a prolific author whose work touched a wide range of prophetic and theological issues. In addition to six books, he published regularly in several Advent Christian

47. Oral history interview, David A. Dean and Freeman Barton, August 4, 1994. Dean related two incidents connected to the tension between Aurora College and the evangelical community in Chicago. The first focused on a student of Jenks, R. L. Peterson, who after completing a course of study at Moody Bible Institute was refused a diploma because he was unable to sign the Institute's doctrinal statement. Jenks threatened Moody with a lawsuit and apparently afterwards, Peterson was awarded the diploma.

Another incident occurred soon after Jenks became president of the newly moved Aurora College. Jenks accepted an invitation to offer the invocation at the inauguration of the new Wheaton College president. That invitation was withdrawn after someone from Moody Bible Institute protested Jenks's inclusion and threatened not to appear.

48. Jenks's disposition toward what he considered non-intellectual approaches to Christian faith and theology is best illustrated by his response to the tragic death of an Aurora student who was run over by a train in 1922. The student, Wallace Armstrong, while on a trip to Chicago, "had come into contact with a group of people who hold extreme views in regard to Christian experience. They had taught him that if he would seek the baptism of the Holy Spirit he would receive the gift of healing, tongues, and various other gifts which would endow him with almost unlimited power."

Jenks concluded that Armstrong had run out in front of the train "because he was obsessed with the idea that he had power to stop the train." Therefore, "we cannot hold him responsible for the sad ending of his life." The responsibility must rest in Jenks's view with those who teach these extreme Pentecostal doctrines. These views lead to folly, fanaticism, and division within churches. "The safe road," according to Jenks, "leads in the way of moderation." See, Jenks, "The Aurora Tragedy," 15.

49. For a biographical sketch of Clarence Hewitt, see Dean, "Echoes," 402–3.

periodicals. Due to premature death at age 62, Hewitt was unable to finish a task that he longed to complete: a systematic theology written from a distinctively Advent Christian viewpoint.[50]

In terms of his view of inspiration, Clarence Hewitt follows his mentor, Orrin Roe Jenks. "The Bible is primarily a religious book," in Hewitt's words. "Its field is that of moral and spiritual truth . . . It is not, and makes no pretense to be, infallible in scientific matters."[51] The Bible's accuracy and reliability, in Hewitt's view, is limited to the field of its own specialization. "It is inerrant as a revelation of God and his saving truth."[52] However its claim to infallibility does not extend to matters of science and history. For Hewitt, the notion of verbal inspiration was synonymous with dictation.[53] While verbal inspiration is an ancient and honorable position, "it has largely served its purpose. Just as there is progressive revelation, so there is progressive thinking about revelation, and there is a more modern—not modernistic—explanation which fits the facts really better than the old opinion."[54]

That explanation Hewitt termed the "dynamic" theory of inspiration. "Dynamic inspiration means that the men, not the words, were inspired. It supposes that God gave the ideas, leaving the writers free to express the truths they had received each in his own way . . . It is inspiration of thought rather than of wording."[55] Because inspiration focuses on the writer, not his words, Hewitt postulates certain kinds and degrees of inspiration. "The words of Jesus the Christ . . . must embody a higher kind of inspiration than the proverbs written and collected by Solomon."[56] Theological treatises like

---

50. Hewitt did complete the first part, titled *A Classbook in Eschatology*, which focused on doctrines relating to individual and general eschatology. The book was reprinted under a different title. See, Hewitt, *What Does the Future Hold?* Hewitt's booklet, *The Conditional Principle in Theology*, was completed the night before his death and provides some hints as to what his completed systematic theology may have looked like. See Hewitt, *Conditional Principle*.

51. Hewitt, *Faith for Today*, 60.

52. Ibid., 61.

53. Ibid., 62. Hewitt wrote, "Put somewhat crudely, God dictated word for word to men who served as stenographers, and they wrote down what God said."

54. Ibid.

55. Ibid.

56. Ibid., 63–64.

Romans and Hebrews must require a higher degree of inspiration than the records of events reflected in the chronicles of the Israelite kings.[57]

In terms of theological method, Hewitt sees in the Bible not so much the source for doctrine and theology, but "the touch-stone by which we test the truth or falsity of theological doctrines. No doctrine can be held as a fundamental of faith which cannot be proved by certain warranty of Scripture, and no theory can be true that is contrary to Bible statements."[58] The formation of Christian doctrine for Hewitt combined examination of theological concepts, of historical theology, and of biblical and extra-biblical statements.[59]

Advent Christians, in Clarence Hewitt's view, were neither liberals nor fundamentalists.[60] They needed a theological focus that would distinguish them from both parties. For Hewitt that focus was found by elevating the doctrine of conditional immortality to what he termed "the conditional principle." This principle, in Hewitt's words, "in its simplest terms may be defined as follows: All the blessings of God are conditioned upon human factors. The blessings are from God, and God only, but man must do something in order to receive them."[61] After citing a variety of Scripture passages in support, Hewitt declares "it is a basic principle of Biblical theology that all the mercies of God are conditioned upon human factors: attitudes, choices, or actions."[62] In Hewitt's theology, human autonomy and freedom become central and conclusions in all areas of Christian theology, especially Advent Christian theology, must be shaped by the conditional principle.[63]

Hewitt followed Miles Grant in attempting to create a distinctive Advent Christian theology by elevating the doctrine of conditional immortality to center stage. For Hewitt, "Conditional Immortality is but one phase of

---

57. Ibid., 64.

58. Ibid., 65.

59. Dean, "Echoes," 425.

60. Oral History Interview, Dean and Barton, August 4, 1994, 11.

61. Hewitt, *Conditional Principle*, 8.

62. Ibid., 13.

63. Ibid., 8. The occasion for writing *The Conditional Principle in Theology* was Hewitt's alarm over the growth of Reformed theology within the Advent Christian Church. On pp. 60–61, he writes, "From the beginning of our history we [Advent Christians] have recognized that our theological position is Arminian in character. To depart from that stand, and to try now to crawl under the Calvinist umbrella, would be in my considered judgment . . . not only a betrayal of our heritage but also a grave threat to our future."

the general principle of Conditionalism in theology."[64] In Hewitt's view, the conditional principle gave Advent Christian theology a strong Arminian character.[65] His understanding of Scripture as dynamically inspired provided Advent Christians, he thought, with a mediating position between Fundamentalism and liberalism.

By the mid-1930s, the Fundamentalist-Modernist controversies within the Northern Baptist and Northern Presbyterian denominations were winding down with the progressives in control not only of the denominational machinery but of the key divinity schools and seminaries that trained clergy in those denominations. Under the direction of Orrin Roe Jenks and Clarence Hewitt, by the outbreak of World War II, the theological approach of Aurora College was positioned comfortably within the sphere of this emerging liberal Protestant mainline.[66]

NEST and Biblical Inerrancy

While Aurora College identified with the emerging Protestant mainline, a different trend took shape among Advent Christians in New England. For the first thirty years of its existence, the New England School of Theology was theologically eclectic, especially in terms of its understanding of the nature of God.[67] While the school was generally conservative in its understanding of inspiration, the focus of the first thirty years was more on institutional survival than on constructing a coherent biblical and theological orientation.[68] That began to change in 1927 with the arrival of James Albert Nichols, Jr. Born in 1899 in Old Orchard, Maine, Nichols was the

64. Ibid., 8. See also, Dean, "Echoes," 449. Dean writes, "To employ human reason rather than the Scripture as the source and touchstone of doctrine is the 'Rationalistic Principle.' By means of it, Hewitt is able to transform 'Conditional Immortality' into the 'Conditional Principle.'"

65. Ibid., 60. For Hewitt, Arminian theology "is a system which is practically based upon the Conditional Principle, and which makes room for it . . . at every point."

66. Yet with this conclusion, it is important to note the efforts of Clarence Hewitt to define a mediating position between Fundamentalism and Modernism. Hewitt wanted to articulate a position that was in touch with modern sensibilities in regard to how the Bible was inspired while at the same time maintaining some semblance of the uniqueness of Jesus Christ and the necessity of repentance and faith in him as a condition of salvation.

67. Fillinger, "Berkshire Christian College," 65.

68. Ibid., 35.

son of an active Advent Christian pastor. A graduate of the University of Maine (B.A. in English, 1924), Nichols would later complete two degrees at Gordon Divinity School (B.D., 1935; Th.D., 1949), and, while continuing his teaching ministry, would serve the Advent Christian Church as editor of the *World's Crisis* from 1945–1952.[69] His love was teaching and the subject he loved most was systematic theology. His teaching would not only impact the lives of scores of Advent Christian pastors, but would move New England School of Theology toward a distinctively Reformed, evangelical theological posture.[70]

For Nichols, the source for Christian theology was the infallible standard of Scripture. Through the Bible, Christians throughout history have possessed "an objective standard of truth that enables them to judge the varying teachings and opinions of men. This standard reveals truths which men could never discover themselves."[71] The Bible is not one source of revelation among many. Although Nichols believed that the facts "revealed in geology, physics, biology, and psychology, are a part of the divine revelation as surely as those recorded in the Bible,"[72] the chief source of truth regarding man's relationship to God is the Bible.

The Scriptures are an infallible standard and for Nichols, their inspiration guarantees inerrancy.[73] The human authors of the Bible "were inspired by the Spirit of God to recognize the divine revelation as from God and to record its truths accurately."[74] Inspiration is both verbal and plenary. Inspiration, for Nichols, extended to the words of Scripture. The Holy Spirit guided the authors so "that they expressed the revealed facts and thoughts in words that accurately conveyed the facts and thoughts."[75] Inspiration also extended to every part of Scripture. While there are many methods

69. For a biographical sketch, see Dean, "Echoes," 404; and the foreword by Roger Nicole in Nichols, Jr., *Christian Doctrines*.

70. Fillinger, "Berkshire Christian College," 66–68.

71. Nichols, *Christian Doctrines*, 4. While the publishing of this book came after Dr. Nichols retired from active teaching, it was prepared from his earlier lecture notes and syllabi. His former students and colleagues Oral Collins, David A. Dean, Fred Ehle, and Robert Fillinger directed the project.

72. Ibid., xi.

73. Ibid., 4.

74. Ibid.

75. Ibid., 5.

of revelation within Scripture, "All is God's revelation; all is inspired and therefore authoritative."[76]

Nichols was sensitive to the charge that the notion of verbal, plenary inspiration meant that the authors were stenographers through whom God mechanically dictated the words of the Bible: "[T]he Holy Spirit did not work in a mechanical way upon the authors of Scripture, ignoring their personalities, distinctive abilities, and previous training. On the contrary, the Spirit so used these men that they freely wrote sober prose, poetry, allegory, symbols, laws, and predictions."[77] The authors wrote in their own languages and used their own styles and idioms. Yet, God's spirit acted on them in such a way that while the words are authentically those of the author, "they are also God's; hence authoritative and free from error."[78]

Because the Bible is the source of Christian theology, for Nichols, the proper development of a theological system must be based on proper exegesis. "Exegesis must preclude theological formulas and doctrinal statements. Theology should not start with doctrinal presuppositions and then attempt to reconcile the Bible with them."[79] Developing a Christian theological system in Nichols' view should "take into account all the facts, especially those of divine revelation, if it is to succeed in giving a faithful and complete world view."[80] For Nichols, the task of theology was not constructing an apologetic for the doctrinal distinctives of a particular denomination. Nor was it to start with the presuppositions of philosophers or theologians. Theology starts with an objective consideration of the data of Scripture. "This data, when defined, explained, and systematized becomes theology."[81]

While James Nichols, Jr. would develop a theology that was moderately Reformed and distinctively Advent Christian, he did so not in an attempt to prove either, but to produce Christian theology that was faithful to what he saw in the Bible, properly interpreted. Unlike Grant or Hewitt, who attempted to use the Advent Christian doctrinal distinctive of conditional immortality as the starting point for their theological efforts, for Nichols, the heart of Christian theology was found in God's revelation through Holy Scripture. And unlike Hewitt, Nichols declared that "Advent

76. Ibid.
77. Ibid., 6.
78. Ibid.
79. Ibid., 17.
80. Ibid.
81. Ibid.

Christians should classify themselves with the conservatives, because these people take the Bible as God's Word, as authoritative in all matters of faith and doctrine, and as supernaturally inspired."[82] If Advent Christians were to abandon the Scriptures as the source and starting point of Christian theology, then two unfortunate consequences would occur. First, Advent Christians could not argue that the resurrection of the body, the personal return of Jesus Christ, and the doctrine of conditional immortality are true. Second, many Advent Christians, especially young people, would abandon the Christian faith first for theological liberalism, then for secularism.[83]

Nichols saw the consequences of modernist theology much in the same way as John Gresham Machen. Nichols saw no mediating position between Fundamentalism and Modernism. Therefore Advent Christians should think and act like conservatives because, "those who leave this position, as Walter Lippmann has clearly indicated, logically have no stopping point until they land in humanism, which is definitely non-Christian."[84] When the Bible is abandoned as the source of Christian revelation; speculation, human philosophy, and "a necessary ignorance" become its replacements.[85]

For over forty years until his retirement in 1968, James A. Nichols Jr. taught systematic theology at New England School of Theology and Berkshire Christian College.[86] More than anyone else, Nichols was responsible for defining the theological direction of NEST/Berkshire. Through Nichols' influence, the school was moving toward teaching Advent Christian doctrine within a Trinitarian and Reformed context. It became strongly committed to a verbal, plenary understanding of Scripture that stressed biblical inerrancy.

During this time, Advent Christians in the northeast began to enjoy a productive relationship with other evangelicals in New England, at least at the leadership level. Evangelicalism in New England was less separatistic than its Midwestern counterpart. Part of that probably stems from the influence of Clarence Macartney on one of his young associate pastors

82. Nichols, "Adventism's Theological Position," 4.

83. Ibid.

84. Ibid.

85. Ibid., 3.

86. James A. Nichols Jr. would stay with the institution through two moves. The first, in 1939, was from Roxbury to Brookline, Massachusetts. The second move, from Brookline to Lenox, Massachusetts in 1957 coincided with the name change to Berkshire Christian College.

who would move on to become a leader among New England evangelicals, Harold John Ockenga.[87] In larger part, New England evangelicalism was less dispensational in doctrine and outlook than evangelicalism in other parts of the country.[88] So while New England evangelicals emphasized the inerrancy of Scripture and the importance of world missions, the drawing of theological lines over issues relating to eschatology did not take place to the extent that it did in the Midwest and other parts of the country.[89] Advent Christians and other evangelicals in New England shared a common commitment to world missions.[90] The New England School of Theology enjoyed a good relationship with Gordon Divinity School.[91] By 1950, Advent Christians were perceived by many as part of the evangelical coalition in New England.[92]

87. Longfield, *The Presbyterian Controversy*, 217. In Longfield's words, "Macartney advanced conservative Christianity both in the Presbyterian Church and the broader Christian community by nurturing over a dozen assistant pastors, including Harold J. Ockenga, founder of the National Association of Evangelicals, during his ministry in Pittsburgh. Macartney wielded enormous influence over these young men during their tenure under him and maintained relationships with them even after they left Pittsburgh."

88. Oral History Interview, Dean and Barton, August 4, 1994, 9. In Dean's words, "I think one of the differences is certainly the shadow of A.J. Gordon here in New England. And [what] I would see [in] the lengthening of that shadow would be that evangelicalism in New England was non-dispensational, where evangelicalism in the Midwest was dispensational. And that is largely [because] A.J. Gordon was premillennial in the classical sense of the term. [He] was mission minded . . . solidly committed to Scripture, but . . . had no interest in the dispensational themes of secret raptures and dispensationalist futurism."

89. Ibid.

90. Ibid. In Dean's words, "The first Advent Christian missionary to go to Africa is a former student of A. J. Gordon."

91. Oral History Interview, Carlyle A. Roberts, August 3, 1994. See also, Oral History Interview, Dean and Barton, August 4, 1994, 10.

92. That does not mean that relationships between Advent Christians and other evangelicals were always harmonious at the local level. In an oral history interview conducted for this project, David McCarthy describes growing up in an Advent Christian congregation in Portsmouth, NH, during the late 1940s and early 1950s. He describes some of the Advent Christian preaching at that time as "polemic preaching against the Baptists." While the young people from both congregations were attempting to engage in a unified witness for Christ on their local high-school campus, the pastors appeared to be point men in a verbal war that was "Scofield Bible against the 'sleep-of-the-dead conditionalism.' And our church and the Baptist church spent a great deal of time making sure their people understood the differences between the Advent Christians and the Baptists." In 1994, David McCarthy returned home to Portsmouth to serve as Pastor of the Advent Christian congregation that he grew up in. See Oral History Interview, David

Two Divergent Theological Approaches

While the impact of the Fundamentalist-Modernist controversy on the Advent Christian Church was not immediate, it was substantial. The two schools of higher learning founded by Advent Christians in the late 1890s were impacted in dramatically different ways. As a liberal arts school, Aurora College provided a hospitable environment for faculty and students open to exploring new vistas of learning in a variety of academic disciplines, especially after World War II when the college shifted its focus to serving the Fox River Valley community surrounding Aurora. The bulk of its graduates would not enter the Advent Christian ministry, but would seek employment in the burgeoning professional market. Its theological faculty remained open to the conclusions of modern theologians and academics, and sought to guide their students (and the Advent Christian Church) away from what they perceived as narrow-minded Fundamentalism. In their view, Advent Christians were neither liberal nor fundamentalist. Therefore, their theology should be characterized by a broadly Arminian approach that retains an emphasis on Advent Christian distinctives while allowing room for different understandings of issues like the authority of Scripture and the nature of God.

As a theological school, the New England School of Theology maintained a narrower focus than Aurora by stressing the training of men and women for vocational Christian service within the Advent Christian Church, especially within its Eastern region. Though theologically eclectic in its early years, by the late 1940s, the school was becoming more consciously evangelical and Reformed in its theological approach. In the view of those who taught at New England School of Theology, Advent Christians were not liberals but conservatives. While they disagreed with dispensationalists regarding eschatology and with most evangelicals regarding the nature of eternal punishment, Advent Christians should share their understanding of Scripture as the verbally inspired Word of God.

By the late 1940s, the doctrinal issues dividing the two schools were becoming increasingly clear. The New England School of Theology was becoming strongly committed to verbal, plenary inspiration of Holy Scripture. Aurora College allowed for various theories of inspiration and was open to insights from liberal and neo-orthodox theologians. James Nichols Jr. was successful in focusing NEST toward a Reformed theological

---

S. McCarthy, November 24, 1995, 23.

emphasis which allowed little room for human autonomy. The Aurora theologians, especially Clarence Hewitt, were much more Arminian in approach and more concerned with the place of human freedom in theology. In terms of theological method and formulation, for the Aurora theologians, the Bible represented one of several sources of God's revelation. While at NEST, the Bible was seen as the primary source and starting point for Christian theology.

One fascinating aspect of this theological divergence between the two schools is that each at a particular point adopted a stance that ran counter to the bulk of opinion and tradition within the Advent Christian Church. While William Miller was a Calvinist, the Advent Christian Church had been mostly Arminian in theology since its founding. NEST's move toward a Reformed posture began to place it in tension with many Advent Christians, especially outside of New England, who were historically Arminian. At the same time, Advent Christians had traditionally been conservative in their view of the Bible as the written Word of God. The openness of Aurora College to the modernist/liberal impulse in Protestant theology placed it in tension with many Advent Christians whose understanding of Scripture was conservative.

As a small denomination, Advent Christians have tended to view themselves as a large extended family. Many of its members have roots within the denomination that extend back several generations. At the same time, as we saw earlier in this chapter, the understanding of what it meant to be an Advent Christian was subject to some subtle regional and sectional differences. As Aurora College and New England School of Theology graduates returned to Advent Christian congregations in positions of pastoral or lay leadership, they shaped the understanding of what it meant to be Advent Christian in increasingly diverse ways.

During the 1920s and 1930s, most Advent Christians were at best interested bystanders in the controversies that divided the Northern Baptist and Northern Presbyterian denominations. Little could they have imagined how those controversies would impact their two schools and set the stage for pending conflict within the Advent Christian Church a generation later. The stage is almost set for us to explore that conflict in more detail. But first, we must look at the mainline and fundamentalist coalitions that emerged during the 1940s and 1950s in the aftermath of the fierce controversy between the two. As Robert Wuthnow cogently argues, American Protestantism in the aftermath of World War II increasingly became a two-party system,[93] with the mainline and fundamentalist coalitions each representing one pole of a bi-polar Protestant axis. Both desperately sought to define not only the shape of American Protestantism but the direction of postwar American culture. Both also experienced significant theological change and reform.

93. Wuthnow, *Restructuring of American Religion.*

CHAPTER FOUR

A Divided Protestantism
Competes for America's Soul

WITH THE DEATH OF John Gresham Machen in 1937, the end of an era seemed at hand. By all outward appearances, Machen was the last of a long line of intellectuals for whom Protestant orthodoxy formed the core of their academic work and reflection. With Machen's death, the triumph of the modernist impulse both within the major Protestant denominations and academia seemed complete. At most state colleges and universities, the movement toward secularization was well advanced. Even at most older church-related colleges and seminaries, the core of the educational project had moved from Christian orthodoxy to an emphasis on scientific method and academic freedom.[1] Only at a handful of small schools like Wheaton College, Westminster Seminary, and Gordon Divinity School did a traditional Christian emphasis at the core of the educational task survive into the 1940s.

Despite their triumph, those who had embraced the modernist impulse were forced to confront several stark realities that deeply challenged the progressive notion that God was at work through human cultural development and that society (especially western society) through human effort was moving toward realization of the Kingdom of God. With the

1. For an understanding of how secularization developed both in public and private institutions of higher learning, see Marsden, *Soul of the American University.* Note on pp. 30–59, Marsden's summary of the 1915 Report of the Committee on Academic Freedom and Tenure of the American Association of University Professors.

advent of the 1930s, the economic depression that had nearly destroyed the economies of Western Europe hit the United States with such force that by 1933, almost one-quarter of Americans were without work. The seeds of worldwide conflict and war were already being sowed by the rise of fascism in Italy, communism in Russia, nazism in Germany, and military dictatorship in Japan. By 1945, the progressives who fifteen years earlier had celebrated their triumph within the mainstream of American Protestantism, now confronted the harsh terror of six million Jews slaughtered by the very nation where Protestantism's modernist impulse was given birth.[2]

The events of the period between 1930 and 1945 forced liberal and progressive Protestants throughout the western world to rethink their almost uncritical embrace of much of the modernist impulse. Mainline Protestant theologians and leaders continued to embrace the higher critical approach to the Bible that had been evolving for more than one hundred years. On the whole they remained committed to adapting religious ideas to the realities of modern culture. But their reflection caused them to focus their work in two directions— the drive toward ecumenism and an effort to craft theological approaches in harmony with the grim reality of a world that had faced economic collapse, genocide, and world war.

Academic theology played a vital role in mainline Protestantism during the 1940s and 1950s. The progressive triumph of the 1920s and 1930s had not only brought control of the major Protestant denominations, but dominance within the seminaries that trained the bulk of mainline Protestant clergy. The nature of academic theology meant that the voices of theological reform were many and not always cohesive. Four voices for theological reform seem to have had the most impact within the American Protestant mainline. Ironically, three of those four voices were German— Karl Barth (a Swiss-German), Rudolf Bultmann, and Oscar Cullmann. The fourth was an American intellectual of German descent at home in both theology and political theory, Reinhold Niebuhr.[3] Their project was to articulate how twentieth-century Protestant Christians could take seriously both the intellectual canons of modernity, especially in terms of Darwinian evolution and biblical criticism, and the Bible's witness that God had acted

2. There are numerous volumes that chronicle the history of Western society during the depression and World War II years. One book that describes both the events and the ideological currents of those years is Johnson, *Modern Times*, 203–431.

3. In focusing on these four theologians, this writer does not wish to minimize the contributions of Paul Tillich, Dietrich Bonhoeffer, and others. See, Hughes, ed., *Creative Minds*, for summaries of their lives and work.

in human history through Jesus Christ. Each of the four would express the results of that project in his own unique way.

Theological Reform within Mainline American Protestantism: Four Approaches

As Protestant progressives in the United States were consolidating their gains during the 1920s, European academic theology, especially in Germany, faced a dramatic challenge from a Swiss-German clergyman whose pastoral experiences forced him to seriously question the essence of what he had learned as a student of the German theological establishment. "I absorbed [Wilhelm] Herrmann through every pore," wrote Karl Barth. "I thought I had acquired a sound theological foundation by an intensive study of Schliermacher and Kant."[4] But the demands of pastoral work forced Barth to question his theological mentors. "The more I began to preach and teach, the more the pursuit of academic theology began to become "in some way" alien and puzzling to me."[5] As Barth observed the real-life struggles of people in his Aargau, Switzerland congregation, his attention turned away from academic theology toward "factory acts, safety laws, and trade unionism, and my attention was claimed by violent local and cantonal struggles on behalf of the workers."[6] As early as 1912, Barth had begun to be influenced by his reading of John Calvin's *Institutes of the Christian Religion*. But World War I "brought concretely to light two aberrations: first in the teaching of my theological mentors in Germany, who seemed to me to be hopelessly compromised by their submission to the ideology of war; and second in socialism."[7]

Barth's theological crisis drove him to a fresh study of the Pauline epistles, especially the apostle's letter to the church at Rome. Out of that, in Barth's words, "the concept of the Kingdom of God in the real,

---

4. Bromiley, *Barth, Bultmann: Letters 1922–1966*, 150–58, contains a fascinating autobiographical reflection by Karl Barth of his early pastoral and theological career. In it, Barth describes the shape of his theological pilgrimage away from an enthusiastic embrace of the idealistic-romantic theological posture taught by the major German academic theologians of the late nineteenth and early twentieth centuries.

5. Ibid., 154.

6. Ibid.

7. Ibid.

transcendent sense of the Bible became increasingly more insistent."[8] As the force of that observation became more and more apparent, Barth realized and declared his "open opposition to Schliermacher" and his theological heirs who dominated the German academy. "Directly out of the problems of my pastoral ministry, I found myself compelled—at about the age of thirty—to revise my theological formulations insofar as I had received them at the universities."[9]

While Barth retained a belief that higher criticism of the Bible was necessary,[10] his theological direction became much more oriented toward stressing both the transcendence and hiddenness of God, the validity of Reformed dogmatics, and the importance of concrete biblical exegesis and preaching; all themes minimized in German academic theology. In response to the theologians of the academy, Barth was once again willing to equate Holy Scripture with the Word of God, although in a different way than Benjamin Warfield, John Gresham Machen, and other American conservative scholars. "In calling Holy Scripture the Word of God," according to Barth, "we mean by it Holy Scripture as the witness of the prophets and the apostles to this one Word of God, to Jesus, the man out of Israel, who is God's Christ, our Lord and king in eternity . . . . In Him God meets us. And when we say, I believe in God, the concrete meaning is that I believe in the Lord Jesus Christ."[11] For Barth, God has revealed himself directly to humanity in Jesus Christ. The Bible is the witness to that revelation. "Holy Scripture is the document . . . of the manifestation of the Word of God in the person of Jesus Christ."[12] Thus, while Scripture is the standard by which the church measures its proclamation of the Christian faith and while no other document can claim the uniqueness of Holy Scripture, it is not proper to call the Bible the Word of God apart from its witness to the events surrounding the person and work of Jesus Christ. The Bible can be properly

---

8. Ibid.

9. Ibid., 157.

10. Ibid., 158. To quote Barth, "I learned also to put criticism (which is, of course, necessary) more in the background than positive exposition." Barth wrote this in 1946.

11. Barth, *Dogmatics in Outline*, 17. This volume consists of lectures given in 1946 by Barth "in the semi-ruins of the once stately Kurfursten Schloss in Bonn [Germany] . . . the hour seven a.m., always after we had sung a psalm or a hymn to cheer us up." From Barth's description, we get a glimpse at conditions in post-World War II Germany. He based this series of lectures on the Apostle's Creed and as such they provide us with a concise tool for understanding Barth's theological tone and direction.

12. Ibid., 13.

called the Word of God, but only in an indirect sense in that it witnesses to the direct revelation of God through Jesus Christ.[13]

Barth's understanding of the Bible as the Word of God in an indirect sense is an essential component of his strategy to express what he sees as historic Christian faith within the context of modernity. "The truth of Jesus Christ," in Barth's words, "is also in the simplest sense a truth of facts. Its starting point, the resurrection of Jesus Christ from the dead, is a fact which occurred in space and time, as the New Testament described it."[14] But that truth comes to humanity in the context of God's hidden nature. "The hiddenness of God necessarily reminds us of our human limitation. We do not believe out of our personal reason and power."[15]

For Karl Barth's German contemporary, Rudolf Bultmann, the relationship between the claims of historic Christian faith and the intellectual canons of modernity was radically different. Like Barth, Bultmann's father was a pastor. Unlike Barth, Bultmann's career took place almost entirely within the confines of the academy. Unlike Barth, while Bultmann clearly saw the need for a reformation of German Protestant liberal theology, he did not believe that such reform meant repudiation of that tradition.[16] While Bultmann's work focused primarily on exegesis, during his years at the University of Marburg (1921–51), he was strongly influenced by his teaching colleague, the existentialist philosopher Martin Heidegger. Heidegger's presence at Marburg led to, in Bultmann's words, "an extraordinary surge of intellectual life" on the campus.[17] "I enjoyed lively interaction with him, and the relations between theology and philosophy led to students and doctoral candidates attending lectures and seminars in both disciplines

---

13. For his extensive dogmatic treatment of the doctrine of Holy Scripture, see Barth, *Church Dogmatics*, 1/2:457–740. Geoffrey Bromiley, the English translator of Barth's *Dogmatics*, has provided a summary of Barth's theological positions in which he comments about Barth's view of the Bible, "In no sense does he think of a constitution of Scripture as God's word by subjective experience of it. He has little time for inerrancy, which he seems to regard as both irrelevant and even misleading. On the other hand, while thinking that the possibility of error must be accepted, he can see no absolute position from which to establish actual errors and he sets no store by the emphasizing of alleged mistakes or difficulties." See Bromiley, *Introduction*, 43–44.

14. Barth, *Dogmatics in Outline*, 25.

15. Ibid., 20.

16. Two sources provide autobiographical sketches of Bultmann's life and theological career: Bromiley, *Barth, Bultmann Letters*, 158–62; and Ogden, *Existence and Faith*, 283–88.

17. Bromiley, *Barth, Bultmann Letters*, 162.

. . . . The link between theological and philosophical work was for some time a good old Marburg tradition"[18]

That link showed up in Bultmann's exegetical and theological work, especially in his 1941 lecture, *New Testament and Mythology*. In this clear, concise, and controversial essay, we discover how Heidegger's existential philosophy shaped Bultmann's view of the relationship between the Christian proclamation and modernity. For Bultmann, the real message of the New Testament is what he terms the "salvation occurrence" in its proclamation of the death and resurrection of Jesus Christ.[19] However, the events described by the New Testament writers are "mythological talk, and the individual motifs may be easily traced to the contemporary mythology of Jewish apocalypticism and of the Gnostic myth of redemption."[20] Modern men and women cannot possibly be expected to embrace Christian proclamation based on a mythical world picture such as this. "We cannot use electric lights and radios and, in the event of illness, avail ourselves of modern medical and clinical means and at the same time believe in the spirit and wonder world of the New Testament."[21]

Therefore, the task of Christian theologians and proclaimers is to "demythologize" the New Testament, to reinterpret its mythological events in a way both faithful to its essential message and compatible with modern scientific thought.[22] For Bultmann, the older liberal theology failed in this task because it eliminated mythological representations as time conditioned and not essential to the great religious and moral ideas common to all religious expression. Such a strategy is flawed in Bultmann's view because it ignores the kerygmatic essence of the New Testament. The New Testament does

18. Ibid.

19. Bultmann, *New Testament and Mythology*, 12.

20. Ibid., 2.

21. Ibid., 4.

22. Ibid., 95. In Bultmann's words, "Myth is the report of an occurrence or an event in which supernatural, superhuman forces or persons are at work (which explains why it is often defined simply as history of the gods.) Mythical thinking is the opposite of scientific thinking. It refers certain phenomena and events to supernatural, 'divine' powers, whether these are thought of dynamistically or animistically or are represented as personal spirits or gods."

On Bultmann's understanding of science, Bloesch comments, "He accepted uncritically the presuppositions of Newtonian science, which portray the phenomenal world as a closed continuum of cause and effect." See Bloesch, *Holy Scripture*, 237.

not simply proclaim Jesus as a great moral teacher, but claims that in his person, we discover the decisive event of God's salvific strategy.[23]

So how do we demythologize the New Testament? By interpreting its mythology "in terms of [its] understanding of existence, that is, in existentialist terms."[24] Demythologizing the New Testament in the Bultmannian program means that we regard any notion of supernatural activity as premodern and proclaim the message of the New Testament strictly in terms that harmonize with modern conceptions of facts, objectivity, and science. Once we do that, we capture the essence of the New Testament kerygma— the announcement that God's forgiveness is available to human beings through the ministry and death of Jesus Christ. "To believe in the cross of Christ," in Bultmann's words, "does not mean to look to some mythical process that has taken place outside of us and our world or at an objectively visible event that God has somehow reckoned to our credit; rather, to believe in the cross of Christ means to accept the cross as one's own and to allow oneself to be crucified with Christ."[25] Salvation means that we have allowed God's liberating act to take place in the concrete existence of our daily lives.

Bultmann's existentialist methodology led him in a radically different direction than Barth.[26] Because he saw any sense of the supernatural in Scripture as scientifically impossible, Bultmann ultimately wound up divorcing the person of Jesus Christ from the kerygma of the New Testament. Moreover, for Bultmann, it appeared impossible for God to intervene in the space-time continuum of human history. While Barth argued that the way we treat both Christian faith and modernity seriously was through

---

23. Bultmann, *New Testament and Mythology*, 12–14.

24. Ibid., 15. Bultmann writes, "The task, then, is also to interpret the dualistic mythology of the New Testament in existentialist terms. Thus, when the New Testament talks about demonic powers that rule the world and under whose power we human beings have fallen, is there in such talk a view of human existence that offers even to us today, who no longer think mythologically, a possibility for understanding ourselves?"

25. Ibid., 34. Earlier, Bultmann writes, "If we follow the objectifying representations of the New Testament, the cross is indeed understood as a mythical event: the crucified one is the preexistent Son of God who becomes man and who as such is sinless. He is the sacrifice whose blood atones for our sins; he bears the sin of the world vicariously, and by taking upon himself the death that is the punishment for sin, he frees us from it. We can no longer accept this mythological interpretation in which notions of sacrifice are mixed together with a juristic theory of satisfaction."

26. For a summary of the significant differences between Barth and Bultmann, see Bloesch, *Holy Scripture*, 239–41. On pp. 223–54, Bloesch offers an analysis of Bultmann's methodology and his impact on twentieth-century theology.

a proper understanding of direct and indirect revelation, Bultmann proposed a program by which revelation must be bounded by the presuppositions of human scientific reason. In other words, the scientific canons of modernity must act as a boundary on what we can proclaim as the message of Christian faith. If we label Barth as neo-orthodox, then we must see the Bultmannian program as essentially neo-liberal.

The third voice for theological reform was a distinctively American one. Although Reinhold Niebuhr was influenced by both Barth and Bultmann, as well as other European theologians, his "Christian realism" was a call to embrace the biblical themes of love and justice in a way that would permit the Christian faith to be seen as meaningful by his contemporaries, especially those in the academy and in the culture-forming institutions of American society: law, government, and the media. Like Barth and Bultmann, Niebuhr grew up in a parsonage. And like Barth, Niebuhr's early career focused on parish ministry. After graduating from Yale Divinity School, Niebuhr served as pastor of Bethel Evangelical Church, a middle-class parish in Detroit, Michigan from 1915 to 1928.[27]

While in Detroit, Niebuhr's confrontation with the realities of life in industrial America led him to question the liberal optimism of the social gospel he had earlier embraced. Out of that came one of his earliest and most significant books, *Moral Man and Immoral Society*.[28] Niebuhr believed that the optimism of the late nineteenth and early twentieth centuries did not account for the personal and systemic evils apparent in modern life. As he moved from the pastorate to a professorship at Union Theological Seminary in New York City, Niebuhr's theological reflection focused more and more on the pervasiveness of human sin and its consequences.[29]

27. Brown, ed., *Essential Reinhold Niebuhr*, xv, 254. Brown provides a brief biographical sketch of Niebuhr's life on pp. xi–xxiv. For an extended biographical account of Niebuhr, see Fox, *Reinhold Niebuhr: A Biography*.

28. Niebuhr, *Moral Man and Immoral Society*.

29. While Niebuhr took seriously the notion of personal and systemic evil, he rejected the Calvinist notion of total depravity. Late in his life, Niebuhr wrote the following: "The mixture of motives in all people, incidentally, refutes the doctrines both of total depravity and of saintliness. In my case, retrospection from the sidelines prompted me to remember many instances in my earlier years when my wife had protested my making an extra trip or going to yet another conference, despite my weariness; I always pleaded the importance of the cause that engaged me, and it never occurred to me that I might have been so assiduous in these engagements because the invitations flattered my vanity." See Brown, *Essential Reinhold Niebuhr*, 254.

Niebuhr resisted all attempts to reduce the meaning of Christian faith into a single coherent system. "The whole realm of genuine selfhood, of sin and grace, is beyond the comprehension of various systems of philosophy."[30] Therefore, authentic Christian faith is not found in rationalism but in the Christian existentialism first articulated by Blaise Pascal,[31] an approach that recognizes both the freedom of God and the autonomy of humanity. But human freedom must be understood within the context of human sinfulness. "The self is free to defy God. The self does defy God. The Christian conception of the dignity of man and of the misery of man is all of one piece, as Pascal rightly apprehended."[32] Once we grasp the mystery of human freedom and the reality of human sinfulness, we are then ready to deal with the fundamental question of Christian apologetics, how the existential realities of Christian faith can be applied to "the structures and forms of nature, life, and history."[33]

Niebuhr does that by what he calls "biblical [or Christian] realism." While some have equated his thought with the neo-orthodoxy of Karl Barth, Niebuhr rejects Barth's approach because in his view, it does not grapple seriously with what Niebuhr terms, the "wisdom of the world."[34] Biblical realism takes human history seriously and rejects a negative attitude towards both philosophy and science. This realism requires departure from the biblical picture of life and history at one crucial point. "The accumulated evidence of the natural sciences convinces us," in Niebuhr's words, "that the realm of natural causation is more closed, and less subject to divine intervention, than the biblical world view assumes."[35] Therefore, "we do not believe in the virgin birth, and we have difficulty with the physical resurrection of Christ. We do not believe, in other words, that revelatory events validate themselves by a divine break-through in the natural order."[36] But we can, through the Bible, see human history as an engagement between man and God and "we can recognize in the course of history

30. Ibid., 220.

31. Ibid.

32. Ibid., 223.

33. Ibid., 225.

34. Ibid., 228–31. In Barth's theology, according to Niebuhr, we find "a religion . . . which is fashioned for the catacombs and has little relation to the task of transfiguring the natural stuff of politics by the grace and wisdom of the gospel."

35. Ibid., 232.

36. Ibid., 235.

particular events which have a special depth and penetrate to the meaning of the whole, that is, revelation."[37] Those meanings must be appropriated existentially and with a spirit of humility that recognizes the truth of the Apostle Paul's admonition that "For now, we see through a glass darkly."[38]

For Niebuhr, authentic Christian existence comes as we learn to appreciate the mysterious character of God's ways. God is our creator, savior, and judge. "Yet He does not fully disclose Himself, and His thoughts are too high to be comprehended by human thought."[39] As Christians, we must learn to appreciate not only the mystery of nature, but the mysteries of human nature, of sin, and of death. "Man is a creature of nature, subject to its necessities and bound by its limits. Yet he surveys the ages and touches the fringes of the eternal."[40] At the same time, the inclination to evil (what Niebuhr terms "the inclination to inordinate self-love") subconsciously permeates our identity.[41] It is here that we discover the real mystery of evil in the fact that "it [evil] presupposes itself."[42] However, despite the mystery of sin, Niebuhr argues that authentic Christian hope rests on the reality that "by reason of the freedom of our spirit, we have purposes and ends beyond the limits of our physical existence."[43] Only divine mercy can heal us of our evil and complete our incomplete lives.

For Reinhold Niebuhr, liberal Protestantism needed reform in two important ways. First, Protestants in the liberal tradition needed to appreciate the mysterious nature of God's work in history. The meaning of that work was often hidden and was to be apprehended provisionally through the eyes of faith. Second, the historical optimism of liberal Protestants needed to be tempered by properly understanding the nature of sin and evil, two realities grounded not only in biblical realism but in human experience. Despite these two important propositions, the Niebuhrian epistemology

37. Ibid., 232ff. Niebuhr argues that Christians must make a radical distinction between nature and human history and that God's intervention in human history occurs in a way "in which God intervenes to reconstruct the rational concepts of meaning which men and cultures construct under the false assumption that they have a mind which completely transcends the flux of history, when actually it can only construct a realm of meaning from a particular standpoint within the flux."

38. See 1 Cor 13:12.

39. Brown, *Essential Reinhold Niebuhr*, 240.

40. Ibid., 242.

41. Ibid., 244. Niebuhr writes, "We seem to be betrayed into it."

42. Ibid., 245.

43. Ibid., 248.

bears significant resemblance to that of Bultmann. Niebuhr rejects God's direct intervention in human history because of what he sees as the accumulated evidence of modern science. Therefore, like Bultmann, Niebuhr defines authentic Christian faith in existential categories. Although there are significant differences between the Bultmannian and Niebuhrian programs, the description of each by the term "neo-liberal" is appropriate.

The final strategy for theological reform within mainline Protestantism is well represented by the German theologian, Oscar Cullmann.[44] A colleague of Karl Barth at Basel, Cullmann reacted strongly against Bultmann's efforts to demythologize the New Testament.[45] In Cullmann's view, the Bultmannian program failed to take seriously the historical character of the New Testament proclamation and essentially stripped Christian proclamation of any distinctive message. Bultmann's problem, in Cullmann's view, was that he ignored how the New Testament writers themselves understood the historical character of revelation. Christian faith, for Cullmann, cannot be stripped of historical content, because "the Christian absolute norm is itself also history and is not, as in the philosophical norm, a transcendent datum that lies beyond history."[46]

Cullmann's theological approach, called by its German name "heilsgeschichte" meaning "salvation history," was shared by a host of post-World War II American and European biblical scholars and theologians. For Cullmann, Christian theology must start by recognizing that for Christians in the first century, the whole of God's revelation, not just certain parts of it, was expressed in historical terms. Moreover, the New Testament writers, indeed the entire first-century church, knew nothing of the distinction between history and myth that preoccupied many of the theologians and critics of Cullmann's day.[47] Like his colleagues, Cullmann accepted Martin Kahler's distinction between "historisch" (events which are verifiably historical) and "geschichtlich" (events which are beyond the realm of historical verification).[48] Events in the latter category, even though they may be mythical in character, are still an essential part of the entirety of God's revelation and must not be excluded from our understanding of Christian

---

44. For biographical information regarding Oscar Cullmann, see Wallace, "Oscar Cullmann," 163–66.

45. Cullmann, *Christ and Time*, 28–32.

46. Ibid., 21.

47. Cullmann, *Christ and Time*, 94–97.

48. Ibid., 99.

faith. "At the outset it must be made clear that between these various items [history and myth] Primitive Christianity makes no distinction. In this respect it considers Adam to be upon the same plane as is Jesus of Nazareth. The historical sense is completely lacking in the authors of the Primitive Christian writings, and hence for them a distinction between history and myth is *a priori* remote."[49]

For Cullmann, history and myth function on a single redemptive continuum and the entire scope of redemptive history is best described by the term "prophecy." "We have to do with prophecy not only in the "mythical" stories of the beginning and the end [creation and consummation], but even in the "historical" sections we are dealing not simply with history but with *history viewed from the prophetic point of view*."[50] All of the events described in the New Testament, even those subject to historical verification, "are presented in the Primitive Christian writings not as 'history' but as 'revealed prophecy concerning history.'"[51] Therefore, while twentieth-century Christians, according to Cullmann "know that Adam was not a historical personality in the same sense that Jesus was; what is essential is for us to perceive that the entire redemptive history, in both its historical and non-historical parts, presents a single coherent process" that does not permit us to demythologize or reinterpret it.[52]

When we look at the early Christian proclamation, we discover that the kernel of Christian faith lies not in a kerygma divorced from the person of Jesus Christ (as in Bultmann) but in the primitive Christian notion of Jesus Christ as the midpoint of salvation history. "The chronologically new thing which Christ brought for the faith of primitive Christianity consists in the fact that for the believing Christian, the mid-point [of time], since

---

49. Ibid., 94.

50. Ibid., 97. Cullmann writes, "Martin Kahler, who discerned the problem here treated, uses the word 'saga' in approximately the sense that we here are giving to the word 'prophecy.' The expression 'prophecy' is more in keeping with Primitive Christian thought than are the terms 'saga' and 'myth.'"

In this context it is important to note a distinction that points to the problem evangelical scholars have found in using the "salvation history" approach, indeed any approach that distinguishes between verifiable and non-verifiable events. Are non-verifiable events historically true and simply not subject to investigation? Or should they be seen as legends designed to teach larger truths essential to the whole of Christian revelation? This problem points to what in this writer's view continues to be one of the fundamental issues in Christian theology—how to understand God's activity in human history.

51. Ibid., 98.

52. Ibid., 100.

Easter, no longer lies in the future" but in the past.[53] It is here we find the fundamental difference between primitive Christianity and Judaism. While Judaism locates the midpoint of history in the future, for Christians, that midpoint was reflected in the events surrounding the incarnation of Jesus. "The midpoint of time is no longer the future coming of the Messiah, but rather the historical life and work of Jesus Christ, already concluded in the past."[54] The task of Christian proclamation is then to help people understand time in a Christian way and hence to see that Jesus Christ stands at the center of history.[55]

Cullmann's approach offered mainline Protestants perhaps the most attractive way to reconcile Christian faith with what they saw as the reality of modern intellectual life. For even while much of the Bible could be seen as outside the realm of historical investigation, the entirety of its message could be studied and proclaimed.[56] For mainline Protestants uncomfortable with the radical distinction between faith and history offered by Bultmann (and to a lesser degree by Niebuhr), Cullmann and other "salvation-history" scholars provided a methodology that allowed them to study and embrace the whole of biblical revelation while at the same time maintaining the modern distinction between verifiable history and unverifiable event.

The Ecumenical Impulse

The programs for theological reform articulated by Barth, Bultmann, Niebuhr, and Cullmann demonstrate clearly the eclectic nature of post-World War II mainline Protestant theology. While the Protestant liberalism articulated so well by Harry Emerson Fosdick, Henry Sloan Coffin, and others during the first quarter of the twentieth century remained viable, the fact that it became one of several options among post-World War II

53. Ibid., 81.

54. Ibid., 82.

55. Ibid., 93.

56. Cullmann's theological approach also found a warm welcome among several important evangelical theologians including the noted Fuller Seminary New Testament scholar, George Eldon Ladd. In embracing Cullmann's conclusions, Ladd writes, "The God who reveals himself in redemptive history is both Lord of creation and Lord of history, and he is therefore able not only to shape the course of ordinary historical events but to act directly in ways that transcend usual historical experience." See Ladd, *Theology of the New Testament*, 25–33.

mainline Protestants points to the struggles that coalition wrestled with in their attempt to forge a Christian faith in tune both with modern sensibilities and the witness of Scripture to the nature of God and the nature of humanity.

Those struggles were exacerbated by the cultural situation mainline Protestants found themselves in during the fifteen years following the close of World War II. First, they confronted a new religious climate marked by a growing Roman Catholicism and a more assertive American Judaism.[57] Mainline Protestants now spoke of the spiritual heritage of the United States in the broader scope of a "Judeo-Christian ethic." Despite a strong residual anti-Catholicism (that mainline Protestants shared with their despised fundamentalist Protestant counterparts), more within the Protestant mainline were comfortable with Jewish sociologist Will Herberg's notion that the ethical and spiritual heritage of the nation could best be described by the title of his influential book, *Protestant, Catholic, Jew.*[58]

Not only was the United States becoming spiritually diverse, it was also becoming more suburban and affluent. Urbanization had been under way in America since the 1870s and with it had come a dramatic shift in the cultural ethos of the country. Now, as the 1950s emerged, population in the suburbs was growing three times as fast as in the central cities[59] and a new cultural shift had begun to emerge. The growth of American suburbs coincided with [and perhaps precipitated] what church historian Martin Marty terms "a gap between intellectual centers and lay religion."[60] Popular religion was increasingly being driven, not by intellectual formulations of doctrine and theology, but by the power of raw experience. "The mainstream churches and synagogues," in Marty's words, "were not necessarily denying such experience, but they did not promote it effectively, so the church members and the public smuggled it in through the inspirational religion that was becoming a large market item."

57. Marty, *Under God Indivisible*, 413. Marty quotes the words of sociologists Eugene Lipman and Albert Vorspan, "American Protestants have suffered a severe historic jolt. This is no longer 'their' country." Despite outward appearances of increased church attendance and renewal among mainline Protestant congregations in the 1950s, it became apparent to perceptive observers like Will Herberg that Protestant hegemony over American culture was drawing to a close.

58. Herberg, *Protestant, Catholic, Jew*. For a summary of Protestant anti-Catholic attitudes, see Marty, *Under God, Indivisible*, 157–79.

59. Marty, *Under God, Indivisible*, 401.

60. Ibid., 317.

What mainline Protestants did promote was ecumenism. The best way to combat the growing forces of secularism in public life and pluralism in religious life was through an intentional, conscious effort to unify Christians and their competing denominations. Since the Protestant reformation 450 years earlier, many Christians had struggled to reconcile the growing theological and organizational fragmentation of the church with Jesus' prayer for his disciples in John's gospel, "that they may become perfectly one, so that the world may know that thou has sent me and hast loved them even as thou hast loved me."[61] Now, many mainline Protestant leaders were ready to put their energies into forging two new institutions, the National Council of Churches and the World Council of Churches. It was time, in their view, to rise above an embarrassing sectarianism and propagate a Christian faith characterized by justice, commonality, and attention to the larger purposes of God.[62] Their cooperative efforts, in their view, were imperative if Protestant influence in the intellectual, governing, and popular life of post-World War II America was to remain strong.

While the Protestant mainline leadership hoped that ecumenism would solve the embarrassment of sectarianism, there was another, even larger embarrassment that they had hoped would simply disappear. Unfortunately for them, Protestant Fundamentalism showed no signs of doing so. Fundamentalism had for all purposes dropped off the radar screen of the American intellectual and governing elites during the 1930s. However during that period, it retained a strong reservoir of support among the American people.[63] Ironically, despite the motifs of separatism and withdrawal that Fundamentalism had embraced in the 1920s and 1930s, ecumenism was something that some fundamentalist leaders were willing to explore well before their mainline Protestant counterparts. In that context, the fundamentalists had a distinct theological advantage. While the theological direction of mainline Protestantism was fragmenting in several directions, Protestant fundamentalists shared essentially common understandings of what they saw as core doctrines of the Christian faith. They were unified in

---

61. John 17:23 (RSV).

62. For a description of the organization of the National and World Councils of Churches, and of the drive toward ecumenism within mainline Protestantism during this time, see Marty, *Under God Indivisible*, 248–73.

63. For an account of Protestant Fundamentalism in the twenty-five year aftermath of the Fundamentalist-Modernist controversies, see Marsden, *Reforming Fundamentalism*, 13–52.

how they understood God's revelation through Holy Scripture and in their declaration that individual faith in Jesus Christ was essential for salvation.

Fundamentalists practiced ecumenism on two levels. On one level, they organized new agencies—schools, para-church organizations, and mission societies that were essentially task oriented. These agencies were in many cases entrepreneurially driven and organized to accomplish specific functions that local churches and even denominations could not accomplish on their own. Then, they attempted to organize umbrella organizations that would focus on unifying individuals, churches, and denominations that identified with their theological core and on representing their interests within the larger spheres of American life. Many Americans were attracted to Fundamentalism because of the powerful critique of modern society that it offered. While Fundamentalism was a movement that reached across a broad spectrum,[64] at its theological core was a group of men who had been influenced by John Gresham Machen and the old-school Presbyterian tradition that had shaped Princeton Theological Seminary until the reorganization of the school in 1929.

One of those men was Harold John Ockenga. Born in Chicago in 1905, Ockenga was raised a Methodist and attended Taylor University, an evangelical Methodist college in Indiana. Upon graduation from Taylor in 1927, he entered Princeton Theological Seminary and two years later joined with a group of students who left Princeton to follow Machen in the organization of Westminster Seminary. Soon after graduation, Ockenga joined the staff of First Presbyterian Church in Pittsburgh, a congregation led by conservative Presbyterian and Machen ally Clarence Macartney.[65]

---

64. Marsden, *Fundamentalism and American Culture*, 184–95. Marsden writes that Fundamentalism took three principal forms. "Considerable groups within the major denominations identified themselves with the Fundamentalist tradition . . . Second, there were substantial Fundamentalist influences outside of the traditional dominant structures of American culture but within denominational traditions that were not purely Fundamentalist [for example, in Holiness and Pentecostal movements and in various pietistic traditions] . . . Finally, some of the extreme Fundamentalists separated into their own denominations or into independent traditions. These were mainly dispensationalists for whom strict separation was an article of faith."

65. While Clarence Macartney and John Gresham Machen shared much in common in theology, their outlooks on American culture were significantly different. Machen's Southern libertarianism caused him to focus almost singlemindedly on doctrine, while because of his Reformed Presbyterian heritage, moral and social reform was, for Macartney, as equally important as doctrinal integrity. Macartney was also more adverse to schism within the church and refused to leave the Presbyterian Church with Machen in 1936. See, Longfield, *Presbyterian Controversy*, 114–25.

By 1936, the young pastor had assumed the pulpit of Boston's Park Street Congregational Church where his pulpit ability, organizational skills, and leadership aptitude enabled the historic church to flourish. Then in 1939, Ockenga completed his Ph.D. at the University of Pittsburgh.

Park Street Church provided Harold Ockenga with opportunities to extend his ministry in two important ways. First, like his mentor, Clarence Macartney, Ockenga began to look for ways to strengthen the conservative wing of the church by building inclusive coalitions of evangelical Christians. He played a pivotal role in the founding of the National Association of Evangelicals,[66] and in his 1942 keynote address before the fledgling association's first gathering, Ockenga argued that an inclusive organization of evangelical Christians was essential if the gospel was to make a significant impact in American society. Most fundamentalist pastors and leaders were like "lone wolves" who served in isolation from each other and from any larger fellowship of like-minded believers. Even though God had blessed their individual efforts, Ockenga declared that he saw "on the horizon ominous clouds of battle which spell annihilation unless we are willing to run in a pack."[67] Fundamentalists had been attacked and frozen out of many denominations and organizations, and unless they organized nationally, they would be shut out of any opportunity to receive free radio broadcasting time on the three major networks, NBC, CBS, and Mutual.[68]

"Look about you at individuals in our churches," Ockenga challenged his hearers. "They are defeated, reticent, retiring, and seemingly in despair."[69] Scriptural unity was essential if evangelicals were to once again discover hope, power, and purpose. But for that to happen, "this millstone of rugged independency which has held back innumerable movements before, in which individual leaders must be the whole hog or none, must

66. Matthews, *Standing Up, Standing Together*, provides a sympathetic account of the founding of NAE.

67. Ockenga, "Unvoiced Multitudes," 10.

68. Matthews, *Standing Up, Standing Together*, 289. In Matthew's words, "NBC's policy was to recognize three faith groups: Catholic, Protestant, and Jewish, and to divide its sustaining (free) time religious programs between them. The trouble with that, from the evangelical point of view, was that NBC considered the Federal Council of Churches as the sole representative of Protestantism. The network refused to sell time to religious broadcasters, so those not picked by the Federal Council had no access to NBC. The Columbia Broadcasting System (CBS) had a similar policy. The third major radio network of that day, Mutual, sold some time to Charles E. Fuller, (among others) but it was sending signals that it might stop that practice."

69. Carpenter, *New Evangelical Coalition*, 29.

be utterly repudiated by every one of us."[70] Unlike the separatist American Council of Christian Churches, organized a year earlier by Carl McIntire, NAE reflected an inclusive approach to evangelical unity. Fellowship would be marked not by denominational affiliation nor by one's willingness to "separate" from others deemed heretical, but by commitment to the doctrinal essentials marked by the NAE statement of faith.[71]

Reforming Fundamentalism: The Emergence of New Evangelicalism

Like their mainline Protestant counterparts, some Protestant fundamentalist leaders were beginning to see the need for reform and renewal within their coalition. Fundamentalism, in their view, had become theologically stagnant and organizationally fragmented. The motifs of withdrawal and separatism had isolated the movement from society at large and if that direction continued, the belief that Fundamentalism was irrelevant and obscurantist would continue to grow more powerful. Harold Ockenga's willingness to build a broad-based coalition of theologically conservative Christians reflected the first of four currents of reform that emerged within the fundamentalist coalition during the 1940s and 1950s.

Ockenga was aware that even in the early 1940s, biblical Christianity could not be solely defined by one faction or party within the larger fundamentalist movement. Fundamentalism was in reality a coalition of several theologically conservative parties of which two, those who gravitated around the classic Presbyterian confessionalism as defined by the Princeton theology, and dispensational premillennialists, were the most prominent. Ockenga's strategy was to broaden Fundamentalism into a larger evangelical coalition that included theological conservatives from ethnic denominations, from Pentecostal and Holiness traditions,[72] from region-

---

70. Ibid., 32.

71. Ibid., 34. In Ockenga's words, "Unless we can have the cardinal evangelical doctrines of Christianity as the fundamental basis of such a program it is impossible for us to unite."

72. Ockenga, "Pentecostal Bogey," 12–13. Evangelicals in the Pentecostal and Holiness traditions played little, if any, role in the Fundamentalist/Modernist controversies of the early twentieth century. Unlike many from the Reformed and dispensational parties within the fundamentalist coalition, Ockenga saw them not as heretics, but as fellow believers with whom he disagreed over certain matters of doctrine. "I have known the Pentecostal brethren from the Assemblies of God, the Church of God, the Pentecostal

ally oriented denominations like the Southern Baptist Convention,[73] even from evangelicals who had chosen to remain in denominations associated with the theologically liberal Federal Council of Churches.

The second direction for reform within the Fundamentalist coalition emerged from the pen of Carl F.H. Henry[74] with his 1947 book, the *Uneasy Conscience of Modern Fundamentalism*. Henry argued that fundamentalists had forgotten the dual nature of their Christian citizenship as well as their mandate to engage and influence the larger culture in which they lived. The motifs of separatism and withdrawal were combined with a hyper-premillennialism in a way that made it difficult for fundamentalists to, in Henry's words, "work out a positive message within [their] own framework."[75] Henry declared that it was time for theologically conservative Christians to "reawaken to the relevance of [their] redemptive message to the global predicament" and "discard elements of [their] message which cut the nerve of world compassion as contradictory to the inherent genius of Christianity."[76] Evangelicals were not only called to proclaim the historic Christian gospel, but they needed to use biblical truth to address serious national and international concerns.

Carl Henry's call for evangelicals to recognize the social consequences of their core beliefs was warmly received in some circles and bitterly opposed in others, especially by fundamentalists associated with the separatist movement led by Carl McIntire. McIntire's moves during the 1930s and 1940s had further fragmented an already divided Fundamentalism,

Holiness Church and other similar theological groups, which are in fellowship with the NAE. They are evangelical, Bible-believing, Christ-honoring, Spirit-filled brethren, who manifest in character and life the truths expressed in the statement of faith of the NAE. Set in ethical contrast with some of the fundamentalist brethren they shine brilliantly. I testify to precious fellowship with these men, though I disagree with their doctrine of the work of the Holy Spirit."

Ockenga's understanding of how these traditions relate to evangelicalism addresses two issues that evangelicals continue to wrestle with today. First, which doctrines are essential and form the core of Christian faith? Second, how broad can the evangelical coalition be and still be called evangelical?

73. One of the most interesting discussions among students of American Christianity focuses on the relationship of the Southern Baptist Convention to both evangelical and mainline Protestantism. Numerous books and articles have dealt with this issue, including Dockery, *Southern Baptists and American Evangelicals*.

74. The best source for information about Carl F. H. Henry's life and thought comes from his own memoirs. See, Henry, *Confessions of a Theologian*.

75. Henry, *Uneasy Conscience*, 32.

76. Ibid., 76.

and the veteran separatist argued that the Bible taught not only separation from unbelief but from fellow evangelicals who cooperated in any way with progressive or modernist Christians.[77] In the early 1950s, one of his loyal students began to seriously question the direction not only of McIntire's leadership, but the whole tone of his separatist movement. Francis August Schaeffer had followed Carl McIntire out of Westminster Seminary and had sided with McIntire in his opposition to the National Association of Evangelicals during the 1940s. While twenty years later Schaeffer would become widely known as the intellectual conscience of evangelicalism with books like *Escape from Reason*,[78] the early 1950s found Francis Schaeffer and his wife, Edith, in Switzerland attempting to develop a ministry called "Children for Christ."

Schaeffer carried on an extensive correspondence with friends in Europe and the United States and it is through this correspondence that we not only detect a significant shift in Schaeffer's thinking about the church, but a distinct call for reform in how Fundamentalism viewed Christian spirituality. "I am sure "separation" is correct," Schaeffer wrote in a 1951 letter. "But it is only one principle. There are others to be kept as well. The command to love should mean something."[79] By 1955, Schaeffer was ready to openly break with McIntire and offered a four-point criticism of separatist varieties of Fundamentalism. In these separatist movements, there was very little waiting on God and very little of the love of God exhibited. Moreover separatist leaders demanded a loyalty from their followers that was unscriptural. And separatist leaders had forgotten that the purpose of the church was to preach the gospel.[80]

For Schaeffer, the real problem in Fundamentalism was spiritual. "I have come to realize that you were right," Schaeffer writes to a Mr. Lohmann on August 29, 1956, "as you wrote of the lack of love as 'the driving motive' in the personal attacks made on other Christians . . . . It is as important to show forth the love of God as to show forth the holiness of God."[81] For Schaeffer, the essential weakness of Protestant Fundamentalism was

---

77. Marty, *Under God, Indivisible*, 106.

78. Schaeffer, *Escape from Reason*. For a concise account of Schaeffer's life and his impact on evangelicalism, see Hamilton, "Dissatisfaction of Francis Schaeffer," 22–30.

79. Dennis, ed. *Letters of Francis Schaeffer*, 39.

80. Ibid., 52. This critique was written by Schaeffer in a letter dated February 12, 1955 to, in the editor's description, "a Finnish Christian leader and coworker of the Schaeffers."

81. Ibid., 67.

the temptation toward a dead orthodoxy, an orthodoxy that minimizes the work of the Holy Spirit.[82] This was a problem that had plagued earlier Protestant generations and that had set the stage for the emergence of theological liberalism. "Increasingly I believe that after we are saved we have only one calling, and that is to show forth the existence and the character of God. Since God is love and God is holy, it is our calling to act in such a way as to demonstrate the existence and character of God."[83] Christian faith for Schaeffer, became much more than intellectual assent to doctrine. True spirituality was desperately needed among fundamentalists and the only way for authentic spirituality to be expressed was for Christians to live in a way that demonstrated God's love and holiness simultaneously.[84]

Schaeffer's concern for Christian love was expressed in a different context by a young intellectual who by 1950 had emerged as one of the brightest minds among theological conservatives. Edward John Carnell had not only published an attention-getting text on Christian apologetics, he had completed doctoral degrees at Harvard Divinity School (Th.D.) and Boston University (Ph.D.). The young scholar's meteoric rise culminated in his selection in the fall of 1954 as the second president of Fuller Theological Seminary.

Fuller Seminary had been established by Harold Ockenga and the radio evangelist Charles Fuller with the goal of establishing intellectual credibility for theologically conservative Christian scholars. Ockenga was convinced that in order for evangelicalism to once again impact American culture significantly, it needed an intellectual renaissance. As early as 1944, he had gathered a group of evangelical theologians to, in his words, "discuss the need for the writing of a new evangelical literature, based upon evangelical principles, and, in particular upon an inerrant Scripture."[85] With the close of World War II, Ockenga's vision came into sharper focus. He had become convinced that a new evangelical seminary was needed—a seminary that would function not only as a place to train the coming generation of evangelical pastors and missionaries but as a scholarly center that

82. Ibid., 70–71.

83. Ibid., 71.

84. Later in his career, Schaeffer would develop these themes in two of his most influential books *Mark of the Christian*, and *True Spirituality*.

85. Ockenga, in Lindsell, *Battle for the Bible*, 12. In the foreword to Lindsell's controversial book, Ockenga reflects on the importance of the doctrine of biblical inerrancy in the founding of Fuller Seminary and in the intellectual core of the emerging new evangelicalism.

would produce the type of literature that would have to be noticed by the intellectuals who shaped government, academia, and the professions.[86] Edward John Carnell shared Ockenga's vision for intellectual renewal among American theological conservatives. As the 1950s unfolded, Carnell would push that renewal in directions that would not only make Ockenga and others uncomfortable but would expose serious theological disagreements within the emerging new evangelical coalition.

For the first seven years of Fuller's existence, Ockenga had served as president-in-absentia, commuting twice each year to Pasadena while maintaining his Park Street Church pulpit in Boston. By 1954, Fuller Seminary's growth demanded a full-time resident president and in Edward John Carnell, Harold Ockenga found someone who not only shared his vision but his educational philosophy. "A great school," Carnell wrote to Ockenga, "requires a great administrator as head: a master of general educational theory; one versed in educational trends; one who is vigilant to see . . . that every organizational means is being used to convert the school into maximal service for Christ."[87] The president should be a "first-rank scholar and teacher" as opposed to a promotional person who "wins friends for the school without at the same time inspiring the faculty to the type of world scholarship" that would bring favor to the cause of Christ.[88]

One of Fuller Seminary's primary objectives was to create an evangelical institution where scholarly research and writing would be highly valued. Perhaps better than any of the Fuller faculty, Edward Carnell captured that spirit. While he was determined not to allow the administrative demands of the Fuller presidency to deflect his scholarly pursuits, by the late 1950s it became clear that the presidency did affect the shape and direction that his scholarship would take. Carnell had already been wrestling with the existential questions raised by Søren Kierkegaard and was becoming convinced, as he would write toward the end of his Fuller presidency, that Fundamentalism had driven a wedge between revelation as disclosure of God's will (which was objective and propositional) and revelation as disclosure of God's person (which was mystical and inward). "If we drive a wedge between personal and propositional revelation," according to Carnell, "we evacuate Christian theology of its normative elements."[89] Fundamentalism

86. Marsden, *Reforming Fundamentalism*, 24.

87. Edward John Carnell to Harold John Ockenga, March 8, 1953.

88. Carnell to Ockenga, February 12, 1954.

89. Carnell, "Review of," 319.

had come to the point where it equated possession of virtue totally with possession of correct propositional truth. Therefore, it had lost the sense of balance that traditionally characterized Protestant Christianity. Losing that balance, in Carnell's view, had resulted in disastrous consequences not only for people and institutions but for an entire movement.

If the Carnellian critique of Fundamentalism had stopped there, Ockenga and other evangelical intellectuals would have had little reason to feel threatened. But Carnell's administrative, interpersonal, and theological struggles as Fuller president had left him frustrated with what he saw as Fundamentalism's self-destructive tendencies.[90] In the late 1950s, he determined to write a book that would "separate the men from the boys theologically."[91] If Carnell's goal was to infuriate separatistic Fundamentalists like Carl McIntire, he accomplished that. However, he also raised the ire of many of his fellow new evangelicals. In *The Case for Orthodox Theology*, Carnell not only offered a critique of separatism, he called into question the finality of the understanding of biblical inerrancy developed by Benjamin Warfield and adopted by the next generation of evangelicalism.[92] He argued that John Gresham Machen's fixation on combating theological liberalism blinded him to the evils of the separatist mentality that would become the focal point of Fundamentalism.[93]

The most controversial part of the book was its last chapter. Fundamentalism was, in Carnell's words, "orthodoxy gone cultic."[94] Fundamentalists were endangering Protestant orthodoxy by their "ideological thinking, a highly censorious spirit, and a curious tendency to separate from the life of the church."[95] While Fundamentalism was started with the noble intention of defending traditional Christian faith, it evolved into a mentality of separatism that disconnected it from the classic creeds of the church. When Modernism collapsed in the midst of the Great Depression and World War II, Fundamentalism became an army without a cause governed by rigid, inflexible, separatistic ideological thinking.[96] American fundamentalists

---

90. For a description of Carnell's presidency and the frustrations he faced, see Marsden, *Reforming Fundamentalism*, 172–96.

91. Carnell to Ockenga, November 24, 1958.

92. Carnell, *The Case for Orthodox Theology*, 102–11.

93. Ibid., 114–16.

94. Ibid., 113.

95. Ibid.

96. Ibid., 113–14. In Carnell's words, "The mentality of fundamentalism is dominated

were making minor doctrinal points into tests for orthodoxy and were confusing common courtesy and civility with theological compromise. As a result, unbelievers are often more sensitive to justice and mercy than those who call themselves Christians.[97] Therefore, true Christians must reject the fundamentalist mentality by paying attention to the majesty of their tradition and balancing their beliefs with a healthy dose of Christian love. They should remain within the denominational families that nurtured their Christian faith unless their denomination removes the gospel from its statement of faith or moves to expel them.[98]

Carnell's program pushed in directions that Harold Ockenga, Carl Henry, Francis Schaeffer, and other reformers of Fundamentalism saw as dangerous, because the Fuller president appeared willing to negotiate what they saw as the anchor of their movement, indeed of orthodox Christianity—the inspiration and inerrancy of Holy Scripture. Unlike the theological eclecticism that had emerged in mainline Protestantism in the aftermath of the Fundamentalist-Modernist controversy, Protestant Fundamentalism was much more rigid in its theological core doctrines. New evangelical reformers like Ockenga, Henry, and Schaeffer critiqued Fundamentalism on a methodological, not a doctrinal, level. Theologically, each wished to maintain biblical inerrancy as the core of the new evangelical reform of Fundamentalism.

As the twentieth century progressed from its early to middle stage, the doctrine of biblical inerrancy had become the theological focal point for American theological conservatives. By the 1950s, the divide between mainline and theologically conservative Protestants was essentially defined by this doctrine. Now the issue of biblical inerrancy was becoming the dividing line between two new-evangelical parties, each advocating a different strategy for reforming Fundamentalism. The conservative reformers—Henry, Ockenga, Schaeffer, and their allies now faced a challenge

---

by ideological thinking. Ideological thinking is rigid, intolerant, and doctrinaire; it sees principles everywhere, and all principles come in clear tones of black and white; it exempts itself from the limits that original sin places on history; it wages holy wars without acknowledging the elements of pride and personal interest that prompt the call to battle; it creates new evils while trying to correct old ones."

97. Ibid., 123. "Handing out tracts is much more important than founding a hospital. As a result, unbelievers are often more sensitive to mercy, and bear a heavier load of justice, than those who come in the name of Jesus. The fundamentalist is not disturbed by this, of course, for he is busy painting "Jesus Saves" on rocks in a public park."

98. Ibid., 132–37.

within their own movement from a new progressive party. Carnell's challenge had emboldened several Fuller Seminary scholars—Paul Jewett, George Ladd, and Daniel Fuller among them—to push for an even bolder theological reform: the elimination of biblical inerrancy as the defining mark for how the emerging new evangelical coalition understood the inspiration of Scripture. Carnell's critique of Fundamentalism led them to believe that they could possibly succeed not only at Fuller but over time, within the larger new-evangelical movement.

At this point in the late 1950s, the Fuller progressives (and their allies) were a distinct minority among theological conservatives, most of whom believed that biblical inerrancy was the important doctrinal distinctive of their cause. Perhaps the best statement of how most post World War II theological conservatives (whether they identified themselves as fundamentalist or new evangelical) understood the inspiration and inerrancy of Holy Scripture came from the pen of Dr. Edward J. Young, then professor of Old Testament at the school established by John Gresham Machen, Westminster Theological Seminary. His 1957 book, *Thy Word is Truth*,[99] not only sought to clearly define how theological conservatives should understand the inspiration and inerrancy of Scripture, but to warn against acceptance of any "neo-orthodox" position grounded in higher-critical categories of biblical criticism.[100] To do so, in Young's view, would mean abandoning both the historic Christian understanding of the Bible's inspiration and the Bible's own testimony about itself.

"According to the Bible," in Young's words, "inspiration is a superintendence of God the Holy Spirit over the writers of the Scriptures, as a result of which these scriptures possess Divine authority and trustworthiness and . . . are free from error."[101] That inspiration applied to every part of Holy Scripture including its very words. Because the Scriptures are God-breathed,[102] Young concluded that, "what has been spoken by God, who cannot lie, must be pure and true altogether. Every word which proceedeth from the mouth of the heavenly Father must in the very nature of the case be absolutely free from error. If this is not so, God Himself is not trustworthy."[103] The error-free nature of Scripture, according to Young, ap-

---

99. Young, *Thy Word is Truth*.

100. Ibid., 16.

101. Ibid., 27.

102. See 2 Tim 3:14–17; cf. Ps 12:6.

103. Young, *Thy Word is Truth*, 40.

plied not only to "moral and ethical truths, but to all statements of fact."[104] In other words, biblical inerrancy applied not only to matters of faith and practice, but to historical and scientific matters addressed by Scripture.

A proper understanding of biblical inerrancy, in Young's view, involved grasping two important distinctions. First, inerrancy does not imply dictation. Under the inspiration of the Holy Spirit, the writers of scripture "expressly wrote what he [the Holy Spirit] desired and yet at the same time were responsible individuals whose personalities were not stifled."[105] Human beings were the writers of Scripture, but God was its final and ultimate author. "While the human authors were true authors, nevertheless they were not originators of the words and the thoughts that are found in the Bible. They were holy men . . . who were borne by the Spirit."[106] Second, biblical inerrancy must be confined to the original autographs of Scripture. Although our current copies of Scripture are remarkably accurate, they may contain errors of translation and transmission. But in the original autographs, we find "the actual God-breathed word, true to fact in all its statements. Let no one say that it is a matter of indifference whether this original was inerrant; it is a matter of greatest importance, for the honor and veracity of God himself are at stake. If there are actual errors in the original copies of the Bible . . . the God of truth is guilty of error."[107]

104. Ibid., 48.

105. Ibid., 71. This quotation is in the context of Young's discussion of the mode of inspiration. In response to how the Spirit's superintendence functioned in the context of the human personalities of the writers, Young comments, "Legitimate as such questions are, however, they cannot be fully answered. God has not seen fit to reveal to us the mode by which he communicated His word to His servants, placing that word in their mouths and "carrying" them until the Word was accurately committed to writing. We have come, in other words, to an area of mystery . . . The Scripture is silent as to the mode which God employed to preserve His Word from error."

106. Ibid., 88–89. Earlier, Young comments, "If we examine closely the language of Peter [in 2 Pet 1:21], we shall note that it was while they were in this condition of being borne of the Spirit that men spake from God. The source of their words is said to be God, and they spake these words while they were being borne of the Holy Spirit. While they spoke, they were passive, and God was active. It was He who bore them, and as He bore them, they spoke. It was, therefore, not in the void, but rather through the instrumentality and medium of men who were borne by the Spirit, that God spoke."

107. Ibid., 88.

Struggling With the Limits of Reform

Young spoke for a large majority of fundamentalists and new evangelicals (and for James Nichols, Jr. and other faculty at the New England School of Theology) who saw the doctrine of biblical inerrancy as the dividing line between biblical Christianity and theological liberalism. "We are convinced," Young wrote, "that the Scriptures do indeed claim to be the Word of God, and since they are from Him and find their origin in Him, are therefore infallible and entirely free from error of any kind. Since their author is Truth and cannot lie, so His Word, the Sacred Scriptures, is truth and cannot lie. The Biblical evidence to support this thesis is very clear and cogent."[108] Moreover, in Young's view, biblical inerrancy was pivotal for the future of the church. Many (including some evangelicals) were not aware that the church was at a crossroads and that those who fail to embrace inerrancy have not only had "their vision obscured by the dense fog of modern theology," but "will travel on taking the wrong turning, until the road leads them at last into the valley of lost hope and eternal death."[109]

It was clear that as the 1960s dawned, the reform of Fundamentalism envisioned by Ockenga, Henry, Schaeffer, and even Carnell was having theological as well as ecclesiastical consequences. They had hoped to create a broad-based evangelicalism centered on a doctrinal core grounded in Protestant orthodoxy as interpreted by the Princeton tradition of Hodge, Warfield, and Machen. That would mean, in their view, an evangelical movement capable of maintaining a strong theological distinction from mainline Protestantism and capable of recapturing the initiative for the formation of culture within American society. That would also mean an evangelicalism guided by a strong commitment to the doctrine of biblical inerrancy as the foundation for expressing the truth of historic Christianity in the modern context.

However, what the first generation of new-evangelical reformers discovered was that the theological range within the larger movement they hoped to create was wider than they had foreseen. Therefore, the new-evangelical reformers were beginning to discover what their mainline Protestant counterparts had discovered earlier, that reform was beginning to lead to fragmentation. While post-World War II American Protestantism was clearly divided into two distinct and often warring parties, the theological

108. Ibid., 45.
109. Ibid., 35.

cohesion of both parties had begun to disintegrate with the fragmentation proceeding at a much faster rate within mainline Protestantism. Tensions remained high between mainline and fundamentalist Protestants and both sides had difficulty seeing clearly the efforts toward theological and ecclesiastical reform in the other party. Mainline Protestants were wrestling with how to justify modernity in biblical and theological thought in light of historic Christian faith. Evangelical Protestants were struggling with how to express that faith in a modern context.

It is in this context that the Advent Christian Church struggles with how to understand the inspiration of the Bible. That is the story we will pick up in our next chapter.

CHAPTER FIVE

Advent Christians Engage a Divided Protestantism

THE 1950S EXPOSED WHAT for some were two glaring weaknesses in Advent Christian denominational life. First, the denomination was non-existent in many parts of the United States. With economic prosperity leading to growing migration on the part of many middle-class adults, Advent Christians who moved were more often than not forced to find other congregations. Second, like most restorationist Christian movements, Advent Christians were by nature suspicious of organizations outside the local church. Therefore, their ecclesiastical agencies developed more in a haphazard manner. Leaders of Advent Christian-related ministries found themselves competing for funds not only with each other, but with a growing number of para-church and non-denominational ministries.

The denomination's home missions agency had come up with a plan that they hoped would address the first problem. Large sections of the Midwest and Rocky Mountain states had no Advent Christian activity, and their hope was to build several chains of Advent Christian congregations between east and west. These chains would roughly parallel the emerging interstate highway system and target towns and cities west of the Mississippi River along those corridors. The first chain would cross the Southwest from Dallas to the metropolitan Los Angeles area. Two cities in New Mexico—Albuquerque and Grants—were targeted to provide the first links in the chain. By 1959, Advent Christian home mission activity had already begun in Grants.[1]

In terms of the second issue, the Advent Christian Church had tried to address the problem of organization and funding in the early 1920s when the first attempt at a unified denominational funding plan met with failure.[2] Thirty-five years later, a new generation of Advent Christian leaders was ready to try again. To lead the effort, they turned to an Advent Christian with Canadian roots, Rev. James Howard Shaw. Shaw's Advent Christian upbringing was unique in one important way—his father and stepmother belonged to an Advent Christian fellowship that made up part of the union church in Scotts Bay, Nova Scotia. Hence, as Shaw biographer Ralph Dodge writes, "As a boy growing up in that ecumenical setting, [Shaw] learned what it meant to be loyal to one's religious heritage without becoming intolerant of those with slightly different perspectives."[3] After graduating from New England School of Theology (1933) and Gordon Divinity School (1936), and serving Advent Christian congregations in New Brunswick, Massachusetts, Rhode Island, and Illinois, Shaw was picked in 1958 to serve as the chief administrative officer of the Advent Christian Church,[4] and given a mandate to unify the work of the denomination both organizationally and financially.[5]

Shaw's vision was of a unified Advent Christian Church carrying out its God-given task both locally and globally. What hindered the denomination from doing that was not only a lack of vision, but a lack of organizational cohesiveness that allowed for adequate follow-through on some of the good plans that had been proposed during the 1930s and 1940s.[6] In that context, Shaw was determined not to make the same mistake that an

1. "A New Link." This promotion encouraged Advent Christians to contribute $5,000 toward the opening of church-planting efforts in Albuquerque.

2. Hewitt, *Devotion and Development*, 211–66.

3. Dodge, "God's Statesman," 8–11. Dodge provides the best biographical outline of James Howard Shaw's life and ministry currently available. The biographical details that follow are based on his work.

4. The title given to that position at the time was Executive Secretary.

5. Dodge, "God's Statesman," 9. In writing his article, Ralph Dodge had opportunity to conduct an extended interview with James Howard Shaw before Rev. Shaw's death in 1986.

6. Hewitt, *Devotion and Development*, 275–76. Shaw comments to Hewitt that on several occasions, when plans and strategies were developed and approved, "Two years later we would meet and ride off in a completely different direction."

earlier generation of Advent Christian leaders made during the 1920s. That generation, in attempting to create a unified method for funding Advent Christian agencies and institutions, had not grappled with the reality of a denomination made up mostly of small, fiercely independent local congregations.[7] In Shaw's view, the Advent Christian Church must not only pursue a unified funding mechanism for its ministries but a strategy that would ultimately unify its several national agencies under one organizational umbrella. Only then could the competition and conflict between various agencies be channeled into a common effort to expand the ministry of the Advent Christian Church.[8]

By the early 1960s, Shaw was pressing for acceptance of United Outreach, a funding program by which individual Advent Christian congregations would send their support for Advent Christian ministries to General Conference which in turn would pay it out to Advent Christian ministries and institutions based on a formula established by the denomination's executive committee and ratified by delegates to the biennial General Conference meeting.[9] Such an approach, Shaw and other denominational leaders hoped, would result not only in greater support for Advent Christian work but in less competition for funds between the agencies themselves. "We stand at the crossroads of crucial decision," Shaw wrote in 1963. "The Advent Christian people are now choosing between a program of advance or a return to a policy of 'too little, too late.'"[10] While the bulk of Advent Christian congregations were still opting for the latter, Shaw was hopeful

7. Ibid., 252–53. Hewitt quotes Shaw as remarking that the Forward Movement of the 1920s failed because, "It called for such multiplication of organized groups within the local churches, that it was almost impossible to promote that on a national scale, especially with only one man trying to promote it through the press."

8. Shaw, "Mission and Method," 8. This brief article provides insight into the importance Shaw attached to organizational cohesion. "A significant part of our attention and energy has been devoted during the past four years to the development and promotion of a more effective method of doing our cooperative work for Christ. This improved method . . . is not an end. It is only a means. Yet, if the end to be served is valid and important, then the means is a correspondingly important matter." Later he writes, "Unless we seriously expect to discover that the Advent Christian denomination ought not to exist, we had better get on with the task of making our efforts for Christ more efficient and more effective."

9. At this time, each of the agencies and institutions participating in the United Outreach budget maintained separate administrators and boards of directors. Therefore the process of determining the budget and the proposed reconciliation could be quite involved and usually required much give and take.

10. Shaw, "Mission and Method," 8.

that a growing number of congregations would embrace the new united approach. "The United Outreach churches accept the total program [of the Advent Christian Church] as their responsibility, and they regard the denominational agencies as arms of the local church for fulfilling its responsibility."[11]

Despite the best promotional efforts of Shaw and others, opposition to a unified approach to funding and organization was significant. Opponents' feelings were expressed well by one 1962 letter-writer reacting to General Conference reorganization proposals: "I am a little disgusted about some of them. I, for one, do not like centralized control but it certainly looks like we are heading in that direction . . . . Let us pray—as our church here has been praying at every prayer service—that Christ and the liberty that made us free will reign supreme at this year's General Conference."[12] Opponents like this letter-writer not only could express vocal opposition, they could appeal to Article Eight of the Advent Christian Declaration of Principles which declared that "local church organizations should be independent of outside control, congregational in government, and subject to no dictation of priest, bishop, or pope." Individual freedom (some would say "individual autonomy") and congregational independence were principles enshrined in the theological heritage of the Advent Christian Church and efforts by Shaw and others to promote United Outreach would by their very nature generate controversy.

As controversial as United Outreach was among Advent Christians, Shaw seemed even more troubled by calls for clearer definitions of Advent Christian theology and purpose. "Some would defer a decision as to method until we go back and redefine our mission," according to Shaw. "There is certainly no objection to such a basic reclarification of denominational purpose—although some of us who have freely devoted our lives to this cause had thought we understood the Advent Christian message and mission sufficiently to warrant giving the best energies of our best years to it!"[13]

However, what appeared obvious to J. Howard Shaw was not as apparent at least to some Advent Christians. What was the purpose of the Advent Christian Church in a world of advancing technology and progress? What set Advent Christians apart from other Protestants and were those

11. Ibid.
12. Bunker Jr., "Letters to the PTM Editor," 11.
13. Shaw, "Mission and Method," 8.

differences worth the efforts to maintain a separate denomination? Those questions attracted some surprisingly divergent responses. Some felt that the Advent Christian Church had essentially fulfilled the purpose that God had for it. In their view, a large number of Christians had embraced the early Adventist notion of the soon return of Jesus Christ. Moreover, a growing number of Christian theologians, especially among mainline Protestants, were now seriously considering the Advent Christian doctrinal distinctive of conditional immortality. Therefore, the time was right to explore merger with one or more denominations.[14]

Many others felt that Advent Christian theological distinctives were still important enough (and unpopular enough) to warrant the continued existence of a separate denomination. One Advent Christian leader expressed this view when he declared that God had called the Advent Christian Church to stand for three distinctive doctrines: The unconscious state of the dead, conditional immortality, and the eternal home of the saints here on the earth. "Were it not for these distinctive doctrines, there would be no sufficient reason for maintaining a separate denomination."[15] Therefore, as long as Advent Christians believe it important to emphasize their theological distinctives, "it seems best to maintain our own local churches, our own mission work, and the publishing of our own literature." While Advent Christians share much in common with other Christians, their unique doctrinal views necessitate not only a continued denominational existence but strong support by Advent Christian individuals and churches for distinctively Advent Christian ministries.

This argument captured well and with a gracious tone the traditional Advent Christian posture toward the larger Protestant world, a posture that was still seen as valid by many Advent Christian pastors and laypeople living in the middle of the twentieth century. Advent Christian individuals and congregations, in their view, could cultivate cordial relationships with

14. Oral History Interview, Asa J. Colby, October 19, 1995. Rev. Colby served for over thirty years on the faculty of Aurora College (beginning in Fall 1949) and was a supporter of this strategy. He comments, "Years ago, when there was some discussion about possibly exploring union with another body, I felt this would be a move in the right direction. But of course, it was squelched absolutely."

15. Carter, "One Hundred Per Cent," 56. In Rev. Carter's view, being faithful to the Advent Christian heritage as expressed through its doctrinal distinctives meant that Advent Christians must realize, "We have a message for the times and a corresponding responsibility."

other Christians if they so desired.[16] However, Advent Christians should keep their distance from the controversies and disputes that surrounded the larger Protestant world and focus their energies on building their distinctive ministries.

Still others advocated a third approach. For these Advent Christians, it was not enough to ground denominational identity in Advent Christian distinctive doctrines alone. That distinctive identity was meaningless apart from strong commitment to the verbal inspiration and inerrancy of Scripture, and therefore the Advent Christian Church should position itself squarely within the theologically conservative framework articulated within the larger Protestant world by Billy Graham and Harold John Ockenga. This view found its most prominent advocate in Dr. Edwin K. Gedney, the president and chief legislative officer of the Advent Christian General Conference from 1958 to 1964.

Gedney was a geologist by profession who studied that subject at Brown University (B.A.) and Harvard (M.A.). While studying at Brown, he met Rev. Irving F. Barnes, pastor of the Providence, R.I. Advent Christian Church and noted teacher on the themes of holiness and the deeper Christian life. Through his contact with Barnes, first in Providence and later in Somerville, Massachusetts,[17] Gedney became convinced that Advent Christian doctrinal teachings regarding the nature of humanity were biblical and aligned himself with the Advent Christian Church. After several years in private industry, Gedney, in the words of biographer Robert Craig, "recognized that his real desire was not to mine gold, but to mine souls for Christ."[18] In 1934, he began what was to be forty years of teaching and service at Gordon College, the evangelical school established in 1889 by the New England missionary statesman, Adoniram Judson Gordon.[19] At the

16. Ibid., 6. Rev. Carter suggests that Advent Christians should maintain "friendly relations with other evangelical denominations" and be ready to share in common evangelistic efforts. Others within the denomination continued to take a harsher, more sectarian stance toward the larger Protestant community.

17. For a biographical essay of the life of Edwin K. Gedney, see Craig, "Edwin Kemble Gedney," 1–24. At the same time Gedney moved from Brown University to Harvard to begin graduate work, Rev. Barnes moved from Providence, RI to Somerville, MA to assume the pastorate at the Somerville Advent Christian Church.

18. Ibid., 9.

19. Ibid., 12. Craig writes, "The exploits of Mr. Gedney at Gordon cover several fields. He developed the science department and served as its chair for many years. As more specialized faculty were hired he relinquished his job. When the college required a history department he, along with Dr. Byington, was called upon to organize it. Not only

same time, Gedney would serve the Advent Christian Church in several capacities including pastorates in the greater Boston area, and ongoing teaching and board of regents activities at the New England School of Theology and later Berkshire Christian College. In the midst of his many activities, he found time to pursue theological study and writing, especially in the area of Advent Christian doctrinal distinctives.

Like his counterpart, J. Howard Shaw, Edwin Gedney's formative Christian experiences were somewhat unique, at least among Advent Christians. His focus embraced not only the Advent Christian Church, but the cause of evangelicalism in New England as well. Out of that grew a theological approach which established the justification for Advent Christian doctrinal distinctives in the verbal, plenary inspiration of the Bible. "Our distinctive truths are great because our founders did not create them," wrote Gedney.[20] "They were revealed over the centuries as holy men were moved by the Holy Spirit, buried under years of ecclesiastical perversion and theological incrustation, and rediscovered by simple men who returned to an inspired Bible and searched in faith for truth and light." Biblical inerrancy, therefore, was foundational to the rediscovery of Advent Christian truth and to deny it, in Gedney's view, was to endanger the proclamation of those distinctive truths.

In J. Howard Shaw and Edwin K. Gedney, we find perhaps the two most significant figures in the life of the Advent Christian Church between 1955 and 1965, not only because of their primary leadership roles within the denomination, but because they give voice to the struggle over how to maintain a distinctive Advent Christian identity in a nation and world marked by rapid intellectual, technological, and managerial advance. For Shaw, effective organization based on cooperative effort was the only way that Advent Christians would be able to maximize their ministry. Advent Christians, in Shaw's view, were a theologically diverse people united by common commitment to their distinctive doctrines. Their diversity could be a strength if they could overcome their divisive tendencies and learn to

---

was he responsible for its organization, he taught most of the courses offered in the field for thirteen years. . . .

"As the college continued to grow, the needs for expanded educational opportunities also increased. During the 1940s a need for a psychology and education curriculum became apparent. To meet this need, Professor Gedney became student Gedney and returned to Harvard for 65 credit hours in the School of Education, finishing all the requirements for a Ph.D. except a thesis."

20. Gedney, "Advent Christian Imperative," 3, 13.

work together.[21] While Gedney supported Shaw's goals of effective organization and cooperation among Advent Christians, he viewed much of their theological diversity with alarm. Diverse theological approaches, especially on core issues of Christian doctrine like the inspiration of Scripture, represented a serious danger to the denomination because of their potential to undermine the justification for Advent Christian distinctive doctrines.[22]

Shaw and Gedney had much in common both theologically and culturally. But they differed at one key point—their approach to the diversity that had always marked the Advent Christian Church. Could Advent Christians forge unity out of diversity and address the larger problems that they faced? Could they forge a common mission grounded in their doctrinal identity—a mission that would allow for expansion and growth throughout the second half of the twentieth century? It is in this context that the Advent Christian "Battle for the Bible"[23] would be contested. The issues of Advent Christian doctrinal identity, organizational structure, and missionary expansion form the larger context for the Advent Christian conflict over inspiration. However, that context cannot be limited to events within the denominational structure. Events at Aurora College and the New England School of Theology, the two institutions which continued to train the bulk of Advent Christian clergy who pursued ministerial education, would play an important role as well. Before looking at the conflict itself, we turn to those events.

21. In 1968, Aurora College awarded J. Howard Shaw the honorary degree of Doctor of Divinity. The words of the citation captured well the spirit that Shaw attempted to cultivate within the Advent Christian Church, "He has maintained the highest ethical and moral standards for the ministry without intolerance or prejudice . . . The churches under his care have had their vision lifted to possibilities and potentialities apparently unrealized before. He has taken his place in community and civic affairs as a responsible Christian citizen." See Dodge, "God's Statesman," 10.

22. Gedney, "Advent Christian Imperative," 3. Gedney links the inspiration and inerrancy of Scripture to defense of Advent Christian distinctives with these words, "The Universal confusion of mankind . . . demands the simple truth of an inspired revelation as never before. With the great development of knowledge about man from the fields of anthropology, psychology, biology, and medicine, Man can still look only to that revelation for understanding of his purpose in the world and his ultimate destiny. I know of no other group that has a simple, logical, and believable interpretation of the vital aspects of revelation as that of our people . . . The consistent Biblical teaching of the Advent Christian people should approach the scientific mind with refreshing clarity and be a strong influence in moving that mind toward God."

23. This term was first applied to the Advent Christian conflict over inspiration by Freeman Barton in 1984. See Barton, *Advent Christians and the Bible*, 6.

Aurora College: Expansion and Growth

Because of the Great Depression of the 1930s, many small liberal-arts colleges were forced to close. For others, like Aurora College, continuing to operate was exceptionally difficult. The college had suffered financial hardship through participation in the first abortive Advent Christian attempt at a united budget during the early 1920s.[24] Just as the college was recovering, the 1929 Stock Market crash initiated events that led to the Great Depression. As a result, the college suffered a dramatic loss in endowment income as well as a serious decline in denominational support.[25]

Two important events resulted from the financial crisis. Up until this point, Aurora College had drawn its student body primarily from Advent Christian churches. Now, while not as many Advent Christian students could afford to attend college away from home, the Great Depression was causing more residents of Aurora and the surrounding Fox River Valley to remain at home while pursuing higher education, and Aurora College became the best option for many of them. Economic reality was causing a shift in Aurora College's student population, a shift that the college administration decided to encourage. Also, with the college in financial trouble, the community rallied to its support. In 1934, the first annual City Campaign for Aurora College raised over five-thousand dollars from over five-hundred Aurora based individuals and businesses. A year later, contributions to the college from the Aurora community would exceed denominational

24. Hewitt, *Devotion and Development*, 239–40. Hewitt quotes then president Orrin R. Jenks on the problems surrounding Aurora College's participation in the program. "At the beginning of this year [1922] our college was receiving one-sixth of the original apportionment . . . There are reasons which I cannot disclose in this report which convince me that our school will be strangled financially if allowed to continue as part of the denominational Forward Movement program as at present carried out." The Advent Christian agencies and institutions participating in the United Budget of the Forward Movement had agreed to cease soliciting any denominational monies privately.

25. Anderson, *Building on the Foundation*, 81. Anderson describes in some detail the financial crisis faced by the college during the early years of the Great Depression and the impact of that crisis on the college's relationship with the Advent Christian Church. The gravity of the college's financial situation is illustrated by the following from Anderson's book: "The recent bankruptcy of the W.W. Armstrong Company, which had been the college's agent in endowment fund investing, together with the depression which had impoverished most of the farmers whose mortgages constituted a sizable proportion of the invested capital of the [college] endowment, virtually wiped out the income and endangered the capital of those funds, while unpaid taxes continued to diminish the net values of such mortgages."

support.[26] By the late 1930s, Aurora's new President, Theodore P. Stephens, realized that if the college was to have a future, it could not depend solely on money and students from Advent Christian sources.[27] From that time on, Aurora College would cultivate a regional focus that would by the early 1960s see the school closely identified with the surrounding community.

With the end of World War II, Aurora's focus on serving the Fox River Valley gained even more momentum. By 1947, over half of the student body was from the surrounding community and the percentage of Advent Christian students had dropped below one-quarter.[28] The passage of the G.I. Bill swelled postwar enrollment. For the first time, Aurora College began to accept government subsidy and with those monies came government regulation. The shift in the makeup of the student body also affected the content of the college curriculum with more emphasis on the sciences, business and management, education, and nursing. The college entered into partnerships with the Illinois Institute of Technology in Chicago and the University of Illinois in Urbana—partnerships which allowed Aurora to supply the first two years of study for students wishing to prepare for careers in engineering and occupational therapy.

Although Aurora College's theological posture continued to be identified with mainline Protestantism, with the late 1940s came a significant shift in the college's theological faculty. Clarence Hewitt, the Advent Christian pastor, administrator, and theologian whose work significantly influenced much of the denomination throughout the second quarter of the twentieth century, left the college in 1947 to assume pastoral responsibilities at the Providence, R.I., Advent Christian Church.[29] His replacement was another Aurora College graduate with deep Advent Christian family roots. Moses Corliss Crouse grew up in Northern Maine and was working on the family potato farm when Aurora College president T.P. Stephens visited the Advent Christian congregations in the area. "Mose, you ought to come to

26. Ibid., 15.

27. Stephens believed that a potential constituency of at least eighty thousand people was needed to provide the minimum five hundred students and financial backing necessary for a liberal-arts school like Aurora College to achieve stability and effectiveness. With a total membership of no more than thirty thousand, many of whom seemed indifferent toward higher education, the Advent Christian Church, in Stephens's view, would be unable to sustain and support Aurora College. See Anderson, *Building on the Foundation*, 18.

28. Ibid., 50.

29. He would die five years later at age sixty-two.

Aurora College," Stephens told the young man.[30] As an undergraduate, the young Crouse was initially troubled by the implications of biblical scholarship and struggled with whether or not to transfer.[31] But those struggles were resolved and with encouragement from President Stephens and past president Orrin Roe Jenks, Crouse, after serving as Pastor of an Advent Christian congregation in Kansas City, Missouri, pursued graduate theological study first at Garrett Theological Institute and finally at Northwestern University, where he earned both the M.A. and Ph.D. degrees.

Crouse finished his M.A. dissertation just before joining the Aurora College faculty in 1947.[32] In it, he sought to examine the attempts of two theologians, Herbert George Wood and Paul Tillich, to define a Christian philosophy of history. While the thesis is primarily descriptive, through it we begin to discover the direction that Crouse's theological approach would take. He reacted strongly to what he saw as Tillich's willingness to separate faith from history. "Mr. Tillich affirms that he believes that Jesus was a historical figure," according to Crouse, "But . . . this Jesus is not sufficient for the basis of Christian faith."[33] Later he writes, "It seems that his [Mr. Tillich's] preference for the Christ to the exclusion of interest in the historical Jesus is unwarranted . . . . In the final analysis it is the conformity of the life of the historic Jesus to the intent of the divine revelation that we find in Christ that gives power and meaning to the Christ of faith. I fail to see how there could have been a revelation of God in Christ without this dedicated life of the historic Jesus that was wholly yielded to the will of the Father."[34]

Two themes were already emerging in Moses Crouse's theological direction. First, Crouse was vitally concerned that the link between God's salvific activity and the person and work of Jesus Christ in human history not be severed. Second, the young scholar was unwilling to divorce revelation from history, a trend easily seen in the approaches of Rudolf Bultmann and Paul Tillich. Instead, for Crouse, revelation was seen as essentially historical in character. God had revealed himself (and continues to reveal

---

30. Oral History Interview, Dorothy H. Crouse, May 13, 1995. Mrs. Crouse, the widow of Dr. Crouse, recalled this initial exchange between the two men. The biographical and educational information that follows is based on this interview.

31. Anderson, *Building on the Foundation*, 61.

32. Crouse, "Philosophies of History."

33. Ibid., 121.

34. Ibid., 129. Crouse adds, "What other basis could there be for our faith in Christ?"

himself) through events in human history. While he appreciated aspects of Tillich's work, especially Tillich's view that God can potentially be seen in all areas and activities of human life,[35] Crouse believed that to separate revelation from human history would seriously damage the Christian faith.

After Moses Crouse earned his Ph.D. in 1950, his theological orientation focused on three broad themes. First, much of his teaching and writing addressed the issue of immortality. Crouse was passionate in his view that the Advent Christian understanding of human mortality was consistent with what God had revealed both in scripture and in human history.[36] Second, he believed that Christian ecumenism was vital to the worldwide missionary witness of the church. One of the highlights of his life was the 1961 trip that he and his wife, Dorothy, took to New Delhi, India for the fourth assembly of the World Council of Churches, where Crouse served as an official observer.[37] That journey also provided them the opportunity to visit Advent Christian mission work in southern India, Malaysia, the Philippines, and Japan, and gave him the kind of first-hand experience that would prove invaluable in his service on the board of the American Advent Christian Mission Society (AAMS).

The trip also allowed Crouse time to reflect on two themes—the relationship of Christianity to other world religions and the emergence of new Christian congregations especially in Asia. Humanity is marked with a "restless dissatisfaction" that leads to a longing for immortality. To meet that longing, humans have constructed monuments like the Taj Mahal, and

---

35. With Tillich, according to Crouse, "I am convinced that God is potentially revealed in all things. We only need eyes that are conditioned to see God in them, to ask the questions through which we can become aware of His presence about us." Still Crouse draws a line that he sees Tillich as unwilling to draw. "I am not yet ready to say, however, that there is no difference between the profane and the sacred in the sight of God. This seems to me to cut the nerve of moral endeavor." See Crouse, *Philosophy of History*, 129–35 for his interaction with Tillich's thought.

36. Crouse, *Modern Discussions*, 8. Crouse was convinced that trends in modern scholarship demonstrated that the Advent Christian view was correct and devotes this book to a survey of those. "Contemporary leaders in the field of Biblical studies are joined by those from theology, philosophy, and some of the practical church disciplines in asserting that the Bible teaches that the dead will be resurrected. They assert that the Bible does not teach a doctrine of human immortality. Support for these views can be found from scholars of many backgrounds and from a wide geographic distribution."

37. Moses and Dorothy Crouse, *Starting Point*. This unpublished paper was provided for me by Mrs. Crouse at the time of our interview. See also, Oral History Interview, Dorothy Crouse, May 13, 1995.

developed religious beliefs like Hinduism.[38] "From [the Hindu god Varuna] . . . light emanated. Actually, then this light has metaphysical reality. Here light is God; not God is light. The World Council of Churches in New Delhi confessed that Jesus Christ is the light of the world. Jesus Christ reflected and revealed the true light of the living God."

Therefore, the task of missions is essential because, "in many of the lands we touched, the vast populace know nothing of the true Light revealed in Jesus Christ." However, for the Christian mission to be effective in the developing countries of Asia, American Christians must allow those congregations to develop indigenous approaches to Christian faith and practice. The leaders of the younger churches, according to Crouse, "argue that western thought forms are not wholly adequate to present the Gospel of Christ to the non-western mind . . . . The young leaders are determined to make the faith truly indigenous to their culture."[39] Therefore, an authentic Christian expression of faith in the developing world "cannot be achieved by paternalistic advice or with dogmatic and inflexible encyclicals." It will come as western Christians give these newer congregations "freedom under God to be in their culture what the western man has been in his." In other words, it was time to see the newer churches and their leaders as partners who, once trained, could develop their own indigenous expressions of authentic Christian faith.[40]

The third theological theme on which Crouse would focus attention, especially in the classroom, was the relationship between revelation and human history. Drawing on the work of Oscar Cullman, Crouse's understanding of that relationship shaped how he viewed the inspiration of Scripture and its function in the life of the church. For Crouse, inspiration was not

---

38. Ibid., 14. It is important to see the context in which Crouse uses the term "light" in this passage. Earlier he writes, "Light is another religious symbol expressive of man's yearning for the good, the true, the beautiful." In other words, the symbol of light reflects the human desire to address the "restless dissatisfaction" that God has placed in each human being.

39. Ibid., 15.

40. An essential part of the story of Advent Christian world missions centers on the debate created among Advent Christian leaders and missionaries by the views of Crouse, and the impact of those views on the mission during the second half of the twentieth century. For our purposes, Crouse's views become important in that they reflect another aspect of the tension between Aurora College and Berkshire Christian College and how that affected the Advent Christian Church. For a description of Advent Christian mission work on various fields see, Dean, *Who Will Go for Us?*

grounded in words but in events.[41] "The primary concern is not how God in his infinite wisdom and power chose to inspire men and create a guide for his people, but a clear-eyed vision of the truth that through his living activity in history God has in the Bible given us a valid and authoritative rule."[42] Inspiration, for Crouse, is both historical and dynamic. "I believe that in the midst of life men were confronted with problems, hopes, fears, and anxieties. As they sought to understand their role in these situations, God revealed to them through his Holy Spirit what he was doing for and with them." The Bible is an authoritative guide to faith and practice, not because its words are directly inspired, but because the Holy Spirit illumined the minds of the writers and they were able to speak the word of God into their particular historical context.[43]

For Crouse, the notion of Heilsgeschichte (Holy History) meant that God's revelatory activity could not simply be limited to the texts of Holy Scripture. This allows him to in Craig Bailey's words, "extend inspiration further than any other major Advent Christian theologian."[44] By seeing it in the context of the dynamic activity of the Holy Spirit, Crouse extends the notion of inspiration to include those who participated in the process of selecting the canon of Scripture.[45] "Why are there only sixty-six books in our Bible? This question has been answered with clarity by the church— the

41. Crouse's appreciation for the work of Oscar Cullmann at this point was recalled for me by two of his students, Glennon Balser and Louia Gransee, both of whom remember reading Cullmann's *Christ and Time*, as part of their theological study under Crouse.

42. Crouse, "Sufficiency of the Holy Spirit" (Part One), 4, 13. See also, Bailey, "Various Theories," 13–20. Bailey's work is especially valuable in that he wrote this paper while a student of Dr. Crouse's. From pp. 13–20, we find a concise summary of Crouse's classroom presentation on the issues of revelation and inspiration.

43. Ibid., 13. Crouse sees biblical justification for his understanding of inspiration in 1 Cor 2:9–12, the first part of which reads, "What no eye has seen, nor ear heard, nor the heart of man conceived, what God has prepared for those who love him, God has revealed to us through the Spirit" (RSV). Crouse cites Isaiah's call by God, Hosea's experience with the infidelity of his wife, Paul's response to the Thessalonian believers, and John's concern for the seven churches of Asia as examples of how the Holy Spirit used the activity of history to allow the biblical writers to speak on God's behalf.

44. Bailey, "Various Theories," 16.

45. Crouse, "Sufficiency of the Holy Spirit" (Part Two), 4, 9. Crouse appears ready to extend his understanding of inspiration to include an ever larger circle. "But it is well to point out that if the Holy Spirit had not worked through many instrumentalities: in guiding the transmission of Scripture through centuries, through the illumination of the minds of dedicated translators of the Scripture, the chain of divine authority would have been broken and our understanding of the Word of God seriously limited."

Holy Spirit moved in our midst and led us to choose only these." That means, for Crouse, that the canon of Scripture technically remains open to revision.[46]

In the work of Crouse, we see a view of inspiration that synthesizes several strands of thought. Crouse builds on the work of his Aurora predecessor, Clarence Hewitt, and his notion of dynamic inspiration. To that, he links the principle of Heilsgeschichte—the notion that all of human history is the stage for God's revelatory activity and that God reveals himself through events in human history. Then he integrates two notions we find expressed in the neo-Protestant theological writing of Barth and Reinhold Niebuhr. First, Revelation occurs when people, through the guidance of the Holy Spirit, are sensitive to God's activity in human history. Second, the Bible functions as the word of God in that it witnesses to God's revelation in human history and that revelation is expressed ultimately through Jesus Christ. Therefore, factual accuracy, in matters of science, history, and other areas of human endeavor, lies outside the purview of Scripture's purpose and function within the life of the church. "The living God," according to Crouse, "prepares, guides, and directs weak and imperfect people . . . . As their dreams, frustrations, and hopes are intermingled they are permeated by God's Spirit of truth . . . . Men of faith who read and study their words find them self-authenticating, or more accurately, validated by the Spirit of the living God. He does not leave his inspired witnesses unattested. It is His Word, and that Word is our supreme authority for faith and life."[47] Our confidence in the Bible, according to Crouse, rests not in a mechanical understanding of its inspiration, but "on a deep and settled conviction of the sufficiency of the Holy Spirit."

The theological approach at Aurora College during the twenty years following World War II continued to be an eclectic one where faculty members were encouraged not to pursue a party line, but develop and teach from their own convictions. In that environment, the teaching, scholarship, and graciousness of Moses Crouse made a significant impact both on students and fellow faculty members. Through his work, especially in the area of the relationship between revelation and history, the outlines of an "Aurora approach" began to take shape. Crouse's faculty colleague, Rev. Ronald P.

46. Ibid., 4. "Though I believe that it would be improper for anyone in our day to attempt to revise the canon, on the other hand, I am not willing to say that the Church through its discussions, debates, and councils achieved an infallible grasp of the mind of God."

47. Ibid., 9.

Thomas Sr., expresses that view well: "The real clue to the unity and meaning of the Bible is to read it as a recital, or testimony of what God has done . . . . The New Testament is a witness to God's act in Christ, and the believer assumes his cross because God revealed himself in the <u>act</u> of the cross." Believers also affirm the resurrection "because God acted to raise Christ!"[48] For the Aurora theologians, the proper context for discussing the notions of revelation and inspiration rested in the acts of God in human history.[49] The human authors of the Bible functioned as witnesses to those acts, witnesses who wrote from within their own cultural context. For them, the strengths of the Advent Christian Church rested in their non-creedal approach to Christian theology[50] and their attempt to steer a middle course between the harsh extremes of Fundamentalism and Liberalism.

NEST Becomes Berkshire Christian College

In 1950, the remarkable thirty-year tenure of New England School of Theology president Guy Vannah drew to a close with his official retirement. President Vannah had brought stability to the small school in terms of finance, administration, and faculty, as well as respect from the larger evangelical community in the metropolitan Boston area.[51] The good

48. Thomas, Sr. "By His Works," 7, 23. Six years earlier, longtime Aurora administrator and faculty member Gerald Richardson expressed a similar line of thought to Advent Christian readers. "Yes, the real contents of the Bible, the word or message, of God is guaranteed perfect by the witness of the Holy Spirit through human experience . . . . Only in His Son, the Word made flesh, do we have a perfect medium and a perfect revelation." See Richardson, "All Contents Guaranteed Perfect," 8.

49. Even here, it is important to note that there was not unanimity among the theological faculty. Rev. Asa Colby, who served on the Aurora College faculty from 1949–1980 and who taught Old and New Testament Survey during that time told me the following, "I don't want to speak for others, but I think that my good friend Moses Crouse, was probably less tied to experiential revelation than I. I think he was much more of a biblicist in terms of his understanding of revelation than I am. But that's my interpretation." In Rev. Colby's view, "How does God work? He works through mysterious ways and he works through our conscience, through our senses, through our thought processes, as well as through the written word." See, Oral History Interview, Asa J. Colby, October 19, 1995.

50. Crouse, "Sufficiency of the Holy Spirit" (Part Two), 4.

51. Fillinger, "Berkshire Christian College," 38. Fillinger writes, "Dr. Vannah was well-known and respected at Andover-Newton [where he studied theology] and also at Gordon. He also maintained more than casual acquaintances with pastors of various churches in the Boston area. The New England School of Theology gradually became one

relationship between NEST and the larger Christian community in Boston was one of the primary reasons that Advent Christian people and congregations were welcomed as part of the larger evangelical coalition in New England, something that was not true in other parts of the United States. In the mid-1940s, NEST had been given authority by the Commonwealth of Massachusetts to grant the Bachelor of Arts degree in theology and the four-year degree replaced the earlier three-year diploma. Under Vannah's leadership, NEST focused on training pastors for Advent Christian congregations in the northeastern United States and the Maritime provinces of Canada. In response, support for the small theological college came primarily from Advent Christians in those areas.[52]

The same year that Vannah retired, Ariel C. Ainsworth was named professor of philosophy and apologetics at New England School of Theology.[53] Ainsworth had completed undergraduate studies at Aurora College in 1929 and was working as an electrician when he sensed a call to vocational Christian ministry.[54] He completed his bachelor of divinity degree at Gordon Divinity School while serving as pastor of the Rochester, N.H. Advent Christian Church during the early 1940s. Then in 1946, while pastor of the Waterbury, Conn. Advent Christian Church, Rev. Ainsworth was asked by President Vannah to teach at NEST.

Rev. Ainsworth left the Waterbury pastorate in 1948 to teach full-time. The school encouraged him to complete a graduate degree and he chose to pursue a Th.M. degree at Westminster Theological Seminary. While there, Ainsworth studied under Westminster's renowned professor of apologetics, Dr. Cornelius Van Til. Van Til was one of the original 1929 group of students and faculty who left Princeton Theological Seminary to organize Westminster. Not only did Van Til significantly influence Ainsworth's understandings of philosophy and theology, the two became personal friends.

---

of the accepted Christian schools in the area and frequently participated in cooperative ventures of the Christian community in greater Boston."

52. Before the mid-1950s, many Advent Christians, both inside and outside of New England, viewed New England School of Theology not as a denominational college but as an institution designed to mostly serve the eastern region of the denomination. Fillinger remarks that NEST was "principally sectional in its outreach." See Fillinger, "Berkshire Christian College," 38.

53. Dean, "Echoes," 500.

54. Oral History Interview, A. Cameron Ainsworth, June 1, 1995. A. Cameron Ainsworth is the son of Ariel C. Ainsworth. The biographical sketch and description of Ariel Ainsworth's friendship with Cornelius Van Til is from this interview.

After Ainsworth's graduation in 1949, they remained in contact and on several occasions Van Til visited the NEST (and later Berkshire Christian College) campus to speak in chapel or lecture for one of Ainsworth's courses in philosophy or apologetics.

For Van Til, "man has no excuse whatsoever for not accepting the revelation of God whether in nature, including man and his surroundings, or in Scripture."[55] We do not have to prove God's existence because it is objectively clear both through general revelation in the universe and special revelation through Holy Scripture.[56] Non-Christians however naturally suppress that knowledge[57] and assume "that the human person is ultimate and as such should properly act as judge of all claims to authority that are made by anyone."[58] So the Christian view of life must be set off sharply from all non-Christian views. Christian apologetics must start not by trying to prove God's existence, but with a presuppositional approach.[59] Christians and non-Christians cannot reason together based on "facts" or "laws" because based on their divergent presuppositions, they disagree about their very meaning. Hence, the Christian apologist must "place himself upon the position of his opponent, assuming the correctness of his method merely for argument's sake, in order to show him that on such a position the 'facts' are not facts and the 'laws' are not laws."[60]

Any notion of human autonomy had no place in Van Til's apologetic. Therefore, Van Til rejected the neo-orthodoxy of Karl Barth and others. "In all his thinking Barth is, in spite of his efforts to escape it, still controlled by some form of modern critical philosophy."[61] In the dialectical framework used by neo-orthodox theologians like Barth, Emil Brunner, and others;

---

55. Van Til, *Defense of the Faith*, 255–56.

56. Ibid., 124. "Thus the Bible, as the infallibly inspired revelation of God to sinful man, stands before us as that light in terms of which all the facts of the created universe must be interpreted. All of finite existence, natural and redemptive, functions in relation to one all-inclusive plan that is in the mind of God. Whatever insight man is to have into this pattern of the activity of God he must attain by looking at all his objects of research in the light of Scripture."

57. Ibid., 118. "The Reformed apologist . . . appealing to that knowledge of the true God in the natural man which the natural man suppresses by means of his assumption of ultimacy, will also appeal to the knowledge of the true method which the natural man knows but suppresses."

58. Ibid., 125.

59. Ibid., 116–17.

60. Ibid., 117.

61. Ibid., 147.

God's revelation of himself is bounded by autonomous human religious consciousness.[62]

Ainsworth's use of Van Tilian apologetics is seen in his address to delegates at the 1960 Advent Christian General Conference. Modern humanity faces a profound intellectual crisis, in Ainsworth's view.[63] "The present day theory of relativity as developed by Albert Einstein leaves man in the world without any 'hitching post.'" Idealistic thinking, which Ainsworth defines as "the thinking that glorifies the intellect of man as having priority over material existence," combined with what Ainsworth terms "the new modernism" is, in his words, "even more destructive to the teachings of God's Word."[64] This combination of relativism and idealism leads to irrationalism, the notion that knowledge is intuitive rather than arrived at through logical processes of thought. "This philosophy has robbed God of His sovereignty and has left man without any thing that is absolute and ultimate" and has led to the denial of the verbal inspiration of Scripture and the biblical notion of predictive prophecy. Ultimately, for Ainsworth, that would lead to the destruction of the unique doctrines of the Advent Christian Church.

Through Ariel Ainsworth, the Van Tilian apologetic began to impact the New England School of Theology in two important ways during the 1950s. First, it strengthened the role of Reformed theology at the school. NEST was becoming a school with a well-defined theological approach. The school stressed a Trinitarian understanding of God's nature, the importance of seeing the Bible not only as verbally inspired but as the source and starting point for all Christian theology, a consciously Reformed approach to theology and apologetics, and the grounding of Advent Christian doctrinal distinctives within a theologically conservative framework. Second, the school took a stronger apologetic stance against theological liberalism and neo-orthodoxy.[65] The Van Til apologetic allowed no compromise with any philosophy or ideology that used human autonomy as a starting point. That made any Christian attempts to do theology or apologetics from a human starting point inconsistent at best and dangerous at worst.

---

62. Ibid., 146–48.

63. Ainsworth, "The Potentiality of Our Present," 34, 21.

64. Ibid., 3. "The new modernism," in Ainsworth's view "adds the thinking of Hegel and Heidegger to that of Kant."

65. Oral History Interview, Carlyle B. Roberts, August 3, 1994. See also Dean, "Echoes," 500n3.

In the late 1940s, the theological ethos at the New England School of Theology began to change from a more eclectic approach that emphasized Advent Christian doctrinal distinctives to an apologetic approach that defended those distinctives in the context of commitments to Reformed theology and to the verbal-plenary inspiration of Holy Scripture.[66] That was not the only change taking place at the school during the post-Vannah years. Within the ten-year period from 1950 to 1960 the shape of the Advent Christian Church in New England would undergo subtle but significant change.[67] During the Vannah presidency, NEST supplied student and weekend pastors for small Advent Christian congregations throughout New England. President Vannah often served as a resource for Advent Christian congregations seeking pastoral leadership and the school served as a focal point for much of Advent Christian denominational life in New England.

Throughout the first half of the twentieth century, metropolitan Boston was the geographic center of Advent Christian life in the Northeast. By 1960, that was no longer the case. Advent Christian publications left Boston for Concord, New Hampshire. The American Advent Mission Society, the foreign missions arm of the denomination, moved south to Charlotte, North Carolina. Several Advent Christian congregations in the greater Boston area closed. Finally, in 1958, under the leadership of President Ariel Ainsworth, New England School of Theology would leave Boston for Lenox, Massachusetts (a three-hour drive west on the Massachusetts Turnpike).

While the dramatic change in location was motivated partially by the need for more adequate campus facilities and the desire to gain accreditation by the Accrediting Association of Bible Colleges (AABC),[68] the move was part of an even larger change in the ethos of the institution—the change from Bible institute to Bible college. New courses and majors were added. The Bible institute curriculum generally limited general education courses to 16–32 course hours. In the Bible college curriculum mandated by AABC, general education now involved 32–64 course hours.[69] New England School of Theology was renamed "Berkshire Christian College"

66. With this statement, I do not want to suggest that biblical inerrancy was not taught at NEST before the 1940s; only that this doctrine took on added theological and apologetic importance at NEST during the postwar years.

67. This theme was suggested to me during an oral phone interview with David A. Dean, December 4, 1996.

68. Fillinger, *Berkshire Christian College*, 41.

69. Ibid.

and with the change in name came efforts to expand the constituency the college hoped to serve. Before the move to Lenox, NEST had primarily limited its focus to serving Advent Christian congregations in the Northeast and the Canadian Maritimes. The leadership of Berkshire Christian College wanted to broaden that by positioning the school as a Bible college designed to serve both the entire Advent Christian Church and the community of evangelical congregations in New England and New York. In that context, they hoped to ground the theological distinctives of the Advent Christian Church in a conservative-evangelical approach to Christian theology. The strength of the Advent Christian Church, in their view, was its commitment to the Bible as the inspired Word of God. For them, the Advent Christian Church could only prosper if it built on that foundation.

The Stage is Set

The post-World War II years represented a time of significant change for both Advent Christian-related institutions of higher learning. At Aurora College, the institutional focus was shifting toward a much stronger emphasis on serving students in the surrounding Fox River Valley. While the college hoped to retain a sizable Advent Christian presence among its faculty and student body, the denomination was nowhere near the size needed to sustain a private liberal-arts college, especially in an era where government sponsored two-year community colleges and four-year universities were beginning to directly compete with smaller private colleges like Aurora. The change at New England School of Theology was perhaps even more dramatic. The name change to Berkshire Christian College marked an even more significant change in the ethos of the institution from Bible institute to Bible college. With that change came an attempt to broaden the constituency served by the college to include the entire Advent Christian Church.

Significant theological developments also occurred at both institutions, developments that would heighten the tension between the two. At Aurora, with the transition from Clarence Hewitt to Moses Crouse, the college's theological faculty began to reflect a more focused approach to their understanding of the Bible's role and function in the life of the church, an approach in tune with post-World War II neo-Protestant theology. Their understanding of inspiration and revelation became grounded in the notion that God's revelatory activity occurred not in the context of written words, but in specific events in human history. At Berkshire, the emergence of Ariel Ainsworth both as apologist and administrator brought a sharpened theological focus to the institution, a focus grounded in Reformed theology as expressed through the apologetic of Cornelius Van Til. Authentic Christian doctrine and theology could only be practiced when the Bible was seen as the verbally inspired, inerrant Word of God. With both theological faculties, the articulation of Advent Christian doctrinal distinctives continued to remain important. But the way they interpreted and defended those distinctives was dramatically diverging.

That divergence set the stage for theological conflict within the Advent Christian Church. As denominational leaders attempted to address serious organizational and missions-related issues, they would be forced to face a doctrinal conflict with the potential not only to sidetrack their efforts at organizational reform but to divide the already small denomination.

CHAPTER SIX

Cleveland and Montreat

Discussion, Debate, and Decision

As JOHN F. KENNEDY assumed the Presidency of the United States in 1961, the theological conflict and rivalry between Aurora College and Berkshire Christian College began to seriously impact the Advent Christian Church. Many evangelical and fundamentalist Protestants viewed the Kennedy presidency and the emerging liberal ethos that accompanied it with great alarm.[1] As a result, their resistance to the liberal and neo-orthodox theology that dominated the Protestant mainline became more intense. At the same time, mainline Protestant theologians began to embrace an approach that viewed human reason and endeavor as essential to God's progressive design for society.[2] With the Aurora theologians taking their cues from mainline Protestantism and the Berkshire professors identifying with the emerging new-evangelical coalition, especially as it was represented by theologians at Westminster Theological Seminary and Gordon Divinity School, it was no surprise that the theological differences between them became sharper and more influential within Advent Christian denominational life.

"It is a matter of common observation," J. Howard Shaw wrote to Ivan Adams in 1961, "that this spirit of division centers in the activities and

---

1. Marty provides an account of the American cultural and religious mood at the turn of the 1960s. "In the public religion," Marty writes, "as well as in the social ethos and political tilt, it was 'the liberal hour.'" See, Marty, *Under God Indivisible*, 400, 456–76.

2. Ibid., 461. Marty writes, "The grand themes of the Enlightenment—reason, science, and progress—were features in religious vocabularies across a wide spectrum. A semisecular progressive or millennial—even utopian—outlook countered pessimistic premillennialisms in the favored theologies."

policies of our two colleges and is fostered by the thinking and utterances of certain persons who are either college-connected or college alumni."[3] Rev. Shaw, like most Protestant denominational executives, desired to maintain a public image of unity and forward progress. In small denominations like the Advent Christian Church, raising funds for denominational work was difficult even under the best of circumstances. Rivalry and conflict, especially theological conflict, had the potential not only to impede fund-raising but to foster serious division and disruption within a denominational organization highly dependent upon the goodwill of its independent-minded congregations and constituents. At a time when he was working hard to bring fiscal and structural unity to the Advent Christian Church, the conflict between Aurora College and Berkshire Christian College had grown to the point where it represented for Shaw, a serious threat to "the basic unity of our denomination."[4]

Throughout the late 1940s and 1950s, there had been signs that the rivalry between the two colleges was beginning to impact the Advent Christian Church. At the 1950 General Conference, several Advent Christian pastors challenged the theological views of Moses Crouse and his Northwestern University mentors.[5] In addition, two Advent Christian congregations expressed alarm over aspects of college life that they viewed as serious compromises to Christian and Advent Christian faith. Lela Hill Advent Christian Church of Shamrock, Texas passed a resolution deploring "the fact that Aurora College, the only Advent Christian College of liberal arts, has a member of the Roman Catholic Church on the faculty."[6] An even more serious attack came from the church board of the Advent

3. John Howard Shaw to Ivan E. Adams, May 3, 1961. Ivan E. Adams was chairman of the Advent Christian Board of Higher Education. That commission focused on denominational relationships with Aurora College and Berkshire Christian College.

4. Ibid., 1.

5. Anderson, *Building on the Foundation*, 74–76. Anderson, writing from an Aurora-oriented perspective, described the event this way: "[S]ome of the ultra-conservative easterners launched a vicious attack on Crouse's orthodoxy, without ever attempting to determine his personal stand on various matters." Crouse, in Anderson's view, "expressed a belief in creation, though not as a so-called Creationist, the Virgin Birth, and the inspiration of the Scriptures, though not in any formula devised by men, as to how God went about His creative efforts."

6. Anderson, *Building on the Foundation*, 72. The resolution was published in February 1948 and went on to state, "We are a people of the reformation and believe that God's Holy Truth and judgment are against the Roman Catholic Hierarchy." Ironically, the congregation was also known within the denomination for its strong anti-Trinitarianism.

Christian Church in Somerville, Massachusetts. "It was found," according to the board, "that such practices as square dancing were sanctioned by the management of the school to the point of public announcement of the events in the school paper."[7]

NEST felt the impact during the early 1950s as well. The Reformed theological approach espoused by James Nichols Jr. and Ariel Ainsworth at NEST represented a betrayal of Advent Christian heritage in the view of some within the denomination. Longtime Aurora College professor Clarence Hewitt declared that for Advent Christians to be consistent in their theological approach, they must be Arminian. "To depart from that stand," in Hewitt's words, "and to try now to crawl under the Calvinist umbrella, would be . . . not only a betrayal of our heritage but also a grave threat to our future."[8] Opposition to NEST's growing Reformed emphasis led to calls from within the denomination to remove Nichols from the NEST faculty.[9]

7. Ibid., 73. Anderson reports that Aurora College president Theodore P. Stephens responded to the pastor of the Somerville Advent Christian Church by writing, "The issue is one of Christian liberty vs. legalistic and a legalism that is sectional and inconsistent and unlovely . . . there are many laymen and ministers, and some of them are men and women whose spiritual attainments you would not challenge, who feel that our denomination is quite unrealistic in maintaining a list of taboos the people do not recognize."

In addition, the issue was formally discussed at the 1950 Advent Christian General Conference with delegates passing a lengthy resolution that mandated a mild rebuke of the Somerville, Mass. Advent Christian Church and a reaffirmation of General Conference support for the leadership of Aurora College. See "Minutes of the Advent Christian General Conference Executive Committee," 1950, 36; "Minutes of the Advent Christian General Conference," 1950, 11, 28–29.

8. Clarence H. Hewitt, *Conditional Principle*, 60–61.

9. Oral History Interview, David A. Dean/Freeman Barton, August 4, 1994, 7. Dean comments, "My first General Conference was at Charleston, WV, my guess would be 1954. And that General Conference had as one of its unofficial agenda items getting rid of Dr. Nichols . . . And it was a weird kind of thing, because it was really Ariel [Ainsworth] who was the outspoken Calvinist on the faculty. And Carlyle [Roberts] who was much easier to understand than Ariel and so popularized Calvinism. [Dr. Nichols] never taught it directly, but he cornered people and forced them to think their way into it. And he refuted the popular objections to it . . . People were gunning for [Dr. Nichols] for his teaching of Calvinism, predestination, eternal security. And that was why there was a strong, popular opposition to him."

The Christian Education
Curriculum Controversy

At the beginning of the 1960s, the smoldering Advent Christian theological controversy took on a higher public profile within the denomination through a series of controversial events centering on the denominational Board of Christian Education. Those events revolved around two issues. First, a sizable number of Advent Christians, especially those living in New England, were concerned by what they viewed as highly questionable theological content in the Advent Christian Sunday school curriculum prepared under the board's authority. Second, the Board of Christian Education became embroiled in controversy with the Board of Publications over editorial control and responsibility, as well as the division of profits received from production of the curriculum.

Producing Sunday school curriculum was a major enterprise, especially for a small denomination with limited financial resources. Because Advent Christians could not find a curriculum that embraced their unique theological distinctives, many of their leaders felt that producing distinctively Advent Christian Sunday school materials was essential to denominational health and identity. To guide that production, the board selected Esther Reed, a lifelong Advent Christian, Aurora College graduate, and the wife of veteran Advent Christian pastor Gordon Reed.[10] Reed was an Iowa native who spent most of her adult life in Advent Christian parsonages in the southeastern United States. She was known as "Polly" throughout the denomination and had a reputation as a tireless worker on behalf of Advent Christian Sunday schools. Like other directors in the days before a centralized denominational office,[11] Reed worked out of her home and communicated with other denominational directors scattered throughout the country by letter and phone. That would make her job especially difficult in one crucial context. Reed's primary responsibility as director

10. The biographical information for Esther "Polly" Reed is based on oral history interviews with David S. McCarthy and Roland E. Griswold. See Oral History Interview, David S. McCarthy, November 24, 1995, 20–21; Oral History Interview, Roland E. Griswold, August 13, 1996, 68.

11. Centralized denominational offices would not be realized until 1969, when the national agencies of the Advent Christian Church—foreign missions, home missions, stewardship and tithing, Christian education, publications, finance, and administration—were all moved to the current denominational offices in Charlotte, NC. Even with centralization of the offices, the various ministries functioned under separate boards of directors until reorganization was completed in 1975.

of Christian education was the planning and editing of Advent Christian Sunday school curriculum for all age levels. While she performed that task from the Southeast, the printing of the curriculum was done by Advent Christian Publications in New England.[12]

This was an arrangement fraught with difficulty for both parties. Mrs. Reed's denominational experience was based totally in the Midwest and the South with little or no contact with Advent Christians from New England. Moreover, Advent Christians from the Northeast perceived Mrs. Reed as insensitive to their theological and denominational concerns.[13] Even more significant was the rocky relationship between Mrs. Reed and the manager of Advent Christian Publications, Raymond Beecroft.

Like Edwin K. Gedney, Raymond Beecroft came to the Advent Christian Church out of the larger context of evangelicalism in the northeastern United States.[14] A businessman and Certified Public Accountant by profession, Mr. Beecroft came to Christian faith through the "Word of Life" ministry of Jack Wyrtzen. Subsequently he sensed a call to Christian ministry and attended Philadelphia College of the Bible. After reading Advent Christian prophetic literature, Beecroft became convinced that the Advent Christian prophetic and doctrinal heritage was more biblical than the dispensational views he had previously embraced. While his prophetic views may have changed, Beecroft remained a passionate defender of the doctrine of biblical inerrancy and a champion of evangelical causes.[15] After

12. What made this arrangement even more difficult was that Mrs. Reed's husband, Gordon, assumed the directorship of Messenger Press, publisher of the *Present Truth Messenger*, a southern Advent Christian newspaper that remained independent when the other regional publication societies merged with Advent Christian Publications in the early 1950s. Under Rev. Reed's editorship, the *Messenger* was vying for a national Advent Christian readership.

13. Oral History Interview, Carlyle B. Roberts, 3 August 1994. Roberts comments, "Polly Reed was prejudiced against NEST, I'd say. She said to me personally one time that if a person couldn't go to Aurora, she thought they ought to go to NEST. But that was rather a condescending approach." See also, Oral History Interview, David S. McCarthy, November 24, 1995. Pastor McCarthy comments, "She saw Berkshire [Christian College] and the Eastern Region all rolled up in one as being a very divisive group. This denomination, in her view, could go someplace if we could either jettison them or get them on board. All her friends were Aurora people."

14. The biographical information for Raymond Beecroft is from Oral History interviews with David S. McCarthy and Harold R. Patterson. See: Oral History Interview, David S. McCarthy, November 24, 1995, 8; Oral History Interview, Harold R. Patterson, November 21, 1996, 24.

15. Rev. Beecroft was a supporter of the new-evangelical efforts to reform

his ordination and several years of service as Pastor of the Springfield, Massachusetts Advent Christian Church, Rev. Beecroft became manager of Advent Christian Publications and editor of its flagship publication, the World's Crisis in 1951.[16] By the time Reed became Director of Christian Education in 1958, Rev. Beecroft was already well established as manager of Advent Christian Publications. Their dramatically different life experiences combined with their strong personalities would set the stage for a serious conflict that would range across financial, organizational, and theological boundaries.[17]

Under Mrs. Reed's leadership, the Board of Christian Education attempted to develop a graded Advent Christian Sunday school curriculum that would be "Bible Centered in content; Pupil Centered in method."[18] Being Bible centered, meant viewing the Bible as "the record of God's revelation of Himself and his redemptive purpose for man."[19] Being Pupil centered meant "that we must recognize principles of human growth and sound educational philosophy."[20] That educational philosophy recognized

---

Fundamentalism, as seen, for example, in his strong support of Billy Graham's 1957 crusade in New York City. "Here is an opportunity," writes Beecroft, "to show a Christian spirit, and to possibly turn many liberals to the teaching of the simple gospel of Christ . . . The time is short, and men, women and young people need Christ. Let's not refuse any opportunity to lead them to the fountain of living water." See, Beecroft, "Militant Fundamentalists," 20.

16. Rev. Beecroft's selection to this post was due in large part to the financial crisis faced by the Advent Christian Publication Society, a crisis that forced a major reorganization during the early 1950s. Rev. Beecroft's professional skills as a Certified Public Accountant and businessman were seen as vital. See, Oral History Interview, Harold R. Patterson, November 21, 1996, 3. Rev. Patterson served on the board of Advent Christian Publications from 1962 to 1966.

17. McCarthy comments, "Both Polly [Reed] and [Raymond] Beecroft—you almost could take the inerrancy debate and say that this was a battle that wouldn't have happened if it weren't for [them] . . . The differences might have been there but they exaggerated them because of their strong personalities, their intensive stand. They would not bend for anybody." See, Oral History Interview, David S. McCarthy, November 24, 1995, 20. Rev. McCarthy knew both individuals and considered Mrs. Reed a good personal friend. His writing ministry included both articles for Rev. Beecroft and curriculum writing for Mrs. Reed.

18. "Basic Philosophy," 1. On top of the first page is a handwritten note, "June 1960." This document was apparently discussed by the Board of Christian Education at their meeting in conjunction with the Advent Christian General Conference biennial convention held in June 1960.

19. Ibid., 1.

20. Ibid., 2.

the need to understand human physical and emotional development, the need to involve the learner in the learning experience, the need to relate learning to life need, and the need for learning to be satisfying for the learner.

Controversy broke out even before this curriculum philosophy was reviewed by the Board of Christian Education. The Fall 1959 *Living Water* Senior High curriculum contained, according to the minutes of their 1960 meeting, "some suggestions of 'liberal' theology particularly in the Christmas lesson, which raised a storm of protest."[21] The lesson writer, Mildred Singleterry, had described the incarnation of Christ in a way that made evangelicals within the Advent Christian Church very uneasy. "While this [the incarnation] is a necessary part of Christian doctrine," according to Singleterry, "the actual realization of God's love expressed in the Christ Child is an emotional experience, an experience in faith which cannot be expressed in theological definition."[22] After quoting Philippians 2:7–8, the writer added that "we respond to such love by loving, not by reasoning."[23]

In reflecting on this initial controversy, Reed made two observations in her report to her curriculum committee. First, she argued that the questionable statements cited by critics were taken out of context.[24] Several pages later, she writes, "I have made errors in judgment; but today we have a curriculum comparable to that of other denominations." She made clear to the curriculum committee that Advent Christians faced some serious problems. "Early in my administration," Reed wrote, "I submitted a statement of my philosophy of Christian Education which you ordered. Since then a conflict has arisen. Within our denomination there are 1. Conflicting ideologies 2. Differing opinions about interpretation of Scripture 3. Differing educational philosophy."[25] She hoped that the committee would

21. "Board of Christian Education—Advent Christian General Conference. Minutes of meetings held during the 1960 General Conference at Aurora College," 1.

22. Singleterry, Mildred, "Road from Bethlehem," *Living Water*, 46–47.

23. Ibid., 47. The writer added, "God's concern for man came down in human terms in the loving form of a helpless baby—a love helpless until it is accepted in our hearts where it can work wonders in the changing of lives."

24. "Report to the Curriculum Committee," 1. Reed writes, "The material was read carefully and critically (especially *Living Water*) looking for any possible 'liberal' trend because of distrust of editor and lesson writer. The editor was innocent and unsuspecting and allowed the inclusion of statements which were picked out of context and their significance unduly magnified."

25. Ibid., 3. While Reed recognized that theological difference did exist over the doctrine of Scripture, she apparently had difficulty understanding the nature and

help her and the curriculum writers navigate these rapidly rising currents of conflict.

For their part, the Board of Christian Education issued a strong statement of support for Reed and her efforts.[26] In regards to the controversy surrounding the Senior High curriculum, the board counseled Reed and Singleterry to balance a problem-centered approach with a more traditional emphasis on the exposition of scripture and to make sure that the lessons maintain a distinctive spiritual approach in their aims and content.[27] They also looked for ways to foster better communication with the board of Advent Christian Publications, the organization responsible for production of the curriculum. The curriculum controversy not only affected Reed and those responsible for the preparation of the Advent Christian curriculum, it impacted sales to Advent Christian churches and that affected the revenues of Advent Christian Publications.

Despite the efforts of the Board of Christian Education in 1960, the curriculum controversy seemed only to grow more intense. By mid-1961, Raymond Beecroft was reporting to Reed and to denominational leaders that curriculum sales at the Junior, Junior High, and Senior High levels had declined consistently since those publications were first issued in the Fall of 1959.[28] The *Living Water* Senior High curriculum, according to Beecroft, "seemed to be the subject of greatest concern" because "it lacks an adequate Biblical approach in the text." That problem was placing, in Beecroft's words, "this office in the position where a "spot check" of the text is necessary."[29]

significance of the differences. David S. McCarthy comments that Reed "had a mental block" in understanding the theological significance of the inspiration issue. "You could explain it to her, you could write it out . . . on a chalkboard and outline it, and it wouldn't come in. Because what she was hearing was people who do not hold to inerrancy are not Christians." See, Oral History Interview, David S. McCarthy, November 24, 1995, 11.

26. "Reporting for the Board of Christian Education." The phrase "June 1960" is handwritten at the beginning of this one-page document. "The work done by our director, Polly Reed, is outstanding. We would also commend the lesson writers for their share in providing, together with the editor, complete Sunday School materials for every age group in our Church School. Let us remember that this is the first time in the history of our Denomination that such a feat has been accomplished."

27. "Board of Christian Education—Minutes of Meetings," 1960, 12.

28. Raymond M. Beecroft to Elwell M. Drew, n.d., 12. This memorandum was written after the sales report for the Spring 1961 quarter had become available. Rev. Beecroft reported that sales for *Living Water*, the Senior High curriculum had declined from 2,389 in Fall 1959, its first quarter of issue, to 1,727 in Spring 1961. Sales for the Junior and Junior High curriculums showed comparable decreases.

29. Ibid., 24. As an example, Rev. Beecroft cited the following passage from the

As manager of Advent Christian Publications, Beecroft was feeling forced into the editorial realm in order to ensure that the problems "in the text of Living Water that 'get by' Mrs. Reed" do not make it into print. The tone of his memorandum also made it clear that communication between himself and Reed on a variety of matters was becoming a serious problem.

The Cleveland Conference

While the Sunday school curriculum controversy continued, a new battle line emerged. By early 1961, J. Howard Shaw had come to believe that the rivalry and conflict between Aurora College and Berkshire Christian College had become a serious threat to the future of the Advent Christian Church. In Shaw's view, the source of the conflict rested in "the militant expression of distrust and allegation [that] is largely directed against Aurora College and its Biblical department in particular."[30] The primary source of this militant attitude, according to Shaw, centered in Berkshire Christian College.[31] Berkshire Christian College was the source of aggressive action and that had brought an equally aggressive reaction on the part of Aurora supporters.[32] "It is this allegation," in Shaw's words, "that the very integrity of our Christian faith is at stake, being threatened by Aurora and upheld by BCC—it is this allegation which is potentially so destructive of the unity of the Advent Christian people."[33] On the one hand, according to Shaw, the al-

---

Living Water Senior High curriculum that he felt compelled to rewrite: "The Christian Church is an organization for the propagating and self-guarding of the religion of Jesus: It is a means, not an end; it is not holy in itself. It has secular aspects, and its leadership at times has been confused and self-seeking. We have only to recall the period of the Crusades and the Inquisitions and the witch burning to recognize how tragically the church can lose its way. Zeal alone cannot develop righteousness."

After proposing a much different text, Mr. Beecroft commented, "It is our opinion that the writer's presentation of 'What the Church Really Is' to a teen-ager was so negative and inadequate as to not only be questioned but also rejected by many Advent Christian teachers of this class. This contributes further to the present criticism and increasing rejection of Living Water."

30. Shaw to Adams, May 3, 1961, 1.

31. Ibid., 1. Rev. Shaw amplifies this assertion with these words, "I do not mean to say that BCC is the sole source of this anti-Aurora spirit, but in its claims to unequivocal orthodoxy and in well-authenticated utterances of some members of its staff it has become a rallying point for such anti-Aurora bias."

32. Ibid., 1. Shaw's exact words are, "Aggressive action begets reaction, so that feelings of tension are on the increase among many whose sympathies lie with Aurora."

33. Ibid.

legations against Aurora College had aroused the "fears and vague misgivings of many sincere people." On the other, many Advent Christians who are genuinely conservative and evangelical "are disturbed and apprehensive in the face of a spirit which appears to them to be that of a contentious and restrictive Fundamentalism historically alien to the Advent Christian movement."[34]

For Shaw, the best solution appeared to be a denomination-sponsored consultation with theologians and administrators from both colleges, and denominational leaders. Through such a conference, he hoped that four things could be accomplished. He wanted participants to define terms and positions in a way that "each person, in all Christian honesty and humility, may determine wherein he has misunderstood, misrepresented, or otherwise been unfair to the position of a brother in Christ."[35] Shaw also wanted participants to "identify the areas of basic disagreement" and determine the relative importance of those issues. He wanted the conference to foster an attitude of appreciation and respect among the participants. Finally, he hoped that the conference would help those attending to reappraise their positions and attitudes.

Theologically, while Shaw suggested several issues for discussion including ecumenism and neo-orthodoxy, he knew that the crux of the discussions would focus on issues relating to the Bible's inspiration. "Can we experience true reverence for the authority of the Bible," Shaw asked, "and employ the Word with conviction and boldness while respecting the different viewpoints as to <u>how</u> God effected its inspiration?"[36]

Initially, Shaw hoped that the consultation could take place in June, 1961 in conjunction with the denominational board meetings in Aurora. That became impossible partially because of the logistics involved in setting up the conference and partially because of a desire to hold the conference in a "neutral" location.[37] In addition, there was some reluctance on the part

34. Ibid.

35. Ibid., 2.

36. Ibid., 4. How Shaw framed the question is of significance. The general position of the Berkshire Christian College theological faculty was that verbal, plenary inspiration was not simply one of several possible ways to explain the inspiration of Scripture. In their view, it was the historic position of the Christian church. In contrast, the Aurora theologians viewed verbal, plenary inspiration as one of several possibilities for explaining how the Bible's inspiration and authority functioned in the life of the church.

37. During this writer's research, several reasons have been verbally suggested regarding the need for a neutral location. First, because the conflict had a somewhat

of Berkshire Christian College to participate. "When Ivan Adams came to Berkshire Christian College to persuade us to participate," according to Dr. Oral Collins, "we [the Bible faculty members] met with him in the president's office. During the meeting, we agreed to participate with the express stipulation that the conference sessions be recorded, so that all would be public and above-board."[38] Cleveland, Ohio was eventually selected and eleven participants met at the Central YMCA in that city for a weekend conference on March 23–25, 1962.[39] After starting with a time of fellowship and worship on Friday evening, Saturday was given over to the reading and discussion of papers prepared for the conference.

Rev. Collins prepared two papers on behalf of the Berkshire Christian College faculty dealing with the inspiration of the Bible and with what they viewed as the destructive nature of higher biblical criticism.[40] A fifth-generation Adventist, Oral Collins was a New York native who graduated from New England School of Theology in 1950 and subsequently studied at Gordon Divinity School and Brandeis University, where he completed his Ph.D. in 1977.[41] In terms of the Bible's inspiration, Collins argued that

---

geographical context (Aurora in the Midwest and Berkshire in New England), a neutral site would prevent undue influence on the proceedings. Second, a neutral site would mean that all of the participants would share equally in the inconveniences of travel. Third, a neutral site would allow for better control of information from the conference, especially if the results were not positive.

38. Oral Collins to Robert Mayer, January 8, 1997. Collins adds, "He [Ivan Adams] agreed that the sessions would be recorded and seemed to indicate that he felt that that was a reasonable request. At the opening session in Cleveland when we sat across the table from the brethren from Aurora, the first item on the agenda was a proposal presented by the Board of Education, I. Adams in the chair, that we not record the sessions, as that might inhibit free discussion, etc. In the pressure of the confrontation, I was the only one who voted against it. Nevertheless, the other members of the Berkshire delegation also felt we had been double-crossed, though they apparently felt that it was unwise to hold to our condition."

39. "Conference of the Board of Education, Aurora College, Berkshire Christian College; Cleveland, Ohio, March 23–25, 1962." This document lists the following participants: "For the Board of Education: Ivan E. Adams, Chairman, J. Donald Cates, Ariel C. Ainsworth, James E. Crimi. For Aurora College: Gerald F. Richardson, Moses C. Crouse. For Berkshire Christian College: Carlyle B. Roberts, Oral E. Collins. For General Conference: Edwin K. Gedney, J. Howard Shaw. Recorder: Herbert H. Holland, Sr."

40. Collins to Mayer, January 8, 1997. "I believe I failed to mention [in our interview] that [Dr.] Fred Ehle was invited to go from BCC but did not feel able to do the prep work nor to attend. On account of this, I prepared both papers, one on Inspiration and one on Biblical Criticism with Fred's review and concurrence."

41. The biographical sketch of Collins is based on my interview with him. See Oral

the Berkshire Christian College faculty was not "presenting a theory about the Bible or a presupposition by means of which we may account for the phenomena of Scripture," but the Bible's own view of its inspiration.[42] In almost all cases, the current views found within modern biblical scholarship "disavow any return to the traditional doctrine of Inspiration; namely that the words of the Bible are God's special revelation."[43] Their approach is flawed by two fundamental errors. They build on the Kantian distinction between "objects which are known or may be known to our senses" (phenomena) and "objects of thought which have no basis in sensory experience" (noumena).[44] Therefore, supernatural events such as the bodily resurrection of Christ, "can never become the object of scientific investigation." All propositional theology must therefore be "relegated to this dark land of Kant, knowable only to the mystical eye of faith." The biblical writers "knew of no such philosophical distinction between the events of faith and those of historical knowledge."[45]

Modern scholarship also ignores the teaching of the Bible itself. "The Scripture does not allow that its words are often erroneous and unreliable," according to Rev. Collins. "Belief in the divine trustworthiness of the very words of Scripture has its roots, not in philosophy or presupposition about

---

History Interview, Oral Collins, October 15, 1995. Collins comments about his Adventist roots, "My great great grandfather was converted not to Advent Christendom but to Adventism under the preaching of the Millerite preacher up in Quebec."

Collins recalled for me three important theological mentors. Like most students who attended NEST, Collins recalled the influence of James Nichols. "His teaching methods . . . and his manner of teaching theology from the scriptures were very persuasive to me." In a subsequent letter, he also mentioned two Gordon Divinity School professors. "I could have mentioned Roger Nicole, from whom I had several semesters of Systematic Theology. The man is a gem whom I much appreciate. Another course which greatly helped me to understand existential theology was The Theology of Emil Brunner (not the official title) taught by the late Paul King Jewett, who was at the time completing his doctorate from Harvard." See, Collins to Mayer, December 31, 1996.

42. Members of the Faculty of Berkshire Christian College, *Inspiration of the Bible*, 1.

43. Ibid., 2.

44. Ibid., 6.

45. Ibid., 7. Rev. Collins quotes Young at this point: "Does the virgin birth . . . lie beyond the jurisdiction of the historian? . . . It took place here upon this earth at a definite point in time and in history . . . If the virgin birth is not historical, then there was no virgin birth." See, Young, *Thy Word is Truth*, 251. Ironically Oscar Cullmann makes this same point, although in a different context and with a different interpretation. See, Cullmann, *Christ and Time*, 94.

the Bible, but in the teaching of the Bible itself."[46] In defense of that assertion, Collins argued that the apostle Paul specifically affirmed "the inspiration of the writings themselves" in 2 Timothy 3:16. Moreover, Jesus, clearly recognized the authority of the Old Testament as the written word of God.[47] Quoting Matthew 5:18,[48] Collins asserts, "It is precisely to these literary phenomena of the Scriptures that Jesus appeals for moral authority .... The inspiration of Scripture is verbal. It is the <u>words</u> that are the words of God." When we look to Scripture for its own teaching regarding its inspiration, according to Collins, we will clearly see it teaching that "both the Old and New Testaments are sacred scripture; that these writings in their verbal form are indeed the Word of God; and that the words of Scripture, though they were immediately written by human authors, and through human intellect, and though they bear the stamp of human idiosyncrasies, are at the same time the words of God, with divine authority, inerrant and inviolable."[49]

In contrast, Moses Crouse, on behalf of the Aurora College faculty, articulated a different understanding.[50] Those who teach at Aurora, according to Crouse, do not believe that the Bible merely contains God's word or that it is simply a highly-prized human treasure. "A basic affirmation of the Christian Church through the ages has been that the Bible is the Word of God. This we at Aurora College believe and teach."[51] However, in Crouse's words, "When we confess this of the Bible, we do not intend to say that the words of the Bible are the very <u>words</u> of God." Inspiration cannot be reduced to verbal or mechanical theories because those views minimize the incarnational principle that stands at the heart of Scripture.[52]

46. Ibid., 8.

47. Ibid., 111–13.

48. Rev. Collins quotes the passage as follows, "I have come not to abolish them the Law and the Prophets but to fulfill them. For truly I say to you, till heaven and earth pass away, not an iota, not a dot, will pass from the law until all is accomplished (Matt 5:18)."

49. Ibid., 14. Rev. Collins adds, "We believe all this to be true simply because the authors of Scripture affirm it, even our Lord and His Apostles; and having their clear statements, we accept no other authority and have no other court of appeal."

50. Crouse, "Inspiration." This paper is untitled and does not indicate an author. Several of his Aurora College students identified Dr. Crouse as the author. I have assigned the title, "Inspiration," to the paper, as this title appears at the top of page two and is the only title found in the entire document.

51. Ibid., 2. Crouse adds, "And we affirm this truth because we believe that the scriptures are inspired by God."

52. Ibid. Crouse then defines the Incarnational principle in the following way. "God revealed Himself definitively in Jesus Christ as God incarnate in human flesh, as very

The words "inerrant" and "infallible" are not appropriate descriptions of Scripture because "such formulations add confusion in that only God is rightly said to be infallible or inerrant, and the human element associated with the scriptures negates any possibility of the accuracy of such words."[53]

Crouse then offered several justifications for the position that he and his colleagues took. He began with an appeal to traditional Advent Christian disdain for Greek philosophical thought. "I am always uncomfortable," in Crouse's words, "about any formulation that seems to suggest that the "word of God is something of an emanation from the person of God, a portion of his substance—even His breath— and therefore divine even as the source from which it came was divine."[54] Therefore, "to claim for scripture a degree of divinity that the Bible does not claim for itself, as certain Greek views tend to do, is not to be countenanced."[55] From this point, Crouse moved to a discussion of the Holy Spirit's role in the nature of the Bible's inspiration. Citing 1 Corinthians 2:9–11, he argued that, "it is through the offices of God's Spirit that man receives knowledge of Him. God by His Spirit breathes His truths to man—finite and fallible man." After granting Benjamin Warfield's assertion that it is scripture itself, not the human writers, that are inspired, Crouse adds, "Yet it is equally beyond question that a full-orbited biblical doctrine of inspiration has to take note of the fact that God's truth came through men inspired by the Holy Spirit."[56]

For Crouse, "the other side of the incarnational principle" means that we must see the biblical writers as fallible human beings. "Is the result of this belief a view that there is error and discrepancy in the scriptures?" asks Crouse. "The answer must be an unequivocal "Yes." Again we must insist that the Bible as we now have it leaves a careful student no alternative than to

---

God of very God and also very man of very man. This is a basic Christological corner stone."

53. Ibid.

54. Ibid., 4. Crouse adds, "Such aberrations frequently are found in Platonic and Neo-Platonic literatures. They are, so I believe, the very antithesis of the essentially Hebraic concept of creation . . . The Hebrew thought of creation is unlike emanation. Rather than a divine substance issuing from God that is itself divine, the doctrine of creation asserts that something comes into being over against God by His will and purpose—through His word. The product of His creative act frequently is recalcitrant. The biblical affirmation is that God creates and is revealed even through that rebellious creation. He is its Lord and can work out His purpose through it despite its opposition."

55. Ibid., 5.

56. Ibid.

say this."[57] To argue that inerrancy applies only to the original manuscripts not only begs the question, it suggests a "culpable laxity" in transmission on the part of the early church. "I am well aware that this view is deeply disturbing to many lay people," according to Crouse. "Yet there is not a shred of evidence in the scriptures to support the idea that we ought to create a false apologetic in defense of the Scriptures."[58] For Crouse, the evidence weighed strongly against any notion of inerrancy or infallibility. "Very few informed persons would claim the rhetoric of the Bible to be perfect or inerrant when compared with accepted correct usage."[59] Moreover, there are "known discrepancies between archaeology and the scriptures" that can't be glossed over. "The facts, as best as they can be understood at this time, are that there are points with reference to biblical history which are not in harmony with objective facts as best as they can now be interpreted."[60]

For Crouse, the terms "inerrant" and "infallible" are properly applied to God, to his purposes as revealed in Scripture, and to the plan of salvation witnessed to throughout the Bible. "Those principles rightly deserve the adjectives under discussion."[61] An authentic Christian apologetic does not begin in an artificial notion of biblical inerrancy, but by seeing, to quote Fuller Seminary professor Geoffrey Bromiley, that "the theme of the Bible is the incarnate Word in whom alone we can find truth, freedom and salvation,

57. Ibid., 6.

58. Ibid.

59. Ibid., 7.

60. Ibid., 8. As examples, Crouse cites "areas of discrepancy between the world-view of the ancient Hebrews and early Christians, that seem irreconcilable with modern scientific knowledge, for the world cannot be assumed to be flat since the astronauts have circled it. And if it is a world spinning on its axis, it is doubtful if the great city New Jerusalem (Rev. 21:16) could settle on one location without tearing the globe apart through centrifugal force." He then cites what he views as discrepancies in the trial and crucifixion of Jesus between the synoptic writers and the writer of the Fourth Gospel.

61. Ibid., 89. As support for his views, Crouse cites the views of two Fuller Seminary scholars, Everett Harrison and Geoffrey Bromiley. He is especially favorable to Harrison's use of a quotation attributed by Harrison to the nineteenth-century Princeton scholar, Francis I. Patton: "It is a hazardous thing to say that being inspired the Bible must be free from errors; for then the discovery of a single error would destroy its inspiration. Nor have we any right to substitute the word 'inerrancy' for 'inspiration' in our discussion of the Bible unless we are prepared to show from the teaching of the Bible that inspiration means inerrancy—and that, I think, would be a difficult thing to do." Harrison adds, according to Crouse, "One must grant that the Bible itself, in advancing its own claim to inspiration, says nothing precise about its inerrancy."

and to whom the written Word conforms in divine and human structure."[62] Inspiration must be seen in the context of history. God uses human history "as the medium through which He most significantly reveals himself."[63] Through his Holy Spirit, the living God confronts human beings through "a historic word delivered to the alert consciousness of a man of faith," a word by which he reveals to them the spiritual significance and meaning of events within human history.[64] Christians can have confidence in the message of Holy Scripture, not because its words are inspired, but because "it is the living God who has promised to work through these words in such a manner that none of His purposes will fail."[65]

By the end of Saturday, several of the participants knew that the theological differences between the two sides were significant and would be difficult, if not impossible, to resolve.[66] In addition to the significant differences articulated in the Collins and Crouse papers on the doctrine of Scripture, subsequent presentations confirmed that the Aurora and Berkshire theologians held substantially different understandings of the value of higher biblical criticism, the atonement, and even the nature of the incarnation of Christ. On Sunday morning, the group tried to put the best face they could on the conference with remarks from several people and attention to outlining a conference statement. "A high degree of unity," according to the final statement, "was revealed in nearly all areas of Christian doctrine, even in some areas in which there is marked diversity of mind in our denomination." Although the statement noted disagreements "on some aspects of the

62. Ibid., 9. Crouse does not provide a source for his quotation of Dr. Bromiley.

63. Ibid., 10.

64. Ibid., 10–11. Crouse adds, "In this view I am clearly differentiating my understanding from the views of Athenagoras that the Holy Spirit used the prophets as a flute player blows through his flute; of the suggestion of Hyppolitus that inspiration is akin to a musician playing a zither or harp; or of Augustine saying that Christ used the evangelists 'as if they were his own hands.' Such mechanical views are unfortunate in that they seriously limit and pattern the power of the living God although I am sure that such curtailing of God's freedom to act was not the intention of these church fathers. Their concepts were imprisoned within the limiting walls of a substantial concept of reality; our views of life as being essentially relational give us, so I believe, a much better clue for understanding the process of inspired communication. It was a Person-to-person process."

65. Ibid., 11.

66. Oral History Interview, Oral Collins, October 15, 1995. "I also had the feeling that the members of the board [of education] who were not academicians really didn't have a very profound understanding of what was going on."

doctrine of inspiration," these were fully discussed and "representatives of both schools affirmed their strong belief in the Bible as the Word of God ... The discussions resolved numerous problems and clarified questions of interpretation held by the schools."[67]

In reality, the discussions resolved little, if anything. Within days of the conference, the faculty and administration of Berkshire Christian College had rejected the final statement.[68] Moses Crouse returned to Aurora College with the feeling that the conference had been of little benefit.[69] Nothing was said about the conference in the denominational press.[70] Nothing about the conference appeared in minutes of subsequent Executive Committee or General Conference convention minutes. In addition, conference participants were asked not to quote from the papers presented without

67. "Conference of the Board of Education, Aurora College, Berkshire Christian College, Cleveland, Ohio, March 23–25, 1962," Oral Collins remembers that conference participants discussed an outline of the proposed statement while still in Cleveland, but did not see the statement itself until several days after the close of the conference when they had returned home. "I still do not believe that we ever saw the typed edition until later after we left." See, Collins to Mayer, February 14, 1997.

68. There is disagreement as to the nature and scope of Berkshire's response to the statement. Writing from an Aurora viewpoint, Charles Anderson, states flatly that "the administration of Berkshire Christian College repudiated the statement previously signed." Oral Collins argues that neither the college administration nor the college representatives to the Cleveland Conference ever approved or signed the final document. Therefore, their rejection of the final statement should not be seen as a repudiation of something previously agreed to. See Anderson, *Building on the Foundation*, 77; Collins to Mayer, February 14, 1997; Collins to Mayer, February 15, 1997; Mayer to Collins, February 15, 1997; Collins to Mayer, February 17, 1997.

69. Oral History Interview, Asa J. Colby, October 19, 1995. Rev. Colby comments, "I never heard a great deal about the results of that [the Cleveland Conference]. Moses Crouse came back, and I don't think he was very enthusiastic about what he had seen and heard."

70. James Howard Shaw to Raymond M. Beecroft, May 18, 1962. Apparently, in his role as chairman of the Board of Education, Ivan Adams had asked that the papers presented at the conference not be published. Rev. Shaw writes to Rev. Beecroft, "His [Rev. Adams] position, as I understand it, is that it would be unwise to publish papers prepared for a specialized situation, where discussion and interaction was to take place. To release these papers for general reading, without the opportunity for the asking and answering of questions, might indeed be unwise." Beecroft, according to Shaw's letter, had understood Adams's reason for not wanting to publish the papers to be that they could "give the impression that Aurora's position was so radical and unorthodox that it would be tragic or fatal for it to be known." Shaw wrote, "This is not the case" and later added that he hoped that "the degree and nature of the differences will not be exaggerated in the minds of those who can only guess what it is all about." This writer hopes to publish these papers at some future time.

express permission from the author.[71] Although the events surrounding the Cleveland Conference were (and still are) important to the life of the Advent Christian Church, those events remain shrouded in mystery to most within the denomination.

The Controversy Explodes

If J. Howard Shaw and other denominational officials hoped that they could somehow minimize the impact of the controversy on the Advent Christian Church, those hopes were soon shattered. By the Fall of 1962, the Eastern Regional Association was asking the Advent Christian General Conference to affirm, "that the historical position of the Advent Christian Church has been evangelical and conservative in its beliefs, and on this basis [it] has advanced its ministry to the world. Specifically . . . the constituents of our denomination have believed the traditional position of the church on the Inspiration of the Scriptures, namely that the written words of the Bible, being the words of God, are without error in the original writings."[72] A few months later, the Southern Region passed a similar call at its annual meeting. Their resolution expressed concern over "varying and dangerous views concerning the doctrine of inspiration, the origin of man, the virgin birth and literal bodily resurrection of Jesus Christ . . . as held in some quarters of the Advent Christian denomination" and asked the Executive Committee of General Conference "to give serious consideration to these basic doctrines and to take the necessary steps to define and propagate our theological position on these important issues."[73]

With resolutions from two of the five Advent Christian regions, the Executive Committee was placed in a difficult position. Acting on the resolutions could mean a serious floor-fight at the 1964 General Conference. Not acting ran the risk of appearing insensitive to what many Advent Christians, especially in the denomination's Eastern region, felt were serious matters of Christian doctrine and belief. Either course of action could

71. Oral History Interview, Oral Collins, 15 October 1995. In a subsequent memo, Collins commented, "The point was that we were not to publish nor quote from them without the author's permission . . . I was the only one who voted against this provision, which had the effect of sweeping the results of the conference under the rug." See "Editorial Notes on the Robert Mayer Oral History Interview with Oral Collins, Oct. 15, 1995."

72. "Minutes, Eastern Regional Convention, Somerville, Massachusetts; October 19–20, 1962."

73. Barton, *Advent Christians and the Bible*, 33.

lead to significant conflict, even division within the small denomination. The Executive Committee decided to act. In addition to appointing a committee of three people to suggest "possible changes in the articles necessary for the reaffirmation of our historic doctrinal position," they voted to recommend to the 1964 General Conference delegates the following revision of Article One of the Advent Christian Declaration of Principles: "We believe that the Bible is the inspired Word of God, being in its entirety a revelation given to man under Divine supervision and providence; that its historic statements are correct, and that it is the only Divine standard of faith and practice."[74] The Executive Committee revision made two significant changes. The word "inspired" was added as an adjectival description of the phrase "Word of God." In addition, the phrase "being in its entirety a revelation" replaced the phrase "containing a revelation." Both changes, the Executive Committee believed, would satisfy all of the parties involved.

That might have happened if the Christian education curriculum controversy had not once again exploded. In September 1963, the Plainville, Connecticut Advent Christian Church discontinued use of the Advent Christian curriculum and informed Mrs. Reed and the Board of Christian Education of their decision in three separate letters.[75] "After discussing the weaknesses of the A.C. Material," according to Pastor Roland Griswold, "It was the unanimous vote of the [Church School] Council that we change to a more evangelical, conservative curriculum until such time as the necessary improvements could be made in the Advent Christian materials." According to Griswold, the Sunday school teachers had several concerns. In the nursery curriculum, "There is too much "reading between the lines" and make-believe introduced into the Bible story."[76] The primary curriculum does not adequately grapple with the nature of sin. "Here," in Pastor Griswold's words, "the idea is definitely conveyed that the Cross should not be taught to Primaries. This fits in beautifully with the practice of the liberals and modernists." The Junior High curriculum needs more emphasis

---

74. "Executive Committee Minutes, June 21–26, 1963," 5. The original Article One read, "We believe that the Bible is the Word of God containing a revelation given to man under Divine supervision and providence; that its historic statements are correct, and that it is the only Divine standard of faith and practice."

75. Roland E. Griswold to Esther Reed, September 12, 1963; Roland E. Griswold to Elwell M. Drew, 12 September 1963; Roland E. Griswold to Board of Christian Education, September 9, 1963.

76. Roland E. Griswold to Board of Christian Education, September 9, 1963. The subsequent concerns discussed are from this letter.

on vital issues of Christian faith and Bible exegesis. The Senior High curriculum "raises many questions in youth's mind with no suggestions of answer[s]," and the material is "often at variance with historic Christian faith." Perhaps most alarming, "the present A.C. material," in Griswold's words, "has changed from the former Bible-centered emphasis to a pupil-centered emphasis. The patterns of "progressive" education are followed. When we have children and youth for less than an hour a week for Bible instruction, let's give them Bible instruction!"

While the Board of Christian Education was wrestling with a response to Rev. Griswold's criticism,[77] an even more serious challenge came out of the October 1963 meeting of the Eastern Regional Association. Earlier that year, Berkshire Christian College had invited James DeForest Murch, a veteran evangelical leader long associated with the National Association of Evangelicals, to campus for their annual pastors' conference. While there, Murch impressed many of the younger Advent Christian pastors from New England with his challenge to confront the National Council of Churches and champion the banner of evangelical Christianity.[78] Out of that conference, an organized attempt "to swing Polly Reed into an evangelical position" appeared to emerge especially within the New Hampshire conference.

That conference passed a resolution expressing their alarm over "repetition of material on consecutive Sundays, a lack of factual Bible content, and little or no emphasis on commitment to Christian principles of faith and practice" in the Advent Christian Sunday school curriculum.[79] "Teach-

77. Reed prepared for the Board of Christian Education a six-page response to Rev. Griswold's criticisms in which she offered a spirited defense of the curriculum and concluded, "I beg that each of you disregard what Roland has written and what I have written in answer, and that you get the quarterlies for the spring quarter of 1963 . . . and study them for yourself and arrive at your own independent conclusions." See Esther Reed to Board of Christian Education, October 10, 1963.

78. David S. McCarthy to Louia Gransee, December 7, 1963. McCarthy sees Murch's visit to Berkshire Christian College as the catalyst for the Eastern Region's opposition to the Advent Christian Sunday school curriculum produced by Mrs. Reed and the Board of Christian Education. McCarthy comments about Murch, "He is a spiritual giant, and deeply concerned about liberalism. But Murch, recalling his battles in the 40s, fails to see that the Council of Churches has swung quite a bit to the right. He still represents an extreme wing of evangelical thought who would have nothing to do with the National Council."

79. "Advent Christian Curriculum Materials, Recommendation Adopted by the Eastern Regional Advent Christian Association, October 23–24, 1963" The original draft of this resolution was supplied by the New Hampshire Advent Christian Conference as ratified at their 1963 meeting. See Appendix Four.

ings are 'watered down' and extremely weak in some areas pertaining to the inspiration of the Scriptures as the words of God." Moreover, "it is not always what is written but what is either inferred or omitted that causes alarm within our churches." The curriculum should not breed doubt, but confidence in the authority and infallibility of the Scriptures. Based on that, the Conference asked the both the Eastern Region and the Advent Christian General Conference to adopt three measures. Advent Christian curriculum should be based on the outlines of the National Sunday School Association, the Christian Education division of the National Association of Evangelicals. Advent Christian lesson writers and all connected with the planning, editorial, and production of the curriculum should "sign written statements annually subscribing to the belief that the Bible, as originally inspired by the Holy Spirit, is free from error" and correct in its theological teachings. Moreover, if a sufficient number of qualified lesson writers cannot be recruited, then the Board of Christian Education should "edit and rewrite the Sunday School material of another publisher [preferably Scripture Press or Gospel Light] which is in harmony with the above statements."

The adoption of that resolution by the Eastern Region signaled the beginning of several difficult months of anxiety and tension on several fronts within Advent Christian denominational life. Reed and the Board of Christian Education were struggling with precisely how to respond to the Griswold letter and the Eastern Region resolution.[80] At the same time, the relationship between Reed and Rev. Beecroft became strained to the maximum over several issues, editorial control being the most significant.[81]

---

80. It was especially difficult for the Board of Christian Education to respond because they were able to meet face-to-face only once every two years. In the interim, all of their business was conducted by letter and long-distance telephone calls. There was disagreement within the Board and its curriculum committee over exactly how to interpret the second of the Eastern Region recommendations. Several, including Board Chairman Elwell Drew, interpreted the action to mean that a "loyalty oath" should be signed by the director and the lesson writers. Others argued that Rev. Drew had misinterpreted the recommendation. See, Earl Crouse to Elwell Drew, December 12, 1963; Louia R. Gransee to Elwell Drew, December 17, 1963; Donna Johnson to Elwell Drew, January 26, 1964; Clinton E. Taber to Elwell Drew, February 12, 1964.

81. Oral History Interview, David S. McCarthy, 9. "I do remember clearly," according to Rev. McCarthy, "that Ray Beecroft thought this heretical material was getting out to the denomination. And Polly felt that he was taking power that wasn't his [by making editorial changes]." In describing their relationship at that time, Rev. McCarthy said, "Hostile would be perhaps even more accurate. They got to the point where they—if one person would say one thing, one would say the other. They couldn't confront each other logically on these issues."

The Boards of Christian Education and Publications were at loggerheads over how the profits from the sales of Advent Christian Sunday school curriculum should be distributed.[82] The Board of Publications was in the midst of a serious controversy over the management style and philosophy of Raymond Beecroft, a controversy that had overtones stemming from the rivalry between the two colleges.[83] Within the Eastern Region, a seven-person committee was at work on an extensive report that would "document charges directed against Advent Christian Sunday School Materials."[84] To top things off, the controversy over the Bible's inspiration was now the dominant topic in both the *Advent Christian Witness* and the *Present Truth Messenger.*[85]

82. James Howard Shaw to Esther Reed, August 8, 1963. Up until this point, all of the receipts from sales of Advent Christian Sunday school curriculum remained with Advent Christian Publications. Shaw proposed that 50 percent of the gross profits should be assigned to the Board of Christian Education. "At present, the entire gross profits of better than $14,000 per year are allowed to go completely to the Board of Publications. Against this gross profit, Publications allocates a sufficient amount of general administrative expense so that it shows a net loss on the carrying of Sunday School materials by the Board of Publications. This is a fallacious and misleading approach. This $14,000 that I mentioned is the gross profit after paying for the printing and shipping of materials. [In terms of the general administrative expense], I doubt if this work could justify more than $2,000 per year in charges." Naturally, Raymond Beecroft strongly disagreed with Rev. Shaw's analysis. See Raymond M. Beecroft to James Howard Shaw, August 22, 1963.

83. For background, see Oral History Interview, Harold R. Patterson, November 21, 1996, 27; James Howard Shaw to Raymond M. Beecroft, July 23, 1962; Cecil W. Noble to members of the Board of Publications and Executive Committee of General Conference, January 27, 1964; Raymond M. Beecroft to Members of the Board of Publications, April 30, 1964.

84. "Report of the Special Committee Appointed by the Board of the Eastern Regional Association to Document Charges Directed Against Advent Christian Sunday School Materials 1964."

85. The two publications included four major articles, two advocating the verbal inspiration and inerrancy of the Bible, and two arguing that the inspiration of Scripture rested on the centrality of Jesus Christ and the activity of the Holy Spirit in the lives of the biblical writers and in the life of the church. For the first position, see Dean, "Is the Bible the Inspired Word of God?", 12; Merrill, "Advent Christians and the Word of God," 4, 8; (April 16, 1964), 4; (April 23, 1964), 5; (April 30, 1964), 4, 15; (May 7, 1964), 4. For the second position, see Thomas, "Bible: Word of the Living God," 4–5, 15; Crouse, "Sufficiency of the Holy Spirit," 4, 9.

Montreat: The Conflict Debated and Discussed

Less than three weeks before General Conference delegates were due to arrive in Montreat, NC, the committee appointed by the Eastern Region completed their work and reported to a special meeting of the Eastern Regional Association.[86] As a result of their report, the region modified two of its requested actions. Instead of asking the Board of Christian Education to require all connected with the writing and production of curriculum to annually sign an as yet unwritten statement mandating a belief in biblical inerrancy and verbal inspiration, the region now simply asked them to "subscribe . . . in writing, annually without reservation [to] the statement as found in the Advent Christian Catechism "The Scriptures" on page 36."[87] The region also asked that "the Board of Christian Education take steps immediately to correct the Living Water series at the points of weakness delineated in the report" of the special committee. Specifically the region asked the board to "study the feasibility of alternatives, at all grade levels, to the NCC [National Council of Churches] Curriculum including possible arrangement to purchase the right to use Scripture Press Outlines, Gospel Light outlines, or David C. Cook Thematic Graded Series outlines" and that this matter be determined by vote at General Conference.[88]

Seventeen days later, Advent Christians from across Canada and the United States would gather for possibly the most eventful General Conference in the history of the Advent Christian Church. The conference agenda included consideration of reunification with the Life and Advent Union, a small Adventist body that had broken away from the Advent Christian Church in 1863; a proposal for establishing a General Conference Headquarters building that would place the denomination's national agencies in one central location; finalizing the United Budget mechanism for funding the work of Advent Christian agencies and institutions; and resolutions on two national issues—race relations, especially in terms of Advent Christian

---

86. "Minutes, Eastern Regional Association, Special Meeting, Somerville, Mass., May 27, 1964." Since World War II, this appears to be the only time that an Advent Christian regional association has convened a special delegate meeting.

87. Ibid., 1. See also Adams, Hewitt, and Dean, *Advent Christian Catechism*, 36. One of the problems that Advent Christian proponents of biblical inerrancy faced was that the term was not actually used in the Declaration of Principles or in other statements of Advent Christian doctrine and theology like the *Catechism*. While not using the term "inerrant" to describe the Bible, the *Catechism* does declare that Scripture "is in harmony with all truth" especially in terms of history and science.

88. Ibid., 2.

congregational attitudes toward African Americans, and school prayer.[89] As important as each of those issues were, the conflict over inspiration was foremost in the minds of the delegates and the dominant focus of attention throughout the week. The delegates would discuss and vote on a major revision to the first article of the denomination's Declaration of Principles. They would also address the Christian Education controversy.

As President, Edwin K. Gedney, would play an important role in what would transpire throughout the meetings. In the Advent Christian General Conference structure, the President functioned as chief legislative officer, presiding over meetings of both the Executive Committee and the General Conference delegates. In addition, he served as Sunday morning worship speaker. In that latter context, most General Conference presidents used that time to offer a spiritual challenge or call the delegates to unity of purpose. That Sunday morning, Edwin Gedney spoke to an estimated audience of almost 3,000 people that included Ruth Graham, wife of evangelist Billy Graham,[90] and gave an impassioned address focusing on the importance of the doctrine of biblical inerrancy.[91]

A few hours later, J. Howard Shaw would deliver an equally passionate plea for preserving the unity of the Advent Christian Church. One listener remembered Rev. Shaw using the analogy from the Russian Revolution of 1917.[92] While the revolutionaries were taking control of the country, the Russian Orthodox Church was found debating the kinds of columns they would use for their vestments. In the same way, could Advent Christians afford to divide over differing interpretations of how the Bible is inspired, while the world desperately needs the Advent Christian message of life only in Jesus Christ? After the service, committee and board members hurried off to meetings and clusters of delegates gathered in small groups for fellowship and discussion of the events of the day. Rev. David S. McCarthy, at that time the pastor of the New Albany, Indiana, Advent Christian Church, remembered that "there was a feeling in the air that I never felt at General

---

89. "1964 General Conference Minutes," 4, 6, 11, 12.

90. Beecroft, "The Decision," 2, 15.

91. Oral History Interview, David S. McCarthy, November 24, 1995. Rev. McCarthy recalls, "It was almost a political stump speech, in favor of the inerrancy position. And I remember him invoking Billy Graham's name, pointing up the hill where Graham lived, and suggesting that he would support this kind of position. The whole thrust of Gedney's message was, 'Don't you dare do anything that would water down the inerrant scriptures.'"

92. Ibid., 15.

Conference before—like the night before the mother of all battles. You got all the troops in their little squadrons gathering and talking. And you can just feel the tension in the air. It was a great feeling of expectancy and excitement about what was going to happen the next day."[93]

Several weeks before the Montreat convention, Rev. McCarthy had been asked to offer a critique of the senior high Sunday school curriculum. He had emerged as one of several individuals who was trusted by and had the confidence of both theological parties within the denomination. Born in New England and educated at Northwestern College in Minneapolis,[94] he had come to serve the New Albany, Indiana congregation partially to pursue a master's degree in religious education at the Southern Baptist Seminary in Louisville, Kentucky. During the early 1960s, McCarthy not only began to write Advent Christian Sunday school curriculum, he and Mrs. Reed became good friends and she came to appreciate his advice and counsel especially in terms of how Advent Christians in New England understood specific terminology used in the lesson material.

Rev. McCarthy was candid in his assessment of *Living Water*. "A great deal of Bible is used in each lesson. Even the most ardent fundamentalist would be pleased with the amount and selection of Scripture passages that are brought into focus, but—and this is basic—*the Bible is not forcefully injected into the lesson material*" (emphasis his).[95] Moreover, "the use of Bible readings in *Living Water* fail to proclaim that this book is God's unique revelation that speaks to a teen-ager's problems here and now." At that point, McCarthy reflected on apparently contradictory criticisms he had heard from two Sunday school teachers. One insisted that the lessons were not life centered. The other declared that they were not Bible centered. "As I read the manual for myself," in McCarthy's words, "I had the strange feeling that both teachers were justified in their observations. *Living Water* . . . is neither Bible centered nor pupil centered. Instead it seems to center on a moralistic "religious" outlook on life. At times I feared it was "culture" centered."[96]

---

93. Ibid. McCarthy adds, "I can look back on it now because you don't see anything now like this. I've never felt like that at any other General Conference session."

94. Ibid., 4. McCarthy comments, "I went to Northwestern . . . primarily because I wanted to be the world's next great evangelist and Billy Graham was president of the school at that time." The biographical information for Rev. McCarthy is from pp. 1–6 of this interview.

95. David S. McCarthy, "Living Water," June 1964, 1.

96. Ibid., 2.

Rev. McCarthy offered a radical solution. It was not enough to change curriculum outlines. A whole new approach was needed. Because, in McCarthy's view, teenagers were no longer attracted to the traditional Sunday school quarterly, he advocated that the Board "scrap *Living Water* as a pupil book. In its place, why not use a weekly youth publication, imprinting a back page with a Sunday school lesson topic for teens."[97] Now, as the Board of Christian Education finally had opportunity for face-to-face discussion of curriculum issues, McCarthy's solution became one of their primary considerations. As the minutes record it, the Board now began to discuss "a completely new format for Senior High [curriculum that] might combine *Living Water* and *YOURS* [the Advent Christian Youth Fellowship Magazine] into a correlated weekly publication for Sunday School, Youth Fellowship and devotions."[98]

As the Board of Christian Education continued to meet, General Conference delegates were focused on debating the Executive Committee's proposed revision to Article One. That debate almost did not happen. While the Executive Committee's proposed revision represented a significant improvement in the eyes of most General Conference delegates,[99] especially for those concerned that the Declaration of Principles reflect a commitment to biblical inerrancy, it was not enough. Proponents of that position were caught off-guard when the Executive Committee's proposed Article One revision was brought to the General Conference floor. An attempt to secure quick passage was made, and according to the minutes of the session, the delegates approved the revision without dissention.[100] "There was a real uproar," remembered Rev. Nelson Melvin, "because the vote had been taken so quickly" and no opportunity had been provided for discussion.[101] Although he favored and voted for the revision proposed by the Executive Committee, Rev. Melvin felt that short-circuiting a much-needed debate

97. Ibid., 78.

98. "Board of Christian Education, Advent Christian General Conference, June 16–25, 1964," 3. At that time, all of the boards and committees of the General Conference met concurrently with the General Conference convention.

99. See earlier discussion in this chapter.

100. "1964 General Conference Minutes," 8.

101. Oral History Interview, Nelson A. Melvin, October 24, 1994, 2. Rev. Melvin was a prominent pastor within the Advent Christian Church during the 1950s and early 1960s. For several years, he served as pastor of the Aurora, IL. Advent Christian Church and in 1965 succeeded Raymond Beecroft as manager of Advent Christian Publications and editor of the *Advent Christian Witness*.

could seriously damage the denomination. "I felt," in Rev. Melvin's words, "that it would be terribly wrong to let that vote pass and so, I made the motion to reconsider."[102]

After the delegates voted to reconsider, an amendment was proposed that would add the word "inerrant" immediately after the word "inspired" in the first phrase was proposed.[103] The debate then became impassioned. The minutes record that, "Vice President Ivan Adams was called to the chair in order that President Gedney might participate in the debate on this amendment."[104] Some recall the tone of the debate as civil and constructive. Others viewed it as divisive and mean-spirited.[105] Some who spoke provided arguments that were thoughtful and intelligent. Other comments seemed emotional, even ridiculous. One person asked, apparently tongue-in-cheek, if this discussion was actually about the inerrancy of the King James Version.[106] As the delegates adjourned for lunch, emotions were high and the atmosphere tense.

The delegates returned at 4:00. Before that, efforts to work out a compromise had been going on informally throughout the afternoon.[107] The focal point of that effort was Rev. Robert Hewitt. An individual known

102. Ibid., 2.

103. "1964 General Conference Minutes," 8. With the amendment, the first phrase now read, "We believe that the Bible is the inspired, inerrant Word of God." In subsequent correspondence, David A. Dean confirmed that he was the individual who offered the amendment at that time. "As the debate began, we Inerrantists "in the know" waited for a specific person to introduce our position before we spoke to the issue. But that person . . . did not introduce the planned motion and the moment was almost lost. When reconsideration carried, I was the one who . . . offered from the floor an amendment to insert the word "inerrant" into the proposed revision of Article I." David A. Dean to Robert Mayer, February 18, 1997.

104. Ibid., 8.

105. Unfortunately, no recording the debate is known to currently exist. One debate participant later wrote, "I had little time at Montreat to enter into the discussion but did a great deal of listening as I recorded the entire argument on tape." See J. Kenneth Andrews, "Liberal or Conservative," 2. Efforts on my part to locate these tapes were unsuccessful.

106. Ibid., 2. While Rev. Andrews does not identify who this individual was, there is evidence to suggest that it was Gerald Richardson, an administrator from Aurora College. Oral Collins remembers that Rev. Richardson, at the Cleveland Conference, made similar statements regarding the King James Version in that context. My judgment is that Rev. Richardson used this line of argument as part of his debating tactics. See Oral History Interview, Oral Collins, October 15, 1995, 9.

107. The Executive Committee met from 2:40 until 4:00 that afternoon but their minutes do not record any discussion of the issue or the debate during that time. See "Executive Committee Minutes, June 15–25, 1964," 6.

well for his careful study of scripture and his pastoral concern for people, Bob Hewitt had the ear of leaders within the denomination and from both colleges.[108] Hewitt suggested deleting the word "inerrant" from the first phrase, and adding the words "and infallible" after the word "Divine" in the last phrase.[109] After more debate and one last attempt to divert the issue by referring it back to the Executive Committee, delegates approved that change and the revision to Article One.

The debate seemed to be over and the General Conference sessions were due to end after lunch the next day. However, one more issue directly related to the controversy over inspiration remained to be discussed—the Eastern Region resolution concerning the Advent Christian Sunday school curriculum. Throughout Wednesday evening and early Thursday morning, the Board of Christian Education had discussed the Eastern Region resolution and struggled to develop an adequate response.[110] As the last General Conference business session was getting underway, the Board of Christian Education agreed that their response would involve a statement with two resolutions and asked one of their members, Pastor Earl Crouse from Sumas, Washington, to present them to the delegates.

The statement expressed strong commitment to the "quantity and quality of work" that had been accomplished in developing distinctive Advent Christian Sunday school curriculum and suggested that given the limitations faced by a small denomination, the development and production of this curriculum was "a monumental achievement." In that context, the

108. Rev. Hewitt is the son of Clarence H. Hewitt, the Aurora theologian whose views were highly influential in the Advent Christian Church during the second quarter of the twentieth century. At the time, he served as pastor of the Waterbury, Connecticut Advent Christian Church and as president of the American Advent Mission Society.

109. With Rev. Hewitt's suggested language, Article One would now read, "We believe that the Bible is the inspired Word of God, being in its entirety a revelation given to man under Divine inspiration and providence; that its historic statements are correct, and that it is the only Divine and infallible standard of faith and practice." Rev. Hewitt's pivotal role in these events was first suggested to me by Philip Anderson, an Advent Christian layman who at that time was a member of the National Advent Christian Church just outside of Washington, DC. A chemist by profession, Mr. Anderson served as a convention delegate.

110. One of the things that hampered the Board of Christian Education during their meetings at General Conference was that several of their members served simultaneously on other boards and committees. By the time of their 9:00 p.m. adjournment on Wednesday evening, June 17, not enough board members were present to conduct business. See "Board of Christian Education, Advent Christian General Conference, Montreat, NC, June 16–25, 1964," 4.

committee recognized that they needed to address the "insistent, thoughtful criticisms and suggestions" they had received from the Eastern Region and from others.[111] In their first resolution, the Board of Christian Education voted to "undertake an intensive re-evaluation of our own Curriculum, and a comparative study of other curricula sources" and to present recommendations to the denomination "for the future of curriculum planning."[112] Then they adopted David McCarthy's recommendation that "immediate consideration be given to the feasibility of combining the functions and replacing *Living Water*, the Senior High quarterly, and the youth [National Youth Fellowship] publications in favor of a weekly paper issued jointly by the Board of Christian Education and the National Youth Fellowship."[113]

Although those two resolutions diffused many of the concerns raised by the Eastern region, there was still the matter of asking all of those connected with the planning and production of the curriculum to annually ascribe to the four paragraph statement on Scripture found in the Advent Christian Catechism.[114] Largely because of their restorationist heritage, most Advent Christians remained suspicious of attempts to mandate conformity to any doctrinal test or standard. With this issue, two bedrock principles of Advent Christian denominational life, the freedom to interpret the Bible according to the dictates of one's individual conscience and the desire to affirm the inspiration of the Bible as the foundation for a distinctive Advent Christian expression of Christian faith, were brought squarely into tension with one another. Those who valued freedom of conscience tended to view annual subscription to a statement regarding Scripture as a "loyalty oath." Those who wanted to insure that Advent Christian faith and practice was grounded first and foremost in the Bible saw annual subscription not as a "loyalty oath" but as a means to ensure that Advent Christian writers would remain faithful to their doctrinal heritage.

The discussion that probably should have happened at this point did not. Time was short and given the response by the Board of Christian Education to the concerns expressed by many, the Business Committee recommended that the Eastern Region's call for annual subscription to the

111. "1964 General Conference Minutes," 9; "Board of Christian Education," 4.

112. Ibid., 9.

113. Ibid. The resolution then read, "This exploration will seek to establish a weekly publication with devotional articles, news, features; as well as correlated Sunday School lessons and youth fellowship programming for each." In their resolution, the Board also expressed hope that the Junior High curriculum could be integrated into this approach.

114. Adams, *Advent Christian Catechism*, 36.

Advent Christian Catechism statement on Scripture be modified by asking the Board of Christian Education to "maintain such procedures as may be required to insure that all editors and lesson writers . . . subscribe to Advent Christian doctrine as set forth and explained in the *Advent Christian Catechism* and published by said Board of Christian Education."[115] The delegates unanimously approved that motion and affirmed the two actions offered by the Board of Christian Education. The discussion and debate on how to reconcile freedom of individual conscience with the need to express and maintain the inspiration and authority of Holy Scripture would have to wait for another time and another place.[116]

With approval of the Business Committee resolution, the debate over inspiration was over, at least at the 1964 General Conference session. Before adjourning, the delegates passed several resolutions and Edwin K. Gedney turned the gavel over to a new incoming president. For J. Howard Shaw, adjournment brought a great sense of relief. What could have easily brought division to the Advent Christian General Conference was instead an opportunity to forge a renewed sense of unity and common mission. "I am deeply convinced," Shaw wrote two weeks later, "that the Lord wonderfully answered prayer in the things that transpired at Montreat, and that we saw the Spirit at work in a very definite way both in the pre-Conference committee meetings and on the floor of the delegate sessions."[117] Shaw was hopeful that spiritual unity would grow out of "the painful processes of vigorous discussion and the interchange of ideas" and that the Advent Christian Church could now "get on with the important work of the Kingdom and press forward to the achievement of hitherto unrealized goals."[118]

Not everyone shared J. Howard Shaw's view. The vote to revise Article One of the Declaration of Principles "was not made by a large majority" according to *Advent Christian Witness* editor Raymond Beecroft, "and it is obvious that a difference exists in our denomination as to the extent of the authority of the Scriptures."[119] Therefore, "we face the future in this mat-

---

115. "1964 General Conference Minutes," 10. The Business Committee motion commended the Board of Christian Education for taking "cooperative and constructive steps to deal with the problems set forth in items 1 and 2" of the Eastern Region statement.

116. In this writer's view, this issue is pivotal in associations and denominations that practice non-creedal approaches to Christian doctrine and congregational forms of church government.

117. Shaw to Beecroft, July 3, 1964.

118. Ibid., 2.

119. Raymond Beecroft, "The Decision," 2, 15. Rev. Beecroft added, "Several no longer

ter with uncertainty as to what may emerge from this action in the total evangelical thrust of our ministry." For one other Advent Christian pastor, while the General Conference debate had resulted in a stronger affirmation of the inspiration of Scripture and a marked change in the direction of the Board of Christian Education, it marked a premature end to a much-needed debate on the nature and function of the Bible's inspiration in the life of the Advent Christian Church. "I remember coming back from General Conference [in Montreat] and realizing how badly we had been beaten," according to Pastor David A. Dean.[120] "And I'm sure the Aurora people came away from General Conference feeling that they had been beaten badly. What everybody did was insist they had won. What else can you do?"

What most Advent Christians did was attempt to carry on as if the controversy had never happened. By 1964, dramatic cultural changes were already beginning to impact Canadian and American society. The assassination of John F. Kennedy had already shocked the United States and brought major change to the direction of the American government. The appearance of the Beatles, the British musical group, signaled the rise of a youth culture that was strange and different in the eyes of many, if not most, adults.[121] American involvement in Vietnam was escalating rapidly. Those involved in the Civil Rights movement were aggressively pressing their case that African-Americans should not be subject to discrimination, legal or otherwise, anywhere in the United States.[122] Because they confronted a dramatically changing culture, it was easy for most Advent Christians to turn their focus elsewhere and simply ignore their differences over theological issues like the inspiration of Holy Scripture.

---

hold to the inerrancy of the Bible that God gave to us in its original form."

120. Oral History Interview, David A. Dean/Freeman Barton, August 4, 1994, 33. At the time of the 1964 General Conference, Rev. Dean served as pastor of the Springfield, MA Advent Christian Church.

121. For a discussion of the Beatles spiritual impact on the emerging youth culture and for a theological assessment of their work, see Turner, *Gospel according to the Beatles*.

122. Division over the scope and goals of the Civil Rights movement remained a source of tension among some Advent Christians. In March 1965, five Aurora College students journeyed to Selma, AL to participate in a Civil Rights march lead by Dr. Martin Luther King Jr. from Selma to Montgomery. Charles Anderson reports, "Letters from irate southern Advent Christians reached the desk of Dr. Crimi [the college president] including one from Mr. Rudolph Mitchell, a member of the South Carolina House of Representatives sharply criticizing both the action of the students and college for permitting them to march." See Anderson, *Building on the Foundation*, 119–21.

Despite that, the controversy did have subtle but significant impact on the life of the Advent Christian Church. In our last chapter, we will look at that impact and make some final observations about the controversy.

CHAPTER SEVEN

Aftermath and Impact

RAYMOND BEECROFT'S JULY 1964 editorial lamenting the "difference [that] exists within our denomination as to the extent of the authority of the Scriptures"[1] brought a strong response from Aurora College Vice-president Gerald Richardson. Rev. Richardson interpreted Rev. Beecroft's editorial remarks as directed squarely against Aurora College. Moreover, those who wanted to argue over biblical inerrancy were drawing attention to an irrelevant issue "because either to doubt or affirm anything about the original autographs has no bearing on the inspiration and authority of the Bibles which we trust as God's word today." In Rev. Richardson's view, "to raise the issue is indeed 'disputing about words with no profit.'"[2] Beecroft's rejoinder to what he perceived as Richardson's misinterpretation of his views was just as direct and forceful. "If the source is not totally reliable, absolute truth, and free from error," Rev. Beecroft wrote in response, "then we have no foundation on which we can confidently build our faith and produce reliable translations."

Unfortunately for Rev. Beecroft, the foundation under-girding his position as manager of Advent Christian Publications began to erode rapidly in the months immediately following Montreat. In J. Howard Shaw's view, Beecroft had neglected a basic principle that many Advent Christians felt was vital; that of "preserving an effective regional voice in the editorial

---

1. Raymond Beecroft, "The Decision," 2, 15.

2. Gerald F. Richardson to Raymond M. Beecroft, July 11, 1964; Raymond M. Beecroft to Gerald F. Richardson, August 21, 1964.

policies and expression through the national publication."[3] At the same time, Beecroft had lost the confidence of at least three members of his board, partially over his management style and partially over his strong identification with the theological party that favored a strong statement on biblical inerrancy as an integral part of Advent Christian theology.[4] By November, Rev. Beecroft had offered his resignation to the Board of Publications, and by the following June had been replaced by Rev. Nelson Melvin.[5] Rev. Melvin shared Rev. Beecroft's commitment to biblical inerrancy. However, because of his prior service as pastor of the Aurora (IL) Advent Christian Church and his friendship with many Aurora College graduates, Rev. Melvin was viewed as someone who would bring a more conciliatory approach to Advent Christian Publications.[6] Immediate changes in management, style, and editorial philosophy were evident by the end of 1965.

3. Shaw to Beecroft, July 3, 1964. For Beecroft's response, see Beecroft to Shaw, 7 August 1964. Beecroft responded that with the beginning of the *Advent Christian News*, a news-oriented Advent Christian publication started in 1963, the focus of the *Advent Christian Witness* had changed to the point where the arrangement suggested by Shaw was unwieldy and therefore not practical.

4. Beecroft to Shaw and the Board of Publications, August 7, 1964. The heightened tension is illustrated by one sentence from Rev. Beecroft's letter: "I would be remiss in my responsibility if I did not point out that it is a most unusual and improper action on the part of a Board member to repeatedly request the Manager's resignation and to circulate that request beyond the board that he serves, particularly when it is circulated in opposition and defiance of a decision of that Board." Mr. Beecroft's remarks were directed toward Mr. John R. Thornton, an Aurora College graduate who had served as the Central regional representative on the Publications board since 1962.

5. Shaw to Beecroft, November 13, 1964. See also, Oral History Interview, Harold R. Patterson, November 21, 1996, 5–6; Oral History Interview, Nelson Melvin, October 24 1994. There is some indication that Rev. Beecroft offered his resignation as a way to force the Board to address the conflict between himself and Mr. Thornton. Rev. Patterson comments, "[Mr. Thornton's] complaints were becoming continuous. And I think that it was a test as to who was going to be boss. Remember, I see Ray as a man who wanted control . . . he realized that he could not continue in the circumstance that he was in. He resigned in hopes—I really think he didn't want his resignation accepted." Rev. Patterson was one of two members of the Board who voted not to accept the resignation.

6. Oral History Interview, Harold R. Patterson, November 21, 1996, 2–3. As often is the case, personality and style can play as important a role as theological posture. In Rev. Patterson's view, Rev. Beecroft practiced a strong, autocratic leadership style. "Later in life," according to Rev. Patterson, "when I interacted with him on at least a weekly basis [when Beecroft served as manager of Vernon Advent Christian Home in Vernon, Vermont], I found him very removed from people. He could talk with people but he was always the boss. People found it hard to talk to him."

The Christian Education controversy took on a different tone in the aftermath of the 1964 General Conference. Based on the mandate adopted by the delegates at Montreat, the Board conducted a thorough evaluation of their curriculum and concluded that it was no longer possible to continue producing a distinctive Advent Christian curriculum on their own. For Polly Reed, this presented an opportunity for Advent Christians to participate in a multidenominational curriculum project that would be more theologically oriented and integrate new insights from the field of education. However, several on her board disagreed with that direction and favored the development of a cooperative agreement with David C. Cook publishing. Under the terms of that agreement, David C. Cook would allow the Advent Christian Church to make editorial changes in areas that touched upon distinctive Advent Christian theology, a practice that the company had permitted for several denominations.[7]

At its 1966 meeting, the Board of Christian Education voted to finalize the arrangement with David C. Cook. The multi-denominational project was not yet to the point where specifics in terms of lesson design and price could be offered. In addition, because several of the denominations involved were clearly identified with the Protestant mainline, there was the feeling that pursuing the course that Mrs. Reed desired them to take could once again intensify the theological controversy that had plagued the small denomination for several years. In the aftermath, while Mrs. Reed did all she could to implement the Board's decision, she was devastated by it. "The more I think about what we have done," she later wrote, "the sicker and sicker I get. We have sold our birthright for a mess of pottage. Somehow I failed in interpreting what we could have had . . . . Educationally, we have just drifted back fifty years."[8] By the end of the decade, Polly Reed would resign her position as Director of Christian Education.

As the Boards of Christian Education and Publications underwent changes in leadership and philosophy, J. Howard Shaw continued to lead the General Conference toward unification both in terms of location and structure. By 1969, a denominational office building was established in Charlotte, North Carolina, and each of the Advent Christian agencies that

7. For a description of the issues involved, see Esther Reed to Nelson Melvin, May 25, 1966; Nelson Melvin to Esther Reed, June 1, 1966; Esther Reed to Nelson Melvin, July 7, 1966. As manager of Advent Christian Publications, Rev. Melvin was responsible to ascertain the financial impact of these proposed agreements. In that context, he supported the proposed association with David C. Cook.

8. Reed to Melvin, August 17, 1966.

operated on a denomination-wide level relocated to the new office. Five years later, those agencies would be consolidated under one organizational structure.[9] With centralization came the end of separate boards of directors for each of these agencies, although some degree of competition between them would continue to exist well into the 1980s. Centralization also brought much tighter control and management of any theological disputes that might emerge.[10]

Impact on Denominational Colleges

For Aurora College, the aftermath of the 1964 General Conference meant an acceleration of their drive to attain a less denominational, more regional focus. By the late 1960s, the theological faculty had been broadened to include scholars from outside Advent Christian ranks. College administrators were taking steps to diversify the student body and to address student concerns during this culturally turbulent period. With changes in 1971 to Aurora College's Articles of Incorporation and to the election of its governing board, all formal organizational ties to the Advent Christian Church were essentially severed.[11] Aurora College continued to participate in the Advent Christian United Budget until 1985, when the denomination's executive board voted to eliminate support of all Advent Christian-related institutions from that program.

9. For an account of these events, see Hewitt, *Devotion and Development*, 297–328. The impact of these events on the Advent Christian Church and the agencies involved, especially in terms of intended and unintended consequences, is an area that deserves study in the future.

10. At its 1981 convention in Wheaton, IL, delegates ratified a process for amending the Declaration of Principles of the Advent Christian Church that involves four steps: Submission of a proposed revision by a church or group of individuals; extensive study by an ad hoc task force appointed by the denomination's Executive Council; passage by a two-thirds vote of General Conference delegates; and ratification by a majority of Advent Christian congregations. The minimal time required to change a specific article of the Declaration of Principles using this procedure is nine years.

11. Anderson, *Building on the Foundation*, 139–40. The occasion for the changes, according to Mr. Anderson, was a 1969 report by Aurora College's legal counsel stating that an organizational structure which placed ultimate control of the College in the hands of a religious denomination would make the school ineligible to receive funds from the State of Illinois. In response, the Board of Directors ratified changes that eliminated the term "Bible Training School" from the College's Articles of Incorporation, and mandated that 50% of the College's nineteen members be residents of Illinois with at least five being members of Advent Christian churches. Those changes were ratified on May 15, 1971.

Most significantly, Aurora College eliminated its Bachelor of Theology (B.Th.) program which meant that it would no longer play a major role in the preparation and training of Advent Christian pastors. Up until the late 1960s, Aurora College had served the Advent Christian Church in two important ways. First, it provided both theological and practical training for pastors, especially for those who served Advent Christian congregations in the Midwest, on the West Coast, and in several areas of the South. The college also graduated a sizable number of Advent Christian laypeople who returned to their communities and took on leadership roles in Advent Christian congregations and in their occupations. The elimination of the B.Th. degree combined with the growing distance between college and denomination meant the loss of both of those functions.[12] Since the late 1960s, the number of Advent Christian pastors educated at Aurora College has declined significantly.

The changing relationship between Aurora College and the Advent Christian Church was not unique. Many private liberal-arts colleges followed the same path, especially as they embraced demands for regional accreditation on the part of parents, academic freedom on the part of faculty, and diverse course offerings and majors on the part of students. In conjunction with the 1968 celebration of Aurora College's 75th anniversary, then President James Crimi remarked that the essence of Aurora College as a Christian college was "the Christian student and the Christian faculty and staff member, consciously bringing to bear on every aspect of college life the spirit of concern, of Christian love, which is the very essence of Christ's revelation of God."[13] Even as those words were spoken, Aurora College administrators like Executive Vice-president Mark Trumbo were wondering how those sentiments could be reflected in the midst of an increasingly diverse faculty, student body, and alumni.[14] While administrators had originally hoped that Aurora College could serve both the Advent Christian Church and the Fox River Valley region of Northern Illinois, the

---

12. Anderson, *Building on the Foundation*, 203. Anderson writes, "In days gone by, a considerable number of Advent Christian young people came to Aurora because, in their minds, going to Aurora and going to college were synonymous." The loss of this second function, the education of Advent Christian laypeople in an Advent Christian-related setting, has meant that a number of Advent Christian congregations have suffered the loss of an important source of church leadership. The impact of this loss has not been fully appreciated.

13. Anderson, *Building on the Foundation*, 165.

14. Ibid.

theological controversy within the denomination combined with dramatic change in American cultural life during and following the 1960s made that ideal, in their view, impossible. By the beginning of the 1970s, it was clear that Aurora College and the Advent Christian Church were moving in two different directions.

For Berkshire Christian College, the effects of the controversy are more complex. After 1964, Advent Christian young people interested in studying for the ministry were more likely to choose Berkshire, especially if they were from one of the three Advent Christian regions that bordered the Atlantic Ocean. By the early 1970s, college enrollment was at a high point with the student population being about equally divided between those from Advent Christian churches and those from congregations affiliated with New England Evangelicalism. While some Advent Christians, particularly outside of New England, continued to view Berkshire Christian College as a regional and not a denominational institution, by the mid-1970s graduates of the college could be found in Advent Christian pulpits throughout the denomination. During this time, the college continued to strengthen its commitments both to Advent Christian doctrinal distinctives and to Reformed theology.

Looking at Berkshire Christian College in the mid1970s, an outside observer would have been hard pressed to find any negative effects stemming from the Advent Christian theological controversy over the Bible's inspiration. If that same observer were to return ten years later, she would have discovered a Berkshire Christian College devastated by organizational and theological conflict with the latter focusing squarely on the issue of inspiration. "Financial Crisis Hits Berkshire Christian College," was the headline on a 1983 special edition of the *Advent Christian News*.[15] That crisis stemmed from an enrollment drop that began in the mid-1970s combined with an administrative policy that called for significant short-term borrowing to cover revenue shortfalls. By January 1983, Berkshire Christian College was over $800,000 in debt, with over half of that being

---

15. "Financial Crisis Hits Berkshire Christian College," 1. This author must acknowledge his personal, although indirect, role in the events described here. This issue was one of the first prepared under his guidance as the Director of Advent Christian Publications, a position he assumed in June of 1982. Because of his indirect participation in the events surrounding Berkshire Christian College, this writer acknowledges the tentative nature of the following section and expresses his hope that at some future time, students and scholars will carry out more extensive research on the crisis and conflict that surrounded the college in the 1980s.

in short-term high-interest notes.[16] Although Advent Christians across the country responded generously to the college's financial emergency, in Freeman Barton's words, "the basic needs remained, more students and more money."[17]

In the aftermath of the financial emergency came a transition in the office of the President. A significant number of Advent Christians felt that Berkshire Christian College needed strong administrative and strategic guidance and for that, the Board of Regents turned to Lloyd Richardson. A lifelong Advent Christian who had served from 1974 to 1978 as President of Aurora College, Richardson was the son of an Advent Christian pastor and nephew of longtime Aurora College administrator Gerald Richardson. Lloyd Richardson's strategy represented nothing less than a complete transformation of Berkshire from Bible college to a broadly focused Christian-oriented university. An integral part of that transformation would be theological. When interviewed for the presidency, Richardson had convinced the presidential search committee that he was comfortable with the college's doctrinal statement, a statement which included a specific affirmation of biblical inerrancy.[18] After he assumed the presidency, it became clear that for Richardson this theological commitment was expendable. In order for Berkshire Christian College to serve all of the Advent Christian Church the college must "come to accommodate the points of difference which exist within denominational ranks," and be willing to accept "as Adjunct Faculty those from within and without the Advent Christian denomination who may hold divergent points of view as to the nature of revelation and inspiration."[19]

16. Freeman Barton, *Mary Queen of Scots*, 10–11. Barton served on the college faculty until 1986 and offers an interpretation of the events surrounding the college crisis that will be invaluable to future researchers. Regarding the financial crisis, he comments, "The college administration, then the rest the college community, had been alerted to the crisis seven months before. Business office personnel had discovered at the end of the fiscal year [1982] that the college was burdened with $450,000.00 in short term debt, two thirds of it incurred during the academic year just ended."

17. Ibid., 11. Implied in Barton's words was the need for greater long-term Advent Christian support both in terms of students and financial giving.

18. Ibid., 12–14. Barton records the first article of the Berkshire Christian College Statement of Faith: "The sixty-six books of the Bible as originally written were inspired by God, hence free from error."

19. Ibid., 41–42. For a comprehensive look at how Richardson understood both the ethos and theological posture of Berkshire Christian College, as well as his strategies for change, see Richardson, "Blueprint for Growth."

In several contexts, Richardson referred to his desire to broaden the theological posture of the college, especially as it related to the college's understanding of biblical inerrancy. Faculty, staff, and administration reacted strongly against both Richardson's theological approach and against what they saw as an attempt to destroy the nature and character of the college itself. Opposition to Richardson's leadership quickly spread among college alumni and among Advent Christians who felt that the college's commitment to the doctrine of biblical inerrancy was vital. At the end of three turbulent years, Richardson resigned and the college was forced to close its Lenox, Massachusetts campus due to several factors including a drop in student enrollment, an increasingly difficult relationship with the town of Lenox, and over one million dollars of debt. While it is still too early to measure its precise impact in these events,[20] it is evident that the issue of the Bible's inspiration was able to raise great passion within the denomination even twenty years after Montreat.

Impact on Theological Beliefs

In the words of one participant in the events at Montreat, "There was acceptance of a compromise position in the Declaration of Principles, but no one changed their minds" as a result of the debate.[21] The truth of that statement is beyond question, at least in the immediate aftermath of the Montreat General Conference. At the same time, we can identify several theological effects that the controversy has had on the Advent Christian Church during the second half of the twentieth century. While the revision of Article One was essentially a compromise, it sharpened the denominational understanding of Scripture in two ways that identified the denomination with the emerging new-evangelical coalition within American Protestantism. First, by adding the word "inspired" as an adjective to describe the Bible as the Word of God, the statement located inspiration in Scripture itself, not just in the events described by the Bible. Second, by replacing the phrase "containing a revelation given to man" with "being in its entirety a revelation given to man," the statement affirmed that the whole of Scripture was God's revelation to humanity. While the revision did not use the

20. Ibid., 146. Barton comments that Richardson "was convinced, that despite substantial evidence to the contrary, that the majority of Advent Christians do not believe in the full truthfulness of Scripture."

21. Oral History Interview, Clio Thomas, November 19, 1996.

term "inerrancy," these two changes reflected the reality that most Advent Christians identified with an evangelical Protestant, as opposed to a mainline Protestant, understanding of the Bible's inspiration and authority.

This result also mirrored the tensions beginning to emerge within Evangelicalism during the late 1950s and early 1960s. The one thing that early new-evangelical reformers of Fundamentalism had insisted on was that a strong commitment to biblical inerrancy was essential to authentic Christian faith. That assertion was challenged by a growing number of self-identified evangelical theologians during the 1960s, especially those connected with Fuller Theological Seminary in Pasadena, CA. Like the Aurora theologians within the Advent Christian Church, the Fuller theologians were attempting to argue that one could be evangelical and faithful to the Bible as the Word of God, and not necessarily accept the notion of biblical inerrancy. Like those same Aurora theologians whose views represented a minority opinion within the Advent Christian Church, the Fuller theologians represented a distinct minority view within the larger evangelical coalition. Both the Advent Christian Church and the larger new-evangelical movement faced the problem of what to do with those who embraced this minority view in regard to the inspiration of Scripture. It is an issue that continues to invite discussion and debate among evangelicals in the twenty-first century.

While the Advent Christian controversy mirrored this growing tension within Evangelicalism, it reflected something unique to Christian denominations born out of the restorationist impulse of the second Great Awakening. As a broad theological and religious movement, Restorationism involved several important principles. Two of those principles are especially relevant to our discussion. First, the notion of "no creed but the Bible" reflects not only a commitment to scripture as the final authority for Christian theology and practice but an almost total rejection of tradition as an important source of Christian reflection. Second, within the democratic-congregationalism of Restorationism was an ingrained notion that individual Christians were ultimately free and responsible for determining their own beliefs. It was these two principles—the final authority of Scripture and the freedom of individuals to determine their Christian beliefs for themselves—came directly into conflict with each other at Montreat.[22] No

22. Oral Collins expressed well the tension and conflict between these two restorationist ideals in my interview with him. "I believe very strongly my view of Scripture—in the inerrancy of Scripture," in Collins's words. "But I think within Advent Christendom, many of us grew up with the conviction that Adventism is capable of considerable

matter how vital the issue, the majority of Advent Christians was reticent to act in a way that might restrict the individual freedom of fellow Advent Christians to follow the dictates of conscience.[23]

Confessional Presbyterians in the 1920s found it difficult, if not impossible, to maintain theological cohesion on the inspiration and inerrancy of Scripture, even with established confessions and creeds. In a denomination or association with a historic aversion to creeds and confessions of faith, that task was even more difficult. That Advent Christians were able to forge a widely-accepted compromise that not only strengthened their position on Scripture but averted a split within their ranks is evidence of good will and Christian grace exhibited by people on both sides of the issue. Still, churches with a strong restorationist heritage like the Advent Christian Church need to recognize and address the different understandings of the role and function of the Bible in the life of the church between their restorationist forebears and the early Protestant reformers. Restorationism represented the rejection of hierarchy in both church and society and its replacement with a democratic, equalitarian approach. The task of interpreting Scripture was not to be left to the clergy nor to the church. Instead, it was the task of each individual to determine for himself, independently of others, what the Bible taught and how it applied to life. Since 1964, there is evidence that at least some Advent Christians are becoming more self-critical of this aspect of their tradition. [24]

Addressing the theological impact of the Advent Christian controversy over the Bible's inspiration involves one more important component—the current views of Advent Christian pastors regarding the issue. During the last thirty years, the willingness of Advent Christian clergy to link the inspiration of Holy Scripture to at least some form of biblical inerrancy appears to have increased.[25] Several factors lie behind this trend, including

diversity. We could still have fellowship and believe in the genuineness of the faith of fellow Adventists even though we might feel their theology was defective." See Oral History Interview, Oral Collins, October 15, 1995.

23. The restorationist tendency to minimize the value of church tradition is still reflected by a sizable number of Advent Christian clergy.

24. For evidence of some rethinking surrounding this issue, see Mayer, "An Account of the Advent Christian Controversy," Appendix Five. Responses to the third question indicated that a slight majority of the Advent Christian clergy surveyed (thirty out of fifty-six) see church tradition as a higher source of authority for Christian theology and ethics than either human reason or human tradition.

25. Ibid. Of the fifty-six clergy who responded to the survey, fifty-one linked the inspiration of Holy Scripture with biblical inerrancy in one of two forms. That includes

the greater role played by Berkshire Christian College in the training of Advent Christian pastors between 1965 and 1985 as well as the tendency of Aurora College graduates that remained with the Advent Christian Church after graduation to integrate a more conservative theological posture into their biblical studies and into their ministries.[26] Would this tendency for Advent Christian clergy to gravitate toward a theologically conservative posture have taken place if the controversy had not happened? That is difficult to answer, although those who identified with the NEST/Berkshire party would surely answer in the negative.[27]

Theology for the People of God

Christians from different denominational and theological perspectives, especially those who work in non-creedal and non-connectional contexts, can learn valuable lessons from these events. Major theological differences continue to exist today, especially within the coalition that comprises contemporary Evangelicalism. Those differences need to be addressed, not by caricatures of opposing views and their proponents, but by the practice of sustained, patient, and constructive interaction and dialogue. Dialogue does not mean surrendering our theological convictions. Nor does it mean pretending that real, substantive, and honest differences do not exist between the participating parties. It does mean a willingness to test our viewpoints and convictions, and a desire to understand the convictions of those

---

sixteen of the twenty Aurora College graduates surveyed.

26. Oral History Interview, Louia Gransee, 3 June 1995, 6–7. The views of Louia Gransee, an Aurora College graduate with over forty years of service in Advent Christian pulpits illustrate this well. "I'll tell you," according to Dr. Gransee, "where I had to wrestle with this [the issue of inspiration]—when I taught membership classes for people who were joining the church. I'd take them through some of these things—our view of scripture, and why the scriptures are important to us and so forth. And in that process I articulate for them my position.

"I believe that the scriptures were inspired by God through men who were extremely sensitive to what was happening in the world around them and who were able to discern in the events of human history the hand of God at work.

"I think that sensitivity itself was inspired by the Holy Spirit working in and through these people so they were able to take out of . . . life itself, history, if you please, and bring together those events that are revealed truth, period. And that truth is true for all time. Therefore, the principles of scripture are true no matter what."

27. Oral History Interview, Harold R. Patterson, November 21, 1996, 11. "I felt then," according to Rev. Patterson, "and I still feel now, that we saved the denomination from a liberal-leaning position."

who see matters differently.[28] This type of honest dialogue gives Christians an opportunity to practice one of the Apostle Paul's marks of Christian maturity, the ability to "speak the truth in love."[29]

This type of interaction and dialogue presupposes something else that evangelicals, mainline Protestants, and those who trace their Christian heritage from some aspect of the Adventist tradition must grasp as we begin the third millennium. Christian theology grounded in the teaching of Holy Scripture is essential to the health and life of Christian churches in the years to come. Scores of writers have discussed and will continue to discuss the impact of a host of trends and movements both on church and society. Their analyses often come down to this: Because of increasing intellectual and sociological pluralism, it is much harder for any Christian community to maintain a clear, cohesive expression of Christian faith grounded in Scripture and framed by tradition. This may be true, but it is no reason to shy away from the task. The core of Christian faith rests in the theological assertion that despite our sinful condition and alienation from God, he has expressed his mercy and grace to us in and through the person of Jesus Christ. Holy Scripture throughout its pages testifies to that.[30] When Christian churches minimize the value and importance of Christian theology, they risk allowing personal and cultural preferences, as opposed to the biblical core of Christian faith, to determine the agenda of the church.

Some Advent Christian leaders in the late 1950s and early 1960s on both sides of the debates discussed here were fearful that open, frank, and honest discussion about theological issues and differences would hopelessly divide the denomination. That is always a risk. But the long-term danger of minimizing or covering over theological and organizational differences is even greater. That strategy results in the marginalization of Christian theology within the life of the church and the danger of the church's mission being compromised or subverted by various cultural agendas. The challenge for Christians is an ongoing one. We are called to articulate Christian theology and praxis that are faithful to the Lordship of Jesus Christ as revealed in

---

28. For an excellent understanding and example of dialogue, see, Klenicki and Neuhaus, *Believing Today*. This writer draws on Klenicki and Neuhaus for his understanding of how dialogue and conversation over substantial theological issues should take place.

29. Eph 4:15.

30. See John 5:39–40.

Holy Scripture. At the same time, we are challenged to do that in a church and society that is geographically, ethnically, and culturally diverse.[31]

Good Christian theology requires a biblically grounded expression of the Lordship of Jesus Christ, faithfulness to good interpretation and teaching of Scripture, and a willingness to allow full participation by all followers of Jesus Christ. It also requires that Christian theologians learn to communicate their work in language that all of God's people, no matter what their intellectual ability, cultural background, or economic status, can understand, benefit from, and apply. The audience of Christian theology is not ultimately the academy, but the church.[32] Theology can and should address academically-oriented issues, but Christian theologians must recognize that their primary audience is the church of Jesus Christ.[33] In addition, churches must attend to the importance of Christian theology and challenge all of God's people to this task.

One final observation. Throughout this work, this writer has labored to demonstrate that the Advent Christian conflict over the Bible's inspiration has deep roots in the history of Adventism and the Advent Christian Church. In the years to come, Advent Christians (and Christians from all traditions) must come to terms with their own history, both in terms of strengths and weaknesses. For those who are part of this small denomination, those questions include the following: What led the Advent Christian Church in the space of one generation to essentially reject the Calvinism of William Miller in favor of a theological approach centered in human free will? What led to the embrace of materialistic views of human nature by many Advent Christians in the late nineteenth century, views that were shared by followers of Charles Darwin and other scientific materialists? How did the Advent Christian church develop a paradoxical understanding

31. The writer of the Book of Revelation reminds us that God's kingdom is and will be made up of people "from every tribe and language and people and nation" (Rev 5:9).

32. In this writer's view, this is something with which the Aurora theologians struggled. In their desire to communicate in a way that demonstrated intellectual integrity to their academic peers, with the exception of Clarence Hewitt [who in his 1942 book, *Faith for Today*, sought specifically to address all Advent Christians], they did not do as good a job in articulating their conclusions and concerns to the churches they felt called to serve.

33. Grenz and Olson, *Who Needs Theology*, 22–35. In commenting on the task of professional theologians, Grenz and Olson write, "At its best professional theology functions in a servant role and not a lordly role. That is, the professional theologian serves the Christian community by helping people to think like Christ so that they can be more effective in witness, work, and service both in the church and in the world."

of the role and function of Christian doctrine—an understanding that allowed great latitude of belief while at the same time attempting to define the denomination in terms of theologically distinctive beliefs? Exploring questions like these will help Advent Christians and Christians from a variety of denominational persuasions understand the theological strengths and weaknesses of their denominational histories and traditions, as well as help them articulate their Christian faith in ways that are faithful to the gospel of Jesus Christ as expressed in Holy Scripture. Hopefully, this study will make a contribution to that worthy goal.

William Miller's Fourteen Rules of Interpretation[1]

1. Every word must have its proper bearing on the subject presented in the Bible.

2. All scripture is necessary, and may be understood by a diligent application and study.

3. Nothing revealed in the scripture can or will be hid from those who ask in faith, not wavering.

4. To understand doctrine, bring all the scriptures together on the subject you wish to know, then let every word have its proper influence, and if you can form your theory without a contradiction, you can not be in error.

5. Scripture must be its own expositor, since it is a rule of itself. If I depend on a teacher to expound it to me, and he should guess at its meaning, or desire to have it so on account of his sectarian creed, or to be thought wise, gives me his wisdom, then his <u>guessing</u>, <u>desire</u>, <u>creed</u>, or <u>wisdom</u>, is my rule, not the Bible.

6. God has revealed things to come by visions, in figures and parables, and in this way the same things are often-time revealed again and

---

1. Banks, "Rise and Growth."

again, by different visions, or in different figures, and parables. If you wish to understand them then you must combine them all in one.

7. Visions are always mentioned as such.

8. Figures always have a figurative meaning, and are used much in prophecy, to represent future things, times and events, such as <u>mountains</u> meaning <u>governments</u>, <u>beasts</u> meaning <u>kingdoms</u>.

9. Parables are used as comparisons to illustrate subjects, and must be explained in the same way as figures by the subject and Bible . . .

10. Figures sometimes have two or more different significations, as day is used in a figurative sense to represent three different periods of time. 1. Indefinite, 2. Definite, a day for a year, 3. Day for a thousand years. If you put on the right construction it will harmonize with the Bible and make good sense, otherwise it will not.

11. How to know when a word is used figuratively. If it makes good sense as it stands, and does no violence to the simple laws of nature, then it must be understood literally, if not figuratively.

12. To learn the true meaning of figures, trace your figurative word through your Bible, and where you find it explained, put it on your figure, and if it makes good sense, you need look no further, if not, look again.

13. To know whether we have the true historical event, for the fulfillment of a prophecy. If you find every word of the prophecy (after the figures are understood is literally fulfilled), then you may know that your history is the true event. But if one word lacks a fulfillment, then we must look for another event, or wait its future development. For God takes care that history and prophecy doth agree, so that the true believing children of God may never be ashamed.

14. The most important rule of all is, that you must have <u>faith</u>. It must be a faith that requires a sacrifice, and, if tried, would give up the dearest object on earth, the world and all its desires, character, living, occupation, friends, home, comforts, and worldly honors. If any of these should hinder our believing any part of God's word, it would show our faith to be in vain.

The 1881 Advent Christian Declaration of Principles[1]

1. We believe that the Scriptures, consisting of the Old and New Testament, contain the only divine system of religious faith.

2. We believe the Bible teaches that there is one God, eternal, almighty, the Father and Creator of all things.

3. We believe the Bible teaches that there is one Lord Jesus Christ, the only begotten Son of God, having glory with the Father before the world was; who died and was buried, and rose again the third day, according to the Scriptures, and ascended to heaven, there to appear in the presence of God for us, from whence he will return to judge the quick and the dead at his appearing and his kingdom.

4. We believe the Bible record of the Holy Spirit, sent as the Comforter to the church, and to convince the world of sin, and of righteousness, and of judgment.

5. We believe the Bible record of the creation of man, and that by disobedience to the divine law he fell from the state of uprightness in which he was created and involved himself and his posterity in death, the penalty of the violated law, which death would have been eternal without a Redeemer: that such Redeemer was provided by God in the person of his Son Jesus Christ, who died on the cross that he might

1. Ibid.

become the author of eternal salvation to all who obey him;—that this redemption is of a two-fold nature; first, the redemption of all men from the penalty of Adam's sin, by the resurrection of the dead; second, the redemption of believers from personal sin and its consequences by the blood of Jesus Christ, as it is written, 'In whom we have redemption through his blood, even the forgiveness of sins', and the gift to them of eternal life, possessing which they shall not be hurt of the second death.

6. We believe in repentance toward God and faith in the Lord Jesus Christ as essential to eternal salvation.

7. We believe the Bible teaches that pardoned sinners should be 'buried with Christ in baptism', this showing their faith in his resurrection and in the resurrection of the dead.

8. We believe in the observance of the Lord's Supper in accordance with the commandment of Christ, thereby showing faith in the Lord's death till he comes.

9. We believe that the Scriptures teach that this same Jesus, who was born in Bethlehem, crucified, buried, and rose again the third day according to the Scriptures, and ascended to heaven, will return personally to this world to raise, judge and reward or punish all the human race.

10. We believe the Bible teaches that the finally impenitent shall be punished with everlasting destruction from the presence of the Lord and from the glory of his power; and in the final extinction of all evil.

11. We believe that the fulfillment of the prophetic Scriptures, embracing the physical, moral, political and financial signs of the times, indicate that the return of the Saviour is near, even at the door and that the time has arrived when the subject should be made prominent by all preachers of the gospel.

12. We believe that this earth will share in the final redemption of men, and will become the eternal home of the redeemed, called in the Holy Scriptures the kingdom of God,— "a new heavens and a new earth wherein dwelleth righteousness."

13. We believe that the entire action of the Church, in council, in missionary labor, in public instruction, social worship, and communion, should be with direct reference to the crowning event, viz., the personal coming of our Lord Jesus Christ.

14. We believe the Bible teaches that Christ is the Head of the church; and that all his disciples are but one body united in Christian love; and that Christian fellowship may exist where there are doctrinal diversities occasioned by lack of light on the points of difference.

15. We believe the Bible teaches that the true standard of Christian fellowship is such as to include all of Christ's disciples; and that the presence of the Holy Spirit is essential in order to secure true and permanent union.

16. We believe the Bible teaches that the churches of Christ should be duly organized by the election of proper officers, such as elders and deacons, and that the government of the church should be congregational.

The 1900 Advent Christian Declaration of Principles [1]

I. Article I: We believe that the Bible is the Word of God containing a revelation given to man under Divine supervision and providence; that its historic statements are correct, and that it is the only Divine standard of faith and practice. 2 Peter 1:21. 2 Tim 3:16.

II. Article II: We believe, as revealed in the Bible—

(a) In one God, our Father, eternal, and infinite in His wisdom, love and power, the Creator of all things, 'in whom we live, and move, and have our being.' Gen. 1:1. 1 Kings 8:27. Deut 4:39. Acts 17:28.

(b) And in Jesus Christ, our Lord, the only begotten Son of God; who came into our world to seek and save that which was lost; who died for our sins, who was raised from the dead for our justification; who ascended into heaven as our High Priest and Mediator, and who will come again in the end of this age, to judge the living and the dead, and reign forever and ever.

John 1:14; 3:16, 17. 1 John 4:9. Rom 4:25. Heb 7:26; 4:14. 2 Tim 4:1. Matt 13:39, 40.

(c) And in the Holy Spirit, the Comforter, sent from God to convince the world of sin, of righteousness and of judgment, whereby

1. Ibid.

we are sanctified and sealed unto the day of redemption. John 17:16, 17; 16:7–11. 2 Thess 2:13. Eph 4:30.

III. Article III: We believe that man was created for immortality, but that through sin he forfeited his Divine birthright; that because of sin, death entered into the world, and passed upon all men; and that only through faith in Jesus Christ, the divinely ordained Life-giver, can men become 'partakers of the divine nature', and live forever. Gen.3:22–24. Rom 5:12. Acts 4:12. 2 Peter 1:4.

IV. Article IV: We believe that death is a condition of unconsciousness to all persons, righteous and wicked; a condition which will remain unchanged until the resurrection at Christ's second coming, at which time the righteous will receive everlasting life while the wicked will be 'punished with everlasting destruction'; suffering complete extinction of being. Eccl 9:10. Ps 115:117. 1 Thess 4:13–17. Matt 25:46.

V. Article V: We believe that salvation is free to all those who, in this life and in this age, accept it on the conditions imposed, which conditions are simple and inflexible; namely, turning from sin, repentance to-ward God, faith in the Lord Jesus Christ, and a life of consecration to the service of God; thus excluding all hope of a future probation, or of universal salvation. 2 Cor 6:2. Acts 2:38. Rom 10: 8–10. Titus 2:11–14.

VI. Article VI: We believe that Jesus Christ, according to His promise, will come again to this earth, even 'in like manner' as He went into heav-en—personally, visibly and gloriously— to reign here forever; and that this coming is the hope of the Church, inasmuch as upon that coming depends the resurrection and reward of the righteous, the abolition of sin and its consequences, and the renewal of the earth—now marred by sin—to become the eternal home of the redeemed, after which event the earth will be forever free from sin and death. Acts 1:11. 1 Thess 4:16. Dan 7:13–14. Rom 8:18–23. Dan 2:44. 2 Pet 3:13.

VII. Article VII: We believe that Bible prophecy has indicated the approxi-mate time of Christ's return; and comparing its testimony with the signs of our times, we are confident that He is near, 'even at the doors', and we believe that the great duty of the hour is the proclamation of this soon coming redemption, the defense of Bible authority, inspira-tion and truth and the salvation of lost man. Matt 24:32, 33, 45–47.

VIII. Article VIII: We believe the Church of Christ is an institution of Divine origin, which includes all true Christians, of whatever name; but that local Church organizations should be independent of outside control, congregational in government, and subject to no dictation of priest, bishop or pope—although true fellowship and unity of action should exist between all such organizations. Matt 16:18. 1 Cor 12;12, 13.

IX. Article IX: We believe the only ordinances of the Church of Christ are Baptism and the Lord's Supper; immersion being the only true baptism. Rom 6:4. Acts 8:38. Matt 26:26–29. 1 Cor 11:23, 24.

X. Article X: We believe that the first day of the week, as the day set apart by the early Church in commemoration of Christ's resurrection, should be observed as the Christian Sabbath, and used as a day of rest and religious worship. Acts 20:7. John 20:19. 1 Cor 16:2.

Advent Christian
Curriculum Materials

Recommendation Adopted by the Eastern Regional
Advent Christian Association
October 23–24, 1963[1]

THIS DOCUMENT WAS PREPARED by Executive Secretary J. Howard Shaw for all members of the Advisory Council of the Advent Christian General Conference in preparation for meetings held in conjunction with the 1964 Advent Christian General Conference convention in Montreat, NC. No date is given on the document. Following the document, the author has listed the two revisions to Item 12 of the 1963 Eastern Region Condensed Minutes as approved by a special meeting of the Eastern Regional Association at Somerville, Massachusetts on May 27, 1964.

****

At its annual convention last October 23–24, 1963, the delegate body of the Eastern Regional Advent Christian Association passed a recommendation pertaining to current Sunday School Curriculum materials as produced under our Board of Christian Education. This recommendation calls for certain basic changes in our approach to the production of curriculum materials and was preceded by a statement of the current situation as

---

1. "Advent Christian Curriculum Materials, Recommendation Adopted by the Eastern Regional Advent Christian Association."

understood by members of the Business Committee of the Convention. The Business Committee made certain unqualified allegations of a derogatory nature concerning present curriculum material, as will be seen from the ensuing excerpt from the Condensed Minutes. Copies of these Condensed Minutes were sent to every church in the Eastern Region, so that these allegations are conveyed to the churches as a statement of fact.

Since the President of the Eastern Region is required by the action to present the recommendations to the Advisory Council, the Executive Committee, and the Business Committee of the 1964 Session of General Conference, it seems essential that members of these bodies be acquainted in advance with the full record of the action.

Item 12 of the Condensed Minutes of the Eastern Regional Convention is as follows:

These are critical days for the Christian faith in America and for the Advent Christian Denomination. The propaganda of false ideas and values threaten our youth with gross materialism and moral compromise. In times like these the Advent Christian Church needs the strongest possible program of Christian Education for its youth. The Biblical message of the priority of spiritual values, the facts of creation and providence, the necessity of purity and godliness, and centrality of Jesus Christ needs strong and affirmative emphasis.

The curriculum material published by the Advent Christian denomination is at points humanistic and lacking in its presentation of a positive evangelical image, and is pupil-centered in its approach, following the patterns of progressive education.

Curriculum outlines now employed in Advent Christian Sunday School lessons are established under the sponsorship of the National Council of Churches, an organization dominated by churches which are liberal in their theology.

There is much repetition of material on consecutive Sundays, a lack of factual Bible content, and little or no emphasis on commitment to Christian principles of faith and practice.

Teachings are "watered down" and extremely weak in some areas pertaining to the Inspiration of the Scriptures as the words of God.

It is not always what is written but what is either inferred or omitted that causes alarm within our churches. For instance, in areas pertaining to the supernatural, positive statements are not made, but occasionally we are left to believe that natural causes explain away the miracles. We must not breed doubt to our pupils but confidence in the authority and infallibility of the Scriptures.

The Eastern Regional Association is concerned that Advent Christian Sunday School lessons should present a constructive alternative to the false ideas and values (whether religious or secular) of our age. We, therefore, request the Advent Christian Eastern Regional Association at its 1963 session to initiate procedures that will anticipate the adoption of the following by the Advent Christian General Conference at its 1964 session:

1. An immediate adoption of the lesson curriculum outlines of the National Association of Evangelicals, which is predominantly conservative.

2. Establish the requirement that the Board of Christian Education, the Director of Christian Education, the Curriculum Committee, and all writers for our Sunday School lessons must sign written statements annually subscribing to the belief that the Bible is free from error in its statements, that its words are the words that God intended even though written by men, and therefore the Biblical record of creation, history, and miracles, as well as theological teachings, are true and must be taught to our youth.

3. In the event that a sufficient number of qualified lesson writers can not be obtained, we urge that the Board of Christian Education edit and rewrite the Sunday School material of another publisher which is in harmony with the above statements. The first two publishers to be considered for this purpose should be Scripture Press and Gospel Light.

4. The action will be carried out by the President of the Eastern Regional Association by the method of his presenting the stated recommendations to the Advisory Council, the Executive Committee, and the Business Committee of the 1964 Advent Christian General Conference of America.

(End of Eastern Regional Resolution)

The following steps are being taken, to the knowledge of the Executive Secretary, to give this recommendation the careful and constructive attention which it requires prior to our forthcoming delegate session at Montreat:

1. The Executive Secretary discussed the action with the Eastern Region Board at a meeting of that body in November.

2. The Board of Christian Education is appointing special committees to (a) gather essential factual data pertaining to an objective consideration of the specific recommendations, and (b) make a thorough analysis of recent Sunday school lessons with reference to specific criticisms set forth in the minutes of the Eastern Regional Convention.

3. The Chairman of the Board of Christian Education has drawn up a "Statement of Clarification" addressed to "All Friends of Christian Education." His statement is positive and helpful in spirit and reflects a desire to fairly evaluate criticisms and recommendations with a view to improving curriculum materials.

4. The Eastern Regional Board, in a recent meeting with Conference Presidents, explored ways of proceeding in this matter in such a manner as to avoid unprofitable tensions and misunderstanding, but to bring about positive results. We can be assured that the desire of Eastern leadership is that this matter be considered at the national level in an atmosphere of objectivity, sound judgment and goodwill.

5. The Executive Secretary is beginning in "Advent Christian News" a series of discussions of "vital issues" likely to come before the delegates at Montreat, and he plans to acquaint our constituency with the recommendations in the above minutes, and the steps being taken to afford an objective and constructive consideration of them.

This report is being sent as a matter of information to the members of the Advisory Council (which includes the members of the Executive Committee) and the members of the Business Committee.

J. Howard Shaw, Executive Secretary
Advent Christian General Conference

Revision to Item 12 of the Condensed Minutes
of the 1963 Eastern Region Convention
Adopted: May 27, 1964

We recommend that article #1 of the Curriculum Proposals adopted at the annual convention in October, 1963 be rescinded, and that it be replaced with the following substitution:

1. That the Board of Christian Education take steps immediately to correct the Living Water series at the points of weakness delineated in the report of the Eastern Region Association Curriculum Study Committee. That the Board of Christian Education or a special committee established at the General Conference level study the feasibility of alternatives at all grade levels to the National Council of Churches Curriculum including possible arrangements to purchase the right to use Scripture Press outlines, Gospel Light outlines, or David C. Cook Thematic Graded Series outlines, and that the Board of Christian Education in consultation with the Executive Committee of General Conference then use such curriculum as they deem best until the matter can be determined by delegate body vote at the next General Conference session.

    It was voted that recommendation #2 under October, 1963 minutes . . . be amended by deleting all after "written statements annually" and adding "as found in the A.C. Catechism 'The Scriptures,' page 36." Then it was voted to further amend recommendation #2 by replacing "must sign" with "must subscribe to." A third amendment to recommendation #2 was passed by vote, adding "without reservation" after "subscribe to annually." The recommendation then reads as follows:

2. Establish the requirement that the Board of Christian Education, the Curriculum Committee, and all writers for our Sunday School lessons must subscribe to annually without reservation the statement as found in the A.C. Catechism entitled 'The Scriptures' on page 36.

Bibliography

Many primary source documents are on deposit in the Adventual Collection at Goddard Library, Gordon Conwell Theological Seminary, S. Hamilton, MA, and at the Advent Christian General Conference offices, Charlotte, NC.

"1964 [Advent Christian] General Conference Minutes."

A Brief History of William Miller. 1st ed. Boston: Advent Christian, 1895.

Adams, Ivan E., Robert C. Hewitt, and David A. Dean. *Advent Christian Catechism.* Concord, NH: Advent Christian, n.d.

"Advent Christian Curriculum Materials, Recommendation Adopted by the Eastern Regional Advent Christian Association, October 23–24, 1963."

Ahlstrom, Sidney E. *A Religious History of the American People.* New Haven, CT: Yale University Press, 1972.

Ainsworth, A. Cameron. Interview by the author, June 1, 1995.

Ainsworth, Ariel C. "The Potentiality of Our Present." *Advent Christian Witness,* July 1960, 3–4, 21.

Anderson, Charles W. *Building on the Foundation.* Aurora, IL: Aurora University Press, 1990.

———. *Upon a Rock: A History of the Founding Years of Aurora University.* Aurora, IL: Aurora University Press, 1987.

Andrews, J. Kenneth. "Liberal or Conservative." *Present Truth Messenger* 24 (1964) 2.

Arthur, David T. "Aurora College: Past and Present." Aurora College Curriculum Revision Document, 1972.

Axel, Larry E. "God or Man at Chicago: The 'Chicago School' of Theology with Special Reference to the Issue of Antecedents and to the Roles of G. B. Foster; E. S. Ames; and H. N. Wieman." PhD diss., Temple University, 1975.

Bailey, Craig. "The Various Theories of Inspiration of the Bible and Interpretation of Scripture Held within the Advent Christian Denomination from 1860 to 1964." Course paper, Aurora College, 1964.

Balser, Glennon C. Interview by the author, August 19, 1996.

Banks, Dwight S. "The Rise and Growth of the Advent Christian Denomination from the Point of View of Its Doctrinal Development." MST thesis, Gordon College of Theology and Missions, 1939.

Barth, Karl. *Church Dogmatics*. Vol. 1/2, *The Doctrine of the Word of God*. Edited by G. W. Bromiley and T. F. Torrance. Translated by G. T. Thomson and Harold Knight. Edinburgh: T. & T. Clark, 1956.

———. *Dogmatics in Outline*. New York: Harper & Row, 1959.

Barton, Freeman, ed. *Advent Christians and the Bible: Theological Discussion and Confessional Change in the Early 1960s*. Rev. ed. Lenox, MA: Henceforth, 1984.

——— *Mary Queen of Scots at Berkshire Christian College: Case Study in the Dissolution of a Christian College*. Lake Wales, FL: Society for Advent Christian Thought, 1987.

Barton, Freeman, ed. *Our Destiny We Know: Essays in Honor of Edwin K. Gedney*. Charlotte: Venture, 1996.

"The Basic Philosophy Underlying the Curriculum of Christian Education." June 1960 (date handwritten on document).

Bass, Clarence B. *Backgrounds to Dispensationalism: Its Historical Genesis and Ecclesiastical Implications*. Grand Rapids, MI: Baker, 1960.

Bebbington, David. *Patterns in History: A Christian Perspective on Historical Thought*. Vancouver, BC: Regent College, 1990.

Beecroft, Raymond M. "The Decision." *Advent Christian Witness*, July 1964, 2, 15.

Beecroft, Raymond M. Letter to Elwell M. Drew, n.d.

Beecroft, Raymond M. Letter to Members of the Board of Publications, April 30, 1964.

———. "Militant Fundamentalists." *Advent Christian Witness*, February 1957, 20.

———. Letter to Gerald F. Richardson, August 21, 1964.

———. Letter to J. Howard Shaw, August 22, 1963.

———. Letter to J. Howard Shaw, August 7 1964.

———. Letter to J. Howard Shaw and the Board of Publications, August 7 1964.

Berkhof, Louis. *Principles of Biblical Interpretation*. Grand Rapids, MI: Baker, 1950.

Blanchard, I. M. "The New Theology and the Personal God." *World's Crisis* 1 (1905) 1.

Bloesch, Donald G. *Holy Scripture: Revelation, Inspiration, and Interpretation*. Downers Grove, IL: InterVarsity, 1994.

Board of Christian Education, Advent Christian General Conference. Minutes of Meetings Held During the 1960 General Conference at Aurora College.

Board of Christian Education, Advent Christian General Conference, Montreat, NC, June 16–25, 1964.

Boston, Leonard L. "Letters to the PTM Editor." *Present Truth Messenger*, 16 April 1964, 2.

Bradley, Sidney. Interview by the author. March 13, 1996.

Bromiley, Geoffrey W. *An Introduction to the Theology of Karl Barth*. Grand Rapids, MI: Eerdmans, 1979.

Bromiley, Geoffrey W., ed. *Karl Barth, Rudolf Bultmann: Letters 1922–1966*. Grand Rapids, MI: Eerdmans, 1981.

Bultmann, Rudolf. *New Testament and Mythology and Other Basic Writings*. Selected, edited, and translated by Schubert M. Ogden. Philadelphia: Fortress, 1984.

Bunker, Frank H., "Letters to the PTM Editor." *Present Truth Messenger*, June 7, 1962, 11.

"Can We Fellowship with One Another." *Our Hope and Life in Christ*, August 2, 1922, 8.

Carnell, Edward John. *The Case for Orthodox Theology*. Philadelphia: Westminster, 1959.

————. Review of *The Case for a New Reformation Theology*, by William Hordern; *The Case for Theology in a Liberal Perspective*, by L. Harold DeWolf. *Journal of Bible and Religion* 18 (1959) 319.

————. Letter to Harold John Ockenga, March 8 1953.

————. Letter to Harold John Ockenga, February 12 1954.

————. Letter to Harold John Ockenga, November 24 1958.

Carpenter, Joel A., ed. *A New Evangelical Coalition: Early Documents of the National Association of Evangelicals*. New York: Garland, 1988.

Carter, Linden J. "One Hundred Per Cent Advent Christian." *Advent Christian Witness*, June 1958, 5-6.

Colby, Asa. J. Interview by the author. October 19, 1995.

Collins, Oral E. Interview by the author. October 15, 1995.

Collins, Ora. Letter to Robert Mayer, January 8, 1997.

————. Letter to Robert Mayer, February 14, 1997.

————. Letter to Robert Mayer, February 15, 1997.

————. Letter to Robert Mayer, February 17, 1997.

Conference of the Board of Education, Aurora College, Berkshire Christian College, Cleveland, Ohio, March 23-25, 1962.

Craig, Robert. "Edwin Kemble Gedney." In *Our Destiny We Know: Essays in Honor of Edwin K. Gedney*, edited by Freeman Barton, 1–24. Charlotte, NC: Venture, 1996.

Crouse, Dorothy H. Interview by the author. May 13, 1995.

Crouse, Ear. Letter to Elwell Drew, December 17, 1963.

Crouse, J. H. "An Expression of the Forward Movement." *Our Hope and Life in Christ* 24 (1922) 7–8.

Crouse, Moses C. "The Atonement." Unpublished paper delivered at the Conference of the Board of Education, Aurora College, and Berkshire Christian College, Cleveland, Ohio, 23–25 March 1962.

————. "A Comparison and Contrast of the Philosophies of History as Developed by Herbert George Wood and Paul Tillich." MA thesis, Northwestern University, 1947.

————. "Higher Criticism." Unpublished paper delivered at the Conference of the Board of Education, Aurora College, and Berkshire Christian College, Cleveland, Ohio, 23–25 March 1962.

————. "Inspiration." Unpublished paper delivered at the Conference of the Board of Education, Aurora College, and Berkshire Christian College at Cleveland, Ohio, 23–25 March 1962.

————. *Modern Discussions of Man's Immortality*. Concord, NH: Advent Christian, 1960.

————. "Our Prophetic Heritage." Unpublished paper delivered at the Conference of the Board of Education, Aurora College, and Berkshire Christian College at Cleveland, Ohio, 23–25 March 1962.

————. "The Sufficiency of the Holy Spirit." *Present Truth Messenger*, May 28, 1964, 4, 13; June 4, 1964, 4, 9.

Crouse, Moses C., and Dorothy H. Crouse. "A Starting Point." Unpublished manuscript from the collection of Mrs. Dorothy Crouse, 1962.

Crouse, Sally. "Psychopannychism: A Study of the Doctrine of the Sleep of the Dead during the Sixteenth Century." *Henceforth* 18, no. 1 (1990) 40–64.

Cullmann, Oscar. *Christ and Time: The Primitive Christian Conception of Time and History*. Philadelphia: Westminster, 1950.

———. *Salvation in History*. London: SCM, 1967.

Dayton, Donald, and Robert K. Johnston, eds. *The Variety of American Evangelicalism*. Downers Grove, IL: InterVarsity, 1991.

Dean, David A. "Echoes of the Midnight Cry: The Millerite Heritage in the Apologetics of the Advent Christian Denomination, 1860–1960." ThD diss., Westminster Theological Seminary, 1976.

———. "The Great Disappointment: No Words Can Express the Feeling" *Advent Christian Witness*, October 1994, 6.

———. "Is the Bible the Inspired Word of God?" *Advent Christian Witness*, March 1964, 12–14.

———. *Resurrection Hope*. Charlotte, NC: Venture, 1992.

———. Letter to Robert Mayer, February 12, 1997.

———., *Who Will Go For Us: People and Passion in Advent Christian World Missions 1860–2000*, Charlotte, NC: Venture, 2005.

Dean, David A. Phone interview by the author, December 4, 1996.

Dean, David A., and Freeman Barton. Interview by the author, August 4, 1994.

Dean, David E. "The Forward Movement of the Advent Christian Denomination, 1920–1932." *Henceforth* 9, no. 1 (1980) 11–29.

Dennis, Lane T., ed. *Letters of Francis A. Schaeffer*. Westchester, IL: Crossway, 1985.

Dockery, David S., ed. *Southern Baptists and American Evangelicals*. Nashville: Broadman and Holman, 1993.

Dodd, C. H. *The Apostolic Preaching and Its Developments*. New York: Harper & Row, 1964.

Dyrness, William. *How Does America Hear the Gospel?* Grand Rapids, MI: Eerdmans, 1990.

Eagen, I. C. "The Church of Christ." *World's Crisis* 3 (1922) 8–9.

"Editorial Notes on the Robert Mayer Oral History Interview with Dr. Oral Collins, October 15, 1995."

Eliot, Charles. *Educational Reform: Essays and Addresses*. New York: Century, 1909.

Erdman, Charles. *The Spirit of Christ: Devotional Studies in the Doctrine of the Holy Spirit*. New York: Doran, 1926.

Advent Christian General Conference. "Executive Committee Minutes," June 21–26, 1963.

Advent Christian General Conference. "Executive Committee Minutes," June 15–26, 1964.

Fillinger, Robert E. "Berkshire Christian College: Its Development and Influence in the Advent Christian Church." MRE thesis, Gordon Divinity School, 1965.

"Financial Crisis Hits Berkshire Christian College." *Advent Christian News*, January 7, 1983, 1.

Fountain, Charles Hillman. "The Case against Dr. Fosdick: A Reply to the Report of the Committee of the New York Presbytery Which Exonerated Him of the Charge of Teaching Doctrines Contrary to the Bible and the Westminster Confession of Faith." Plainfield, New Jersey, 1924.

Frame, John M. *Cornelius VanTil: An Analysis of His Thought*. Philipsburg, NJ: Presbyterian and Reformed, 1995.

Fudge, Edward W. *The Fire That Consumes*. Carlisle, UK: Paternoster, 1994.

Fuller, Donald, and Richard Gardiner. "Reformed Theology at Princeton and Amsterdam in the Late Nineteenth Century: A Reappraisal." *Presbyterion* 21, no. 2 (1995) 89–117.

Gaustad, Edwin S. *Neither King nor Prelate: Religion and the New Nation, 1776–1826.* Grand Rapids, MI: Eerdmans, 1993.

Gedney, Edwin K. "The Advent Christian Imperative." *Advent Christian Witness,* October 1960, 3, 13.

Grant, Miles. *Positive Theology, as Proved by the Eternal Principles of Pure Reason, Facts of Science, Metaphysics, Common Sense and the Bible.* Boston: Published by the Author, 1895.

Grant, Robert M., with David Tracy. *A Short History of the Interpretation of the Bible.* Philadelphia: Fortress, 1984.

Gransee, Louia R. Letter to Elwell Drew, December 17, 1963.

Gransee, Louia R. Interview by the author, June 3, 1995.

Grenz, Stanley J., and Olson, Roger E. *Who Needs Theology: An Invitation to the Study of God.* Downers Grove, IL: InterVarsity, 1996.

Griswold, Roland E. Interview by the author, August 3, 1996.

Griswold, Roland E. Letter to Board of Christian Education, September 9, 1963.

———. Letter to Elwell M. Drew, September 12, 1963.

———. Letter to Esther Reed, September 12, 1963.

Hamilton, Michael S. "The Dissatisfaction of Francis Schaeffer." *Christianity Today* 41, no. 3 (1997) 22–30.

Hatch, Nathan O. *The Democratization of American Christianity.* New Haven, CT: Yale University Press, 1989.

Henry, Carl F. H. *Confessions of a Theologian.* Waco, TX: Word, 1986.

———. *Evangelicals in Search of Identity.* Waco, TX: Word, 1976.

———. *The Uneasy Conscience of Modern Fundamentalism.* Grand Rapids, MI: Eerdmans, 1947.

Herberg, Will. *Protestant, Catholic, Jew: An Essay in American Religious Sociology.* Garden City, NY: Doubleday, 1955.

Hewitt, Clarence H. *The Conditional Principle in Theology.* Boston: C. & R. Hewitt, 1954.

———. *Faith for Today.* Boston: Advent Christian, 1942.

———. *What Does the Future Hold.* Charlotte, NC: Advent Christian, n.d.

Hewitt, Clyde E. *Devotion and Development.* Charlotte, NC: Venture, 1991.

———. *Midnight and Morning: An Account of the Adventist Awakening and the Founding of the Advent Christian Denomination, 1831-1860.* Charlotte, NC: Venture, 1983.

———. *Responsibility and Response.* Charlotte, NC: Venture, 1987.

Hodge, A. A., and Benjamin B. Warfield. *Inspiration.* 1881. Repr., Grand Rapids, MI: Baker, 1979.

Hodge, Charles. *Systematic Theology,* Vol. 1. New York: Scribners, 1872.

Horne, Thomas B. "How Do Advent Christians See Themselves?" *Present Truth Messenger,* 11 June 1964, 2, 15.

Hughes, P. E. *Creative Minds in Contemporary Theology.* Grand Rapids, MI: Eerdmans, 1966.

Hutchison, William R. *American Protestant Thought in the Liberal Era.* Lanham, MD: University Press of America, 1968.

———. *The Modernist Impulse in American Protestantism.* Cambridge, MA: Harvard University Press, 1976.

Jenks, Orrin R. "The Aurora Tragedy." *Our Hope and Life in Christ*, September 27, 1922, 15.

———. *The Last Prophets of Israel*. Mendota, IL: Our Hope, 1909.

———. *The Life and Times of Amos and Isaiah*. Mendota, IL: Our Hope, n.d.

Johnson, Albert C. *Advent Christian History*. Boston: Advent Christian, 1918.

Johnson, Donna. Letter to Elwell Drew, January 26, 1964.

Johnson, Paul. *Modern Times: From the Twenties to the Nineties*. New York: HarperCollins, 1991.

Klenicki, Leon, and Richard John Neuhaus. *Believing Today: Jew and Christian in Conversation*. Grand Rapids, MI: Eerdmans, 1989.

Knight, George R. *Millennial Fever and the End of the World: A Study of Millerite Adventism*. Boise: Pacific , 1993.

Kuklick, Bruce. *Science and Religion in America*. New Haven, CT: Yale University Press, 1985.

Ladd, George Eldon. *A Theology of the New Testament*. Grand Rapids, MI: Eerdmans, 1974.

Land, Gary, ed. *Adventism in America: A History*. Grand Rapids, MI: Eerdmans, 1986.

Lindsell, Harold. *The Battle for the Bible*. Grand Rapids, MI: Zondervan, 1976.

Longfield, Bradley J. *The Presbyterian Controversy: Fundamentalists, Modernists, and Moderates*. New York: Oxford University Press, 1991.

Macartney, Clarence Edward. *Shall Unbelief Win? A Reply to Dr. Fosdick*, Philadelphia: Hanf, n.d.

Machen, John Gresham. *Christianity and Liberalism*. Grand Rapids, MI: Eerdmans, 1946.

Marsden, George M. *Fundamentalism and American Culture: The Shaping of Twentieth-Century Evangelicalism, 1870–1925*. New York: Oxford University Press, 1980.

———. *Reforming Fundamentalism: Fuller Seminary and the New Evangelicalism*. Grand Rapids, MI: Eerdmans, 1987.

———. *The Soul of the American University: From Protestant Establishment to Establishment Unbelief*. New York: Oxford University Press, 1994.

———. *Understanding Fundamentalism and Evangelicalism*. Grand Rapids, MI: Eerdmans, 1991.

Marty, Martin E. *Modern American Religion*. Vol. 3, *Under God Indivisible, 1941–1960*. Chicago: University of Chicago Press, 1996.

Matthews, Arthur H. *Standing Up, Standing Together: The Emergence of the National Association of Evangelicals*. Carol Stream, IL: National Association of Evangelicals, 1992.

Mayer, Robert J. *An Account of the Advent Christian Controversy over the Bible's Inspiration, 1956–1964*. DMin diss., Gordon-Conwell Theological Seminary, 1997.

———. Letter to Oral Collins, February 15, 1997.

McAfee Brown, Robert, ed. *The Essential Reinhold Niebuhr: Selected Essays and Addresses*. New Haven, CT: Yale University Press, 1986.

McCarthy, David S. Interview by the author, November 24, 1995.

McCarthy, David S. "Living Water." Unpublished paper, June 1964.

———. Letter to Louia Gransee, December 7, 1963.

McGrath, Alister. *Christian Theology: An Introduction*. 2nd ed. Oxford: Blackwell, 1996.

———. *The Christian Theology Reader*. Oxford: Blackwell, 1995.

Melvin, Nelson. Interview by the author. October 24, 1994.

Melvin, Nelson. Letter to Esther Reed, June 1, 1966.

Members of the Faculty of Berkshire Christian College. "Higher Criticism." Unpublished paper delivered at the Conference of the Board of Education, Aurora College, and Berkshire Christian College at Cleveland, Ohio, March 23–25, 1962.

———. "The Inspiration of the Bible." Unpublished paper delivered at the Conference of the Board of Education, Aurora College, and Berkshire Christian College at Cleveland, Ohio, March 23–25, 1962.

Merrill, Eugene H. "Advent Christians and the Word of God." *Present Truth Messenger*, April 9, 1964, 4, 8; April 16, 1964, 4; April 23, 1964, 5; April 30, 1964, 4, 15; May 7, 1964, 4.

Minutes of the Advent Christian General Conference, 1950.

Minutes of the Advent Christian General Conference Executive Committee, 1950.

Minutes, Eastern Regional Convention, Somerville, Massachusetts, October 19–20, 1962.

Minutes, Eastern Regional Association, Special Meeting, Somerville, Massachusetts, May 27, 1964.

Murra, Fim. "Encouraging Tokens." *Our Hope and Life in Christ*, February 15, 1922, 2–3.

———. "The Fundamentalist." *Our Hope and Life in Christ*. July 12, 1922, 2–3.

"A New Link in the Chain to the West." *Present Truth Messenger*, October 4, 1962, 9.

Newbigin, Lesslie. *Proper Confidence: Faith, Doubt, and Certainty in Christian Discipleship*. Grand Rapids, MI: Eerdmans, 1995.

Nichol, Francis D. *The Midnight Cry*. Washington, DC: Review and Herald, 1944.

Nichols, James A., Jr. "Adventism's Theological Position." *World's Crisis*, January 10, 1951, 4.

———. *Christian Doctrines: A Presentation of Biblical Theology*. Nutley, NJ: Craig, 1970.

Nicole, Roger R., and Michaels, J. Ramsey, eds. *Inerrancy and Common Sense*. Grand Rapids, MI: Baker, 1980.

Niebuhr, Reinhold. *Moral Man and Immoral Society: A Study in Ethics and Politics*. New York: Scribners and Sons, 1932.

Noble, Cecil. Letter to Members of the Board of Publications and Executive Committee of General Conference, January 27, 1964.

Noll, Mark A., Nathan O. Hatch, and George M. Marsden. *The Search for Christian America*. Westchester, IL: Crossway, 1984.

Noll, Mark A. *Between Faith and Criticism: Evangelicals, Scholarship, and the Bible in America*. San Francisco: Harper & Row, 1986.

Northup, Arthur. Interview by the author, June 5, 1994.

———. *The Scandal of the Evangelical Mind*. Grand Rapids, MI: Eerdmans, 1994.

Numbers, Ronald L., and Jonathan M. Butler, *The Disappointed: Millerism and Millenarianism in the Nineteenth Century*. Knoxville, TN: University of Tennessee Press, 1993.

Ockenga, Harold. "The Pentecostal Bogey." *United Evangelical Action*, February 15, 1947, 12–13.

Ogden, Schubert M., ed. *Existence and Faith: Shorter Writings of Rudolf Bultmann*. New York: World, 1960.

Patterson, Harold R. Interview by the author, November 21, 1996.

Paxton, Geoffrey J. *The Shaking of Adventism: A Documented Account of the Crisis among Adventists over the Doctrine of Justification by Faith*. Grand Rapids, MI: Baker, 1977.

Phillips, Timothy R., and Dennis L. Okholm. *The Nature of Confession: Evangelicals and Postliberals in Conversation*. Downers Grove, IL: InterVarsity, 1996.

Piper, F. L. *Life and Labors of Miles Grant: With New-Year Glimpses from His Daily Journal through Fifty Years.* Boston: Advent Christian, 1915.

Esther Reed. Letter to Board of Christian Education, October 10, 1963.

———. Letter to Nelson Melvin, May 25, 1966.

———. Letter to Nelson Melvin, July 7, 1966.

———. Letter to Nelson Melvin, August 17, 1966.

Reed, Gordon O. "Don't Label Me." *Present Truth Messenger,* April 2, 1964, 3.

———. "Our Next General Conference." *Present Truth Messenger,* February 20, 1964, 3.

———. "Our Theological Diversity." *Present Truth Messenger,* May 14, 1964, 3.

———. "Pardon! The Slip is Showing." *Present Truth Messenger,* April 16, 1964, 3.

———. "The General Conference Session." *Present Truth Messenger,* July 2, 1964, 3.

Reid, Daniel G., et al., eds. *Dictionary of Christianity in America.* Downers Grove, IL: InterVarsity, 1990.

"Report of the Special Committee Appointed by the Board of the Eastern Regional Association to Document Charges Directed Against Advent Christian Sunday School Materials—1964."

"Report to the Curriculum Committee by the Director of Christian Education." June 1960 (date handwritten on document).

"Reporting for the Board of Christian Education." June 1960 (date handwritten on document).

"Revision to Item 12 of the Condensed Minutes of the 1963 Eastern Region Convention Adopted: May 27, 1964."

Richardson, Gerald F. "All Contents Guaranteed Perfect." *World's Crisis,* July 9, 1952, 8.

———. Letter to Raymond M. Beecroft, July 11, 1964.

———."This I Have Never Heard." *Present Truth Messenger,* May 7, 1964, 2.

———., "What is the Purpose of the Advent Christian Denomination?" *Present Truth Messenger,* October 4, 1962, 3.

Richardson, Lloyd M. "Blueprint for Growth: Building for His Kingdom or The Strategic Plan, 1985–1990: Distinctive With a Difference." Submitted to the Berkshire Christian College Board of Regents, September 20, 1984.

Roberts, Carlyle A. Interview by the author, August 3, 1994.

Rogers, Jack B., and Donald K. McKim. *The Authority and Inspiration of the Bible: An Historical Approach.* San Francisco: Harper & Row, 1979.

Rosell, Garth M., ed. *The Vision Continues: Centennial Papers of Gordon-Conwell Theological Seminary.* South Hamilton, MA: Gordon-Conwell Theological Seminary, 1992.

Rowe, David L. *God's Strange Work: William Miller and the End of the World.* Grand Rapids, MI: Eerdmans, 2008.

Sandeen, Ernest R. *The Roots of Fundamentalism: British and American Millenarianism, 1800–1930.* Chicago: University of Chicago Press, 1970.

Schaeffer, Francis A. *Escape from Reason: A Penetrating Analysis of Trends in Modern Thought.* Downers Grove, IL: InterVarsity, 1968.

———. *The Mark of the Christian.* Downers Grove, IL: InterVarsity, 1971.

———. *True Spirituality.* Wheaton, IL: Tyndale House, 1972.

Schaumberg, J. J. "Adventism." *Messiah's Advocate,* March 1, 1922, 60–61.

———. "The Church of Rome Today." *Messiah's Advocate,* April 12, 1922, 108.

———. "Missions and Modernism." *Messiah's Advocate,* May 24, 1922, 156–57.

Shaw, J. Howard. "Both Mission and Method are Vital." *Advent Christian Witness*, June 1963, 8.

———. "Christian Education Policy Subject of Careful Thought." *Advent Christian News*, March 19, 1964, 5, 7.

———. Letter to Ivan E. Adams, May 3, 1961

———. Letter to Raymond M. Beecroft, May 18, 1962.

———. Letter to Raymond M. Beecroft, July 23, 1962.

———. Letter to Raymond M. Beecroft, July 3, 1964.

———. Letter to Raymond M. Beecroft, November 13, 1964.

———. Letter to Esther Reed, August 8, 1963.

———. "Vital Issues Await Consideration at June Session of General Conference." *Advent Christian News*, February 20, 1964, 1–3.

Singleterry, Mildred C. "The Road from Bethlehem." *Living Water: Studies in God's Word for Senior High Youth*, edited by Esther Reed, 46–48. Concord, NH: Advent Christian, 1959.

Sproul, Robert C. *Explaining Inerrancy: A Commentary*. Oakland, CA: International Council on Biblical Inerrancy, 1980.

Stonehouse, Ned B. *J. Gresham Machen: A Biographical Memoir*. Grand Rapids, MI: Eerdmans, 1954.

"Summary of Survey Conduced on Cancelled Orders for *Living Water* and *The Christian Way*." June 1960 (date handwritten on document).

Taber, Clinton E. Interview by the author, February 4, 1995.

Taber, Clinton E. Letter to Elwell Drew, February 12, 1964.

Tenney, C.V. "Daniel's Seventieth Week: Past, Not Future." *World's Crisis*, August 9, 1922, p. 4.

Thomas, Clio. Interview by the author, November 11, 1996.

Thomas Clio E. "The Bible: The Word of the Living God." *Present Truth Messenger*, May 21, 1964, 4–5, 15.

Thomas, Ronald P., Sr. "By His Works We Know Him." *Advent Christian Witness*, June 1958, 7, 23.

Thompson, Horace E. "Measuring Adventism by an Opponent's Yardstick." *World's Crisis*, August 9, 1922, 4.

Tillich, Paul. *The Interpretation of History* New York: Scribner's Sons 1936

———. *Systematic Theology*. Vol. 1, *Reason and Revelation, Being and God*. Chicago: University of Chicago Press, 1951.

Turner, Steve. *The Gospel according to the Beatles*. Louisville: Westminster John Knox, 2006.

Tucker, Ruth A. "From the Fringe to the Fold: How the Worldwide Church of God Discovered the Plain Truth of the Gospel." *Christianity Today* 40, no. 8 (1996) 26–32.

Van Til, Cornelius. *The Defense of the Faith*. Philadelphia: Presbyterian and Reformed, 1955.

Weber, Timothy P. *Living in the Shadow of the Second Coming: American Premillennialism, 1875–1982*. Grand Rapids, MI: Zondervan, 1983.

Wells, David F. *No Place for Truth; or, Whatever Happened to Evangelical Theology?* Grand Rapids, MI: Eerdmans, 1993.

Wellcome, Isaac C. *History of the Second Advent Christian Message and Mission, Doctrine and People*. Boston: Advent Christian, 1874.

Wood, Gordon S. *The Purpose of the Past: Reflections on the Uses of History*. New York: Penguin, 2008.

Woodbridge, John D. *Biblical Authority: A Critique of the Rogers/McKim Proposal*. Grand Rapids, MI: Zondervan, 1982.

Woods, Leonard. *The Works of Leonard Woods*. Vol. 4. Boston: Perkins, 1850.

Wuthnow, Robert. *The Restructuring of American Religion*. Princeton, NJ: Princeton University Press, 1988.

Young, Edward J. *Thy Word is Truth: Thoughts on the Biblical Doctrine of Inspiration*. Grand Rapids, MI: Eerdmans, 1957.

Young, George L. "Destructive Criticism." *World's Crisis*, May 17, 1922; May 24, 1922; May 31, 1922; June 7, 1922.

Youngblood, Ronald, ed. *Evangelicals and Inerrancy: Selections from the Journal of the Evangelical Theological Society*. Nashville: Nelson, 1984.